Introduction to Economics

Introduction to
Economics

STEPHEN DOBSON

SUSAN PALFREMAN

OXFORD UNIVERSITY PRESS

1999

Oxford University Press, Great Clarendon Street, Oxford OX2 6DP

Oxford New York

*Athens Auckland Bangkok Bogotá Buenos Aires Calcutta
Cape Town Chennai Dar es Salaam Delhi Florence Hong Kong Istanbul
Karachi Kuala Lumpur Madrid Melbourne Mexico City Mumbai
Nairobi Paris São Paulo Singapore Taipei Tokyo Toronto Warsaw*

*and associated companies in
Berlin Ibadan*

Oxford is a registered trade mark of Oxford University Press

*Published in the United States
by Oxford University Press Inc., New York*

British Library Cataloguing in Publication Data
Data available

Library of Congress Cataloging-in-Publication Data
Dobson, Stephen.
An introduction to economics / Steve Dobson, Susan Palfreman.
p. cm.
Includes index.
1. Economics. I. Palfreman, Susan. II. Title.
HB171.D74 1999 330—dc21 98–28487

ISBN 0–19–877565–2 (pbk.)
0–19–877555–5

1 3 5 7 9 10 8 6 4 2

Typeset by Graphicraft Limited, Hong Kong
Printed in Great Britain
on acid-free paper by
Bookcraft Ltd.
Midsomer Norton, Somerset

To Effy, Karen, and Claire
S. D.

To William, Alice, and Chloë
S. P. P.

Preface

Economic problems are of central concern to individuals, government, and business. Yet in the face of inflation or unemployment many of us feel powerless; we expect government to 'do something'. This book introduces students to some of the key concepts used by economists when analysing such problems. Economic principles may also be used to examine questions about the allocation of health care resources, the demand for water, profits made by the privatized utilities, the effects of a national minimum wage, and so on. The book will thus give students an insight into how economics can be used to analyse important social and economic issues.

Motivation for the book

Our motivation for this book emerged out of our dissatisfaction with the introductory textbooks that are specifically written for people taking an economics degree (whether it be a single honours programme or as part of a joint degree). For the specialist student of economics, these books do an admirable job. But for people who have chosen a one-year elective in economics, these texts tend to cover too much material in too great a depth, and assume some past knowledge of the subject. In the past few years, we have taught modules in introductory economics to a variety of non-specialists (many of whom are mature students). Typically, these people have extremely diverse interests and, in most cases, they have never studied economics before. Our audience ranges from first-year students doing degrees in the arts, social sciences, and management to final-year students taking degrees in mathematics and engineering. In our view, people who have chosen to 'sample' some economics need a text that is aimed specifically at them.

We have, therefore, written this book for people who are not taking an economics degree. Furthermore, it is aimed especially at those who have not studied economics before. This does not mean it is unsuitable for people taking a specialist course. The book covers most of the principles of economics that are found in mainstream texts, but it does so in a way that recognizes that, even for many specialist students, the subject matter of economics can be quite difficult when encountered for the first time. Clearly, where students have studied economics before some parts of the book will be familiar; for these people the book will serve to reinforce and widen their understanding of the subject. Even so, some of the material is treated differently from the way it is covered in standard introductory textbooks.

When teaching introductory economics to non-specialists, we believe less rather than more should be taught. By focusing on those concepts that make up the economist's basic tool kit, we hope to achieve more through attempting less. For this reason, the book does not cover all of the topics usually found in introductory textbooks. We feel it is more important to cover certain key ideas in depth: after all, a little knowledge of supply and demand theory can take us a long way down the road to understanding a wide range of social and economic problems.

The book also introduces many concepts in the context of real-world applications, and it presents many of the macroeconomic themes in the context of their historical development. The chapters in the book are shorter than is usual in books of this type. By the end of each chapter, students will have met a number of key ideas and been shown how these concepts can be useful in making sense of the real world.

Aims of the book

The book has three main aims: (i) to introduce students to some of the main ideas used by economists, (ii) to show students how economic ideas can be used to analyse social, political, and economic problems, and (iii) to help students to think logically and improve their ability to analyse topical economic problems. By the end of the book, students will appreciate that a knowledge of economic principles is essential for understanding the behaviour of consumers, firms, and government.

Who can use the book?

The book is ideal for undergraduates taking first-level modules in economics, especially if they are not taking an economics degree. It is appropriate for students taking any degree course, as it assumes no prior knowledge of economics. Whether students are taking subjects in social science, business studies and management, arts, European studies, or science, the book is suitable. It can also be used on MBA courses and postgraduate conversion courses that include economics. For specialist students of economics, the book can be used in conjunction with others, especially where students have not studied economics before.

Organization and alternative outlines

We give microeconomics and macroeconomics equal attention (twelve chapters each), in contrast to a number of other books which tend to focus on one or the other. We develop ideas in microeconomics first so that the macroeconomic concepts can be built on micro foundations. Our approach to teaching introductory economics is to develop the ideas quite slowly. To this end, we spend two semesters on this material, meeting students four times per week (three lectures and one class). In our view, the time invested pays off, as many students who approach the modules with fear and trepidation end up coming to terms with the material, and some even develop a taste for more! This gradual approach suits our purposes very well and gives us ample time to cover both the ideas and applications within lectures. In fact, a number of lectures are devoted entirely to particular issues, with concepts being introduced as part of the particular example. For instance, the material covered in Chapter 5 forms three separate lectures and helps to reinforce in students' minds the main ideas (and usefulness) of supply and demand analysis. In our experience, students appreciate this approach.

If our approach does not suit an instructor we suggest the following, depending on whether one or two semesters are available. For a one-semester module in economics (based upon two lectures per week), instructors may wish to make use of Chapters 2–10 in the microeconomics section, and Chapters 13–15, 17–18, and 21–3 in the macroeconomics half of the book. If two semesters are available, and if time allows, we recommend following the structure of the book very closely.

Learning Aids

The book aims to show students how economic principles can be applied to the real world. To help with this process, we have included a variety of learning aids that recur throughout the book.

- Chapter introductions. Each chapter begins with an introduction to help set the stage and make clear where each chapter is heading. The introduction also reminds students of what has been covered previously and indicates how the new chapter aims to take the analysis a stage further.

- Many diagrams and illustrations. Each chapter contains numerous diagrams to help reinforce students' understanding. If students are to understand the key ideas they need to be comfortable with diagrams. To this end, we often use the diagrams to build carefully towards a 'final' picture rather than begin with the end result. It is our experience that many students need time to get to grips with the visual representation of economic ideas. In our view, they benefit from careful attention being paid to the construction of diagrams.

- Detailed chapter summaries. Each chapter ends with a numbered summary that reminds students of the most important ideas that they have just encountered. This will provide a useful revision tool later in the course.

- A list of key terms at the end of each chapter. A list of key terms at the end of each chapter allows students to test their understanding of the new terms that have been introduced. These key terms are highlighted in boldface in the main body of the chapter.

- End-of-chapter questions. At the end of each chapter are a number of questions for review that test students' understanding of the key ideas. These questions can be used once a chapter is finished and in preparation for an examination.

- Numerous examples of topical interest. We want students to get a sense of the usefulness of the economic concepts they are learning. To make the subject more interesting it needs to be applied to an understanding of actual events and policies. The book, therefore, contains numerous examples of how economic ideas can be used to analyse social, political, and economic problems. These examples are drawn from specialist publications in economics as well as newspaper articles.

- Further reading. A number of other books are available at the introductory level. Some of these books have been written with specialist students of economics in mind, while others are aimed specifically at students who are doing economics for the first time or as part of a course which contains some economics. If you wish to read more widely and you have not studied economics before you may wish to look at

  - R. H. Mabry and H. H. Ulbrich, *Economics*, 2nd ed. (Boston: Houghton-Mifflin, 1994).

  If you have already done some economics the following books will be of use to you:

  - R. G. Lipsey and K. A. Chrystal, *Principles of Economics*, 9th ed. (Oxford: Oxford University Press, 1999)
  - J. Sloman, *Economics*, 3rd ed. (Hemel Hempstead: Prentice-Hall, 1997)

Acknowledgements

The book owes its origins to the two introductory modules in economics that we teach to students who are not doing a degree in economics. We thank all those students who have listened patiently over the past few years while we have 'fine-tuned' both the content and the level of the material taught. A special thanks goes to the students who have expressed their appreciation. Not everyone has done this when sober, but we thank you all the same!

We would also like to thank those colleagues in Hull who have taught classes with us over the past few years. In addition, we are grateful to Tracy Mawson, formerly of OUP, for supporting the project in its early stages, and latterly to Brendan Lambon, Business and Economics Editor, for his patience, encouragement, and enthusiasm. We would also like to extend our thanks to Ruth Marshall at OUP for her support and professionalism in seeing the manuscript through production, and to T. W. Bartel for his careful reading of the text and for his many appropriate and useful suggestions. Finally, we owe a debt of gratitude to Carlyn Ramlogan and Andrew Palfreman for their unfailing support during the writing of the book.

S. D. and S. P. P.
Hull
April 1998

Contents

Abbreviations

AC	average (total) cost
AD	aggregate demand
AE	aggregate expenditure
AFC	average fixed cost
AR	average revenue
AS	aggregate supply
AVC	average variable cost
C	consumption
CPI	Consumer Prices Index
CSO	Central Statistical Office
EU	European Union
G	government spending
GATT	General Agreement on Trade and Tariffs
GDP	gross domestic product
GNP	gross national product
I	investment spending
IMF	International Monetary Fund
M	imports
M0	narrow money
M4	broad money
MC	marginal cost
MC_L	marginal cost of labour
Md	demand for money
MEB	marginal external benefit
MPB	marginal private benefit
MPC	marginal propensity to consume
MP_L	marginal product of labour
MPM	marginal propensity to import
MPS	marginal propensity to save
MPT	marginal propensity to tax
MR	marginal revenue
Ms	money supply
MSB	marginal social benefit
NHS	National Health Service
NNP	net national product
NRU	natural rate of unemployment
Oftel	Office of Telecommunications

ONS	Office for National Statistics
PED	price elasticity of demand
PES	price elasticity of supply
PPF	production possibilities frontier
r	rate of interest
RPI	Retail Prices Index
RPIX	Retail Prices Index excluding mortgage interest payments
RR	reserve ratio
S	saving
T	taxes
TC	total cost
TFC	total fixed cost
TR	total revenue
TVC	total variable cost
V	velocity of circulation of money
VAT	Value Added Tax
X	exports
X − M	net exports
Y	income, output

PART I
microeconomics

CHAPTER 1

Making economic decisions

Your introduction to the subject matter of economics begins with an attempt to answer the question: 'What is economics?' You will also discover why it is useful to know some economics, and you will find out how professional economists 'do' economics—the sort of questions they ask and the methods they use in searching for answers. The final part of the chapter explains why graphs and data are so vital to the study of economics.

What is economics?

Economics is the science of making choices. As students you must choose whether to study for another hour or go to the bar for a drink; whether to play football, watch television, or go into town for an afternoon's recreation; whether to go into teaching, accountancy, or computing. The common element in all these decisions is that every choice involves a cost. That is, in choosing anything you must give up something else. Attending an early morning lecture in microeconomics means you must sacrifice staying in bed. When making choices, economists assume that people try to **maximize** the benefit they receive from the sacrifices they make. So, when you understand the process of making choices and the costs that go with them, you will have acquired some useful knowledge.

But why are choices necessary? Choices have to be made because the resources needed to make goods and services are limited, while the competing uses for them are not. Time is one of our limited resources. There are only twenty-four hours in a day, and people do not live for ever. By choosing to go out for a meal, you lose time for some other competing activity. Other resources, such as land and human labour, are also limited relative to their possible uses. Basically, there are not enough resources to produce all the houses, books, food, CD players, clothes, and so on that people want. It is therefore the scarcity of productive resources that makes choices necessary.

So, economics is about making choices under conditions of scarcity. In other words, it is the study of how individuals allocate scarce resources among competing uses to maximize their satisfaction. To help clarify this further, we need to make a number of assumptions about the behaviour of individuals in dealing with the problem of scarcity and choice. These are:

Self-interested behaviour. The idea here is that individuals know their preferences; they know what they like and what they do not like and they act to satisfy those preferences.

In other words, people typically know where their self-interest lies and pursue that self-interest. Economists are not particularly interested in knowing where these tastes and preferences come from; they take tastes as given.

Maximizing behaviour. Individuals are maximizers; that is, they want to get as much satisfaction as possible out of the limited resources they have. Getting the maximum satisfaction (maximizing behaviour) is frequently referred to by economists as **rational behaviour**.

Responding to incentives. Economists assume that people respond to **incentives**. If an employer raises the hourly wage, people will work harder, other things being equal. If the price of a particular product is raised, people will choose to buy a cheaper alternative. But notice that not all individuals respond to the same incentive in the same way or at the same time. In economics, we refer to the behaviour of the 'average' or representative individual rather than to each and every individual.

Deciding at the margin. Individuals choose 'at the margin'. It is rare for an individual to face an all-or-nothing choice. People do not choose whether or not to study or whether or not to go out for a meal. They decide whether to study for one more hour or go out for a meal, or whether to drink one more pint of beer or stay sober enough to drive home. **Marginal decision-making** involves deciding whether the benefits of an extra amount of a good are worth its cost. As you will see, marginal decision-making is very important in economics.

Opportunity cost

When individuals decide how to use scarce resources, they do so on the basis of **opportunity cost**. The opportunity cost of using any good or service is the value of the next best alternative forgone. It is convenient to look at the idea of opportunity cost in terms of consumer decisions. For instance, what is the opportunity cost to you of a new £400 CD player? The answer is the satisfaction you would receive from spending that £400 in some other way, such as buying a brand new mountain bike or a new set of clothes. Although we measure opportunity cost in physical terms, we tend to talk in monetary units because we know other prices. Every scarce good has an opportunity cost, because the production of every good or service uses resources that could have been used to produce something else. For example, human labour could be used in a factory, or on the land, or in a football team. The concept of opportunity cost will be discussed further in Chapter 2.

What is microeconomics?

Microeconomics is concerned with individual decisions and specific markets (micro means small). The transfer market for footballers, the price of running shoes, the demand for office workers, and the effect of petrol taxes on petrol sales are all microeconomic subjects. Economists interested in microeconomic issues answer such questions as: 'Will the abolition of mortgage interest tax relief cause fewer people to own their own homes?' 'How much will the price of coffee increase if a winter freeze destroys half the coffee crop in Brazil?' 'Is it cheaper to build a new airport runway with lots of workers using shovels or with a few workers using state-of-the-art equipment?' 'How many students will choose not to go to university if maintenance grants are abolished?' As you can see, microeconomics deals with very specific questions involving individual markets, firms, and consumers.

Why study economics?

Whether your course requires you to study economics or whether you have chosen it as a free elective, there are a number of good reasons for knowing some economics. First of all, it helps you to understand the marketplace and the economic system. As a consumer, it helps you to understand the impact of economic events on your decisions to spend, save, and borrow. If you need to decide whether to buy a house now or wait until later, your decision will need to take into account house price forecasts, movements in interest rates, and other economic factors. Second, whether you are a worker, an employer, or the owner of a firm, economics is relevant to you. It is essential that you understand the signals from the marketplace, the nature of costs, and the process of making decisions. Whether you are a teacher competing for jobs against other teachers or the owner of a corner shop worried about the opening of a new Tesco or Safeway, you need to know the effects of competition on your income. Finally, as an ordinary citizen you have the opportunity (via the ballot box) to affect public sector decisions about taxation, spending, and borrowing. In order to make intelligent decisions about how much money should be spent on education or the health service you need to understand price signals, opportunity costs, and maximizing behaviour.

By applying what you learn in your economics modules you ought to find that economics influences how you look at decisions, although you have probably been thinking like an economist for a long time without even realizing it. At school you probably swapped the contents of your lunch box for sweets and your spare football stickers for marbles. If you were offered money to do household chores, you almost certainly weighed the value of the money against the unpleasantness of the job. In doing this, you made an economic choice. As you got older, the choices became more complex, but they were still economic decisions based on self-interested behaviour, incentives, and opportunity cost. By the time you have finished studying economics, you ought to realize that you have been behaving like a competent economist for a long time.

The economic method

Economists use a standard tool kit and a method of analysis to answer almost every economic question. The tools economists use are models, graphs, and data. The method they use is based on a blend of scientific method and a technique called **policy analysis**.

Suppose an economist were asked to try to solve the problem of youth unemployment. This is a complex issue that has troubled public policy makers in the UK for a long time. How is the economist's approach to this problem different from that of the sociologist, the psychologist, or the ordinary citizen? An economist tackles the problem in the following way: (i) state the problem, (ii) apply an economic model, (iii) use that model to identify solutions, (iv) use economic tools and some objectives to evaluate each of those solutions, and (v) choose and implement a solution (it is normally policy makers who make the final choice).

State the problem. Although this step sounds easy, we need to make sure we do not state the problem in such a way that it prejudges the solution. Our problem is how to lower a persistently high unemployment rate among young people. The side effects of high unemployment are poverty, high welfare payments, and high crime rates. Unemployment also creates a wasted resource, human labour. This labour could be used to produce more goods and services to raise living standards.

As this is quite a broad statement of the problem, it helps to focus on a narrower aspect of youth unemployment. Suppose the economist discovers that the average unemployed young person does not possess marketable skills. Jobs are available, but the applicants for them are not qualified: they lack appropriate educational and work qualifications. By focusing on this narrower aspect we have defined the problem as one of finding the appropriate incentives to get these young people to 'invest' in themselves—that is, to stay in school longer and/or invest in some vocational skills to enhance their job prospects. It is standard practice in economics to express problems in terms of incentives.

Apply the relevant economic model. The purpose of an **economic model** is to make pre-dictions, such that if A occurs (the weather is hot) then B will follow (ice-cream sales will increase). In order to be useful, models have to be abstract and simplify reality. This means that the analytical models of professional economists leave out details that clutter the picture with-out adding significantly to our understanding of the underlying problem. Economists use a number of analytical models, although the one you will see most often in this part of the book is the supply and demand model (which we look at in detail later). For now, we use a simplified version of the supply and demand model to identify the incentives and disincentives the indi-vidual young person faces. Let us assume the unemployed engage in self-interested, maximiz-ing behaviour, know what they like and dislike, and respond to incentives. From this model, it is reasonable to conclude that any potential solution involves changing the incentives they face.

Identify solutions. In this step the economist lists all the possible ways of obtaining the desired result (more employment). In the case of youth unemployment, possible solutions involve changing the incentives people face so as to prepare them for employment. Positive incentives aim to increase the benefits of devoting more time and effort to improving marketable skills. Negative incentives are aimed at increasing the cost of not devoting more time and effort to developing those skills.

A few possible solutions that focus on positive incentives are: (i) guaranteeing the person a job after completing a training programme, (ii) paying students a modest sum of money while in vocational training, (iii) providing better information on the benefits of staying in school and getting training, and (iv) lowering the cost of leaving school at 16 by providing alternative curricula for vocationally minded students.

There are also some possible solutions that use negative incentives, so raising the cost of not acquiring marketable skills and education. These include: (i) raising the school-leaving age, and (ii) supplying information to make students more aware of the costs of leaving school at 16. For example, telling them about higher unemployment rates and lower lifetime earnings among those without qualifications beyond GCSE; this may give some people an incentive to stay on at school.

Evaluate solutions. In the evaluation stage we are likely to consider some of the more obvious advantages and disadvantages of various solutions. It is here where the work of the economist begins to overlap with the work of the policy maker, who evaluates solutions.

One thing we must consider is cost. The least costly solution is perhaps providing better information to people, but it may also be the least effective. Other solutions will involve the taxpayer, and each has different costs for every 1 per cent reduction in unemployment rates. The tax revenue needed to support these programmes has to come from somewhere. If we devote resources to these programmes, then we have less to spend on other public goods and services. Eventually, spending on benefits and crime prevention should fall as unemployment is reduced. This will make future tax increases less likely.

When evaluating solutions, it is important to consider possible side effects. For example, creating job opportunities for younger people may increase unemployment among older workers (in the same town or city). Introducing vocational programmes in schools may harm the academically gifted students if academic programmes are cut back. Requiring the less academically gifted to spend more years in school may make the job of teachers more difficult. The average quality of schooling may suffer, or it may become more difficult to attract enough good teachers. When making a policy choice these side effects can play an important role.

Select and implement a solution. In the evaluation stage, the politician or policy maker normally takes over from the economist. But in reality, many economists also become involved in choosing and implementing policy as well. This point is important, because it emphasizes the difference between positive and normative economics. **Positive economics** answers factual or predictive questions about 'what is or what if?' rather than 'what is better or what ought to be?'

A positive statement tells you that if A occurs, B will follow. It does not pass judgement on whether result B is desirable or important. For example, 'ending transfer fees for footballers will result in players becoming richer' is a statement in positive economics.

Normative economics, in contrast, involves making value judgements. 'Spending more money on education is better than spending more money on social security' is an example of a normative statement, as is 'income in society should be more equally distributed'. Economists are often expected to leave this type of judgement to politicians or policy makers, who are elected to make normative judgements based on the analyses economists provide.

However, this does not mean that economics is a value-free science. For example, the choice of which problems deserve the attention of economists (a scarce resource) is a value judgement. Sometimes the choice of analytical tools, or the way solutions are identified, will reflect the personal biases of particular economists. Even so, most economists make a conscious effort to separate their personal values and preferences from their professional analyses of economic problems.

We also need to recognize that models have limitations. Models are very useful for focusing attention on the key aspects of a particular problem, but they are limited by their assumptions, by the inability to hold other relevant factors constant, and often by important differences in short-run and long-run effects. We consider each of these in turn.

Limitations of economic models

We need simplifying assumptions in order to make models useful; but the use of assumptions can also introduce error. For example, in the mid-1970s many economists mistakenly predicted that higher petrol prices would sharply reduce petrol consumption. An error was made because the prediction assumed no increases in population and income. As you encounter economic models, try to determine the assumptions that are being made.

When economists look at any question, they assume everything else is held constant while they analyse this one issue. The 'everything stands still' assumption is called *ceteris paribus*, which is Latin for 'other things being equal'. *Ceteris paribus* is perhaps the most important assumption made by economists. For example, suppose an economist wants to analyse the effect of a 10p increase in the price of a pint of beer on the number of pints sold per year. To do this she needs to hold consumers' incomes constant, as well as their tastes for beer and other kinds of alcohol. She predicts that a price increase will lead to less beer being sold, but this prediction may be wrong if other things do not remain constant. If consumer incomes double at the same time, or if the medical profession announce that consuming lots of beer is good for you, beer consumption will go up despite the price rise.

In economics, it is quite often the case that the predictions of a model will differ for the short run and the long run. In microeconomics, the **short run** means a time period in which important conditions cannot be altered. For example, workers often make short-run decisions because they have fixed commitments, such as wanting to stay in a place until their children have finished school. This might mean they will take a pay cut in the short run, but once their fixed commitments have been met, they will respond differently in the long run. The exact duration of the short run depends on the length of the fixed commitment people face in a given situation. For some people the short run may only be a week or a month, while for others it may be years.

The **long run** is a time period in which anything can be altered. That is, it is long enough for people fully to respond to incentives and take advantage of economic opportunities. The long run has no specific time frame; it is simply the time period that is long enough to allow a complete response to changing incentives.

Using graphs in economics

Economists are well known for drawing **graphs** and quoting numbers. Sometimes they do both at the same time. Graphs and statistics enable economists to take abstract ideas about economic relationships and put them in a form they can visualize and remember. The graphs you will see in this book are similar to the ones you learned to draw in your school mathematics lessons. Eventually, you ought to feel quite at home using graphs. Like models, graphs enable us to clear away some of the 'clutter' and visually isolate important relationships. Graphs are used by an economist to demonstrate the principles and theories underlying what happens in the real world.

Some graphs illustrate changes in certain economic **data** over time, for example, the ups and downs of manufacturing production, or the change in the cost of living. These graphs are often found in the (broadsheet) newspapers and on television news programmes to help people visualize what is happening to the economy. Most of the graphs you will meet in this book are not descriptive. They are analytical graphs reflecting an underlying model of an economic relationship between two variables.

Either type of graph is simply a visual representation of the relationship between two quantities that could be written in a table. Consider the relationship between the percentage mark on a mid-semester microeconomics test and the number of hours studied per week (before the test). Hypothetical data for eight students might look like that in Table 1.1. There seems to be a positive relationship between the percentage mark and average hours studied. That is, when the value of one increases, the value of the other also increases. Figure 1.1 plots a graph of these numbers. The idea underlying this graph is that higher marks are the result of more hours of studying.

Table 1.1. A positive relationship

Percentage mark	Average hours studied per week
70	16
65	14
60	12
55	10
50	8
45	6
40	4
35	2

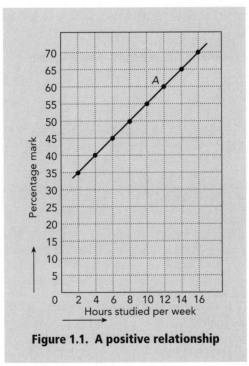

Figure 1.1. A positive relationship

We say hours studied is the **independent variable**, because it causes higher marks. Percentage mark is the **dependent variable**, because (we think) it depends on hours studied, holding innate ability and other relevant factors constant. There is a **positive relationship** between percentage mark and hours studied, meaning that an increase in the independent variable (hours studied) results in an increase in the value of the dependent variable (percentage mark). You can locate combinations from the table as points in Figure 1.1. For example, the combination of 12 hours studied and a percentage mark of 60 is represented by point A. The line sloping upward from left to right that passes through the points represents a visual version of the positive relationship between hours studied and percentage mark.

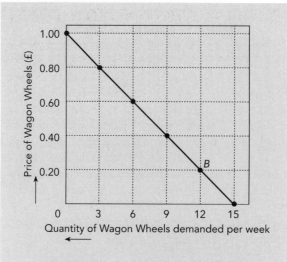

Figure 1.2. A negative relationship

Table 1.2. A negative relationship

Price of Wagon Wheels (£)	Quantity bought per week
1.00	0
0.80	3
0.60	6
0.40	9
0.20	12
0.00	15

We can also illustrate a **negative relationship** by using something economists call a 'demand curve' (which we look at in more detail in Chapter 3). Economists have discovered that the price of any good is the most important single influence on the quantity consumers choose to buy. In this case, price is the independent variable. Consumers buy smaller amounts at higher prices than at lower prices. The demand curve in Figure 1.2 is a plot of the data shown in Table 1.2. Figure 1.2 shows a negative relationship between the price of Wagon Wheels and the quantity consumers wish to buy. At a price of £1 per Wagon Wheel the consumer buys no Wagon Wheels. At a price of 20p each, the consumer buys 12 per week (see point *B*). As you can see in the graph, lines sloping downward from left to right represent negative relationships.

Using data in economics[1]

Economists also like to use numbers to describe what is happening. You will come to realize that economics and numerical data go together in much the same way as fish and chips, Bill and Ben, Lennon and McCartney, Best and Charlton, and Morecombe and Wise! Actually, some of you may wish that economics and numbers were not so closely related. Frequently, students of economics ask why it is necessary to know about numerical data if they are studying economics. To answer this question, imagine what the world would be like without numerical data. We would not be able to observe the way in which consumers react to a change in price or the way a firm responds to a change in the demand for its product.

We could, of course, still study microeconomics by sitting and thinking about economic problems and devising theories of individual behaviour. But we would find it almost impossible to judge whether our theories corresponded to reality, or whether we were addressing the most relevant problems. Basically, data are the economist's link with the real world. Data allow us to verify the results of our analyses. In short, it is not possible to study economics effectively without data.

The most popular economic measure is price. Price measures costs to the producer and value to the buyer. Economists have even found that price gives an answer to the standard arithmetic problem of how to add apples and oranges. For an economist, this problem can be easily solved. If three oranges are 25p each and five apples are 20p each, we have, in total, £1.75 worth of fruit. But how do we compare an apple and an orange? If an orange is 'worth' 25p (that is what sellers are prepared to take for it and what buyers are prepared to offer) and an apple is 'worth' 20p, then one orange is worth 1.25 apples (25/20).

One reason economists are so fascinated with prices is that price acts as a signal. When the price of something rises, it signals to us that the good is scarce and buyers should substitute other, cheaper goods for it. It also sends a signal to producers that they should try to produce more of the good. At the same time, prices send signals from the market to individuals. We use prices to send signals to one another through the market: the prices at which we will sell our goods, or rent our flats, or buy another pair of shoes. But price is not the only number that fascinates economists. In microeconomics, quantities (as we shall see) are also important.

'Data' does not only refer to statistics. While it is true that a lot of information about society comes in the form of numbers, it also comes in many other different forms. For example, information is passed on by word of mouth in the guise of description of economic events or policies in the newspapers or on television. Verbal accounts are data: information about the economy is evidence about the way in which economic decisions are taken. When you are reading a newspaper look for articles covering economic events and try to use them to further your understanding of economics and the economy. Data also come in the form of graphs, as we have seen. These too are important in providing raw material on which economists can work, and they provide crucial tools which help in the interpretation of numbers.

Summary

1. Economics is the study of how individuals allocate scarce resources among competing uses to maximize their satisfaction. Every choice has an opportunity cost in the form of the next best alternative forgone.

2. The choices individuals make in response to scarcity are designed to maximize satisfaction. Individuals pursue their self-interest on the basis of their own tastes and preferences, make decisions at the margin, and respond to economic incentives.

3. Microeconomics focuses on individual prices, markets, and consumer choices.

4. Economists approach issues by stating the problem, applying economic models, identifying solutions, and evaluating solutions. The policy maker chooses and implements solutions.

5. Economics aims to be a positive science (value-free) rather than a normative one (which makes decisions according to the desirability of outcomes).

6. The most popular tools of economists are graphs and numerical data. Graphs provide a visual representation of economic relationships. It is not possible to do economics properly without numerical data.

Key terms

ceteris paribus	maximize
data	microeconomics
dependent variable	negative relationship
economic model	normative economics
economics	opportunity cost
graphs	policy analysis
incentives	positive economics
independent variable	positive relationship
long run	rational behaviour
marginal decision-making	short run

Review questions

1. Economics is often described as the 'science of making choices'. Why are choices necessary?

2. A simple economic model would say that if there are fewer 18-year-old school leavers in 1999, there will be fewer university entrants in 1999. What are the *ceteris paribus* assumptions here?

3. Daisy Cutter has decided to take a job after university as a flight attendant at a salary of £15,000 a year plus unlimited travel. Her dad asks her for an explanation. To what incentives did she respond? What was she maximizing?

4. What is the opportunity cost to you of taking a module in economics?

5. Which of the following are positive statements and which are normative?

   (i) The government should spend more money on the National Health Service.
  (ii) The universe is only 10,000 years old.
 (iii) Aliens exist and have visited the earth.
 (iv) The distribution of income in society should be more equal.
  (v) George Best is the greatest footballer of all time.

6. Given the following information, plot the data on a graph and label the axes. Connecting the points should form a straight line.

Temperature (degrees Celsius)	Sales of ice cream (cones per day)
5	100
10	140
15	180
20	220
25	260
30	280
35	300

Is this a positive or negative relationship? Which is the dependent variable? Which is the independent variable?

Note

1. Some of this material is adapted from Peter Smith, 'Beginning with Data', *Economic Review Data Supplement* (Sept. 1992), 1–2.

Further reading

- Mabry and Ulbrich, chapter 1
- Lipsey and Chrystal, chapters 1 and 2
- Sloman, chapter 1

CHAPTER 2
Scarcity and choice

In Chapter 1, we noted that economics is the study of how people make choices in a world of scarcity. Everything that is valuable is scarce—money, goods, time, human skills—whereas human wants are almost unlimited. With only limited resources available to satisfy our almost endless desire for goods and services, making choices is a fact of life.

At the level of the economy as a whole, society has to decide what to produce, how to produce, and for whom to produce. Not every society answers these questions in the same way. In most Western nations, economic decisions are made mainly through markets, while in countries such as China and Cuba, the government plays a more substantial role in these kinds of decisions. The difference in emphasis largely reflects different attitudes in various societies, but all mechanisms are designed to address the problem of choice in the face of scarcity.

Unlimited wants?

In Chapter 1 we described economics as the science of making choices. Because we live in a world of **scarcity**, choices are necessary. Scarcity means that human wants are infinite but the **resources** available to satisfy those wants are limited. But is it correct to talk about unlimited human wants? You might think that you only want a few things at the moment, such as a car, a new CD player, or a smart place to live. But suppose you win £10 million next week in the National Lottery. As someone who is a maximizing, self-interested individual, you could certainly buy the car, the CD player, and the smart flat. But would you also taken an expensive holiday? Buy presents for your family and friends? Pay off the mortgage on the family home? Would you save a large amount and live for the rest of your life on the annual interest? Would you give some of the money to charity?

So, while you might argue that the list of wants for most people is not infinite, it is likely that most people could produce a reasonably long list of the things they want. Most of these lists involve having more (as well as better-quality) goods and services of all kinds, but they may also include some wants that are not personal or selfish. For instance, some people may want to help other people or give to charity. We can further illustrate the idea of human wants by referring to a specific example: the demand for health care.

The demand for health care

People demand health care for one simple reason: they want to be healthy. The desire to remain healthy has led to a continuous growth in the demand for health care. However, there are also a number of specific reasons why the demand for health care has grown so rapidly in developed countries over the past half-century:

Changes in the age structure of the population. Countries like the UK have an ageing population. In 1948, 10.7 per cent of the population of the UK were over the age of 65; by 1990 the figure was 15.6 per cent, and by 1995 it had reached 16 per cent. A similar picture can be seen by looking at changes in the support ratio (the number of people of working age divided by the number of people of pensionable age). A declining support ratio indicates an ageing population. In the UK in 1970, the support ratio was 3.7; by 1980 it had fallen to 3.5, and by 1991 it was 3.3. It is projected that by the year 2050 the support ratio will be 2.7. Clearly, elderly people require more health care than other age groups. In 1995, about 43 per cent of expenditure in the National Health Service (NHS) went on treating people aged 65 and over, even though they made up only 16 per cent of the total UK population.

Rising real incomes. This has led to people expecting more from the health care system. Many people are no longer prepared to put up with the discomfort associated with some illnesses, such as arthritis. Instead of putting up with the pain we demand treatment, such as hip and knee replacement operations.

Improvements in medical technology. This has meant an increase in the range of treatments possible. For example, the invention of the kidney dialysis machine has largely prevented kidney failure from killing people. Also, there has been continuous development of new and more effective medicines (such as penicillin), which has meant that previously incurable conditions can now be treated successfully.

The concept of scarcity relates not only to unlimited wants, but also to the notion that there is a finite supply of resources. The term 'resources' is used to describe all inputs (or **factors of production**) which are used to produce goods and services. We can divide resources into four types:

Land. This refers to the physical resources of the planet, including mineral deposits. Examples include coal, soil, and trees.

Labour. This refers to human resources in the sense of people as workers. The labour resource includes teachers, doctors, scientists, nurses, social workers, and football managers.

Capital. This is a resource created by humans to make other goods and services: for example, a warehouse, a hospital, a computer, an office desk, or an X-ray machine.

Enterprise. This refers to the human resource of organizing the other factors of production to produce goods and services. Typically, this will be done by people known as **entrepreneurs** (for example, Richard Branson, Anita Roddick, Bill Gates, and Alan Sugar).

We see these factors of production operating in the production of health care. Clearly, the available quantity of these four factors is limited; consequently, there must be some maximum quantity of health care that can be produced at any one time.

Opportunity cost

As mentioned in Chapter 1, we use the concept of **opportunity cost** to decide how to use our scarce resources. The opportunity cost of using any resource, good, or service is the value of the next best alternative. Let us consider an example of this idea.

Consider the opportunity costs faced by Joni, who is thinking about entering Skegness University. Joni's parents want to know the 'full cost' of her spending three years at Skegness.

The items they include when calculating her likely expenditure are housing costs, travel costs, meals, books, entertainment, and other expenses. Doing the calculation in this way is fine if they want to represent Joni's out-of-pocket expenses. However, they have not included all the costs of going to university, while some that have been included are not relevant opportunity costs. One very important item is missing. By going to university, Joni is giving up what she could earn by working; this is the next best use of her time. So, her parents ought to add her lost earnings to the estimation of the cost. Also, they have included some expenses which she would incur whether or not she went to university. For example, the money she will spend on personal items (such as entertainment) is expenditure she would incur whatever she does and wherever she lives.

The production possibilities frontier

One way to represent the choices individuals and societies face is to use a **production possibilities frontier** (*PPF*). The *PPF* looks at how available resources can be used to produce a particular combination of two goods. The *PPF* shows the maximum amounts of these two goods that can be produced when all available resources are being used, including the latest production technology. Thus, the *PPF* shows the various possibilities for allocating scarce resources. We can look at this concept in relation to health care.

The example we use is based on the production of health care within a single hospital, and, in particular, the ability of a specific hospital unit to carry out operations such as hip replacements. Suppose the hip replacement unit has 10 surgeons working in it, and assume that the number of surgeons assigned to hip replacements is the only thing affecting the quantity of operations provided. Let us suppose that if all the surgeons are assigned to hip replacement operations, then the unit can carry out 80 operations per week. If, on the other hand, all the surgeons perform other operations, then the unit can carry out 80 of these other operations per week.

Figure 2.1 shows the *PPF* for this hospital unit. The graph charts all the possible maximum combinations of operations that the unit can achieve given the quantity and productivity of the factors of production available. For example, at point *C* there are 40 of each type of operation being carried out. It is impossible for the unit to produce the combination represented by point *D*. This is because there are not enough resources to produce that combination at the same time. Point *E* shows a combination where the hospital unit could do better; at point *E* the hospital is not getting the most out of its productive resources.

What determines the shape of the PPF? We see in Figure 2.1 that the PPF is a straight line, with a gradient (or slope) of −1. This reflects the fact that when we transfer one surgeon to hip replacement operations from other operations, we get 8 more hip replacements and 8 fewer other operations. There is a one-to-one trade-off between the two possibilities, so in this case the opportunity cost is constant. Clearly, this analysis assumes that all the surgeons (and nurses) are equally proficient at each type of operation, so that it is no more costly to move from 40 to 60 hip replacements (in terms of other operations sacrificed) than it is to move from 0 to 20.

But in reality this is unlikely to be the case (the trade-off is not likely to be one-to-one) because surgeons tend to specialize in particular medical fields. Initially, the most proficient surgeons (and nurses) will be switched from other operations to hip replacements, so that the number of other operations lost will be almost the same as the number of extra hip replacements being carried out (see above). But, at some point, the hospital will need to transfer

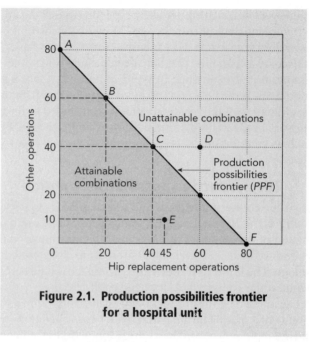

Figure 2.1. Production possibilities frontier for a hospital unit

surgeons (and nurses) who are less capable of making the switch so easily from one type of operation to another. This will mean that the opportunity cost of producing more hip replacements will increase as more hip replacement operations are undertaken. Hence, *PPF*s are normally drawn concave to the origin (they bow outwards), as shown in Figure 2.2.

In this case, the opportunity cost of producing more hip replacement operations changes as more of these operations (and fewer other operations) are carried out. Moving from point C to point D (65 to 75 hip replacements) involves a loss of 20 other operations. Similarly, 20 other operations are lost when we move from point D to point F (75 to 80 hip replacements). So, as we increase the number of hip replacements the opportunity cost of other operations rises; that is, for the same reduction in other operations (20), the incremental increase in the number of hip replacement operations is smaller (5 compared with 10). To put this another way, for the same increase in the number of hip replacements, the unit must give up more and more other operations. The shape of the *PPF* in Figure 2.2 reflects the **law of increasing cost**. This says that the opportunity cost of producing more of one thing increases as more of it is produced. As we move down the curve (from A to F), so producing more hip replacement operations, we require ever larger sacrifices of other operations for the same increase in the number of hip replacements.

Point G in Figure 2.2 corresponds to 45 hip replacement operations combined with 40 other operations. This is clearly a possible combination since the hospital has enough resources to achieve it; but is it an efficient combination? The notion of efficiency used here was introduced by the Italian economist Pareto in the early twentieth century. An allocation of resources is 'Pareto-efficient' if it is impossible to change that allocation to make one person better off without making someone else worse off. We can see this idea more clearly if we look at point G

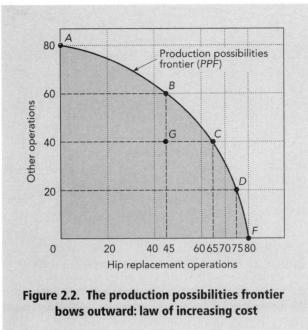

Figure 2.2. The production possibilities frontier bows outward: law of increasing cost

again. It is possible to reorganize the hospital's resources (move surgeons and nurses from one activity to the other) to increase the number of other operations without having to reduce the number of hip replacement operations. This is shown by the move from point *G* to point *B* in Figure 2.2 (a move from 40 to 60 other operations). Moving from *G* to *B* is clearly in society's interests, as we get an extra 20 other operations for the same number of hip replacements. That is, we get more medical care from our scarce resources. In this sense, then, point *G* is not efficient.

Point *B* is, in fact, an efficient allocation: we get a maximum possible combination of operations given the resources available to us. A move from point *B* to point *C* gives us more hip replacement operations, but it is at the expense of 20 other operations. Thus, the move from point *B* to point *C* involves an opportunity cost (equal to a loss of 20 other operations). So, all points which lie on a *PPF* are, by definition, efficient combinations (points *A* to *F* in Figure 2.2), but a move from one efficient allocation to another efficient allocation involves an opportunity cost.

The only ways that society can get more treatment are either by improving the productivity of the factors of production (doctors and nurses working harder, better medical equipment), so that the same amount of resources produces more treatments, or by increasing the quantity of the factors of production. In the former case, if there is an increase in the productivity of surgeons carrying out hip replacement operations, the *PPF* pivots outwards. This is shown in Figure 2.3. Now, a maximum of 90 hip replacement operations is possible, or 80 other operations. In Figure 2.4, more surgeons are allocated to all operations and so the *PPF* shifts outwards (a maximum of 90 hip replacements are now possible, or 90 other operations).

The *PPFs* we have looked at so far relate to choices between different types of health care. But *PPF* analysis can also be used to illustrate the trade-off between health care and all other goods.

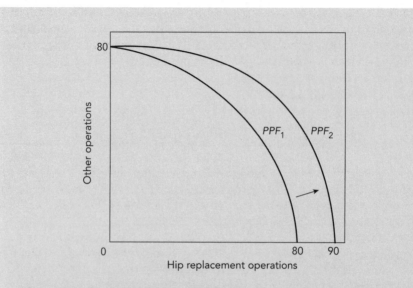

Figure 2.3. The production possibilities frontier pivots outward: increase in the productivity of surgeons carrying out hip replacements

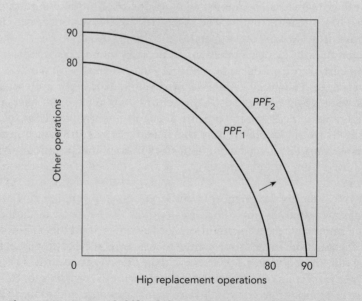

Figure 2.4. Outward shift of the production possibilities frontier: more surgeons allocated to all operations

In terms of Figure 2.2, all we need do is put health care on the vertical axis and all other goods on the horizontal axis. In this situation it is unlikely that society would choose either point *A* (the production of health care only) or point *F* (the production of no health care), but all points in between are feasible. The question is, how does society decide between the feasible points?

Allocation of health care

Society has to solve two basic questions: how much of our scarce resources do we devote to health care, and which type of treatment do we choose? To answer these questions we require an allocation (or decision-making) system. There are three possibilities: the free market, the command system, and the mixed system.

The free market solution allocates health care resources according to consumers' purchasing behaviour. The basis of the command model is to use planning to allocate health care according to some pre-determined 'need'. The mixed system combines parts of the free market with elements of the command model. In order to determine which of these systems is the most suitable in any given case we have to assess the performance of an allocation system. Economists use two main criteria. The first one is efficiency. Does the system produce an efficient allocation (one which is located on the *PPF*)? If the allocation is an efficient one, then it means the economy is producing just the right amount and type of health care that society wants (we have **allocative (Pareto) efficiency**), although the precise point reached on the *PPF* reflects society's preferences to some extent. For example, if it was the case that society preferred hip replacement operations to other operations, then the economy would reach (efficient) point *C* rather than (efficient) point *B* in Figure 2.2. Also, when the economy is operating on the *PPF* it is producing health care at the lowest possible cost (we have **productive efficiency**). In subsequent chapters of the book we develop the economic analysis of markets. In doing so, we will provide a precise way to define allocative efficiency (Chapter 3) and a way of assessing the allocative and productive efficiency properties of markets (Chapters 7, 8, and 9).

The second criterion used by economists is **equity**. Here, we are interested in knowing whether the allocation system is just or fair. This is clearly a normative issue since the decision made depends upon a value judgement. However, it is a crucial question for many countries when they consider the allocation of health care. For instance, it has often been argued that the idea of social justice was of paramount concern when the Labour government set up the NHS in the UK in 1948. The concept of equity is not easy to analyse, but it helps if we distinguish between horizontal and vertical equity.

Horizontal equity is concerned with the equal treatment of equal need. This means that if a health care allocation system is to be equitable it must treat two people with the same complaint in exactly the same way. **Vertical equity**, on the other hand, is concerned with how far we should treat unequal individuals differently. In health care we may see this in the objective of unequal treatment for unequal need: those with serious conditions (heart problems) receive more treatment than those with relatively minor complaints (septic toe).

What does this kind of analysis add to our understanding of health care problems? Take the following report in the *Guardian* newspaper on 11 January 1997:

The Government admitted yesterday that hospitals were seeing unprecedented numbers of emergency patients this winter as doctors warned that the NHS was facing its worst financial crisis for a decade. The British Medical Association (BMA) yesterday issued a fresh list of trouble spots around the country where lack of beds and cash problems meant operations delayed or cancelled, or patients being treated in corridors. Most hospitals have stopped carrying out any routine surgery, such as hip replacements, so as to leave beds free for emergencies, and many health authorities and trusts face overspends running into millions of pounds . . . The National Association of Health Authorities and Trusts has said the NHS needs a cash injection of £150 to £200 million to get hospitals through the winter. The BMA said . . . the requirement for hospitals to make 3 per cent efficiency savings meant many were cutting services.

The problems identified in the report are obviously related to an increase in the demand for health care, especially during the winter months. Also, *PPF* analysis makes it clear that this situation reflects one of two possibilities. Either hospitals are operating on their *PPF*, or they are operating inside it (such as point *G* in Figure 2.2). If they are operating on their frontier, they have to find a way of choosing between two or more efficient allocations (in this case routine surgery—hip replacements—or emergency operations) or more resources need to be devoted to medical care (to shift the *PPF* outwards). If they are inside their *PPF*, we do not need to choose between two efficient possibilities, since the initial allocation is inefficient. All we need to do is remove the inefficiencies so that we can have more of both routine surgery (hip replacements) and emergency operations.

Although this analysis is simplistic, it does relate directly to the ongoing debate about changes in the NHS. The Conservative government under Mrs Thatcher and Mr Major argued that the allocation of resources was inefficient (like point *G* in Figure 2.2), so we could get more from our existing resources. The present Labour government, when in opposition, argued that the problem was (and still is) a lack of resources; in other words, since hospitals are already operating on their *PPF* (they are efficient) they need more resources in order to shift the *PPF* outwards.

Summary

1. Scarcity is the fundamental economic problem, arising from unlimited wants to be met with limited resources.

2. An increasingly ageing population, an increase in real incomes, and improvements in medical technology have all contributed to an increase in the demand for health care.

3. The limited resources or factors of production are land, labour, capital, and enterprise.

4. Scarcity means that choices must be made and that every choice has an opportunity cost.

5. The production possibilities frontier (*PPF*) is a useful analytical tool that shows all the possible combinations of maximum output of two goods when all available resources and the best technology are fully used. The *PPF* reflects the economic concepts of choice, opportunity cost, efficiency, and the law of increasing cost.

6. Systems for allocating resources are judged according to the criteria of efficiency (allocative and productive) and equity (horizontal and vertical).

7. An allocation system is Pareto-efficient if it is impossible to reallocate resources to make someone better off without making someone else worse off.

Key terms

allocative (Pareto) efficiency

capital

enterprise

entrepreneur

equity

factors of production

horizontal equity

labour

land

law of increasing cost

opportunity cost

productive efficiency

production possibilities frontier (*PPF*)

resources

scarcity

vertical equity

Review questions

1. What is the primary opportunity cost to you of:

  (i)   choosing to eat a kebab tonight?
  (ii) studying economics for an hour today?
  (iii) the government doubling its spending on the NHS?
  (iv) the production of a CD player?

2. In St Fagen's hospital the opportunity cost of undertaking one heart operation is four hip replacement operations. If all its resources are used to produce heart operations, the hospital can carry out 100 heart operations. How many hip replacements can it undertake? If 50 heart operations are completed, how many hip replacement operations can the hospital carry out? Draw the hospital's *PPF*, representing the various combinations of heart operations and hip replacements. Why is it unlikely that a real hospital's *PPF* would have this shape?

3. Identify on your diagram in Question 2 the following combinations:

  (i)   60 heart operations and 100 hip replacement operations.
  (ii) 80 heart operations and 300 hip replacement operations.
  (iii) 20 heart operations and 320 hip replacement operations.

Which of these combinations are feasible and which are efficient?

4. Which do you think is more important—that we treat all patients with kidney failure in the same way or that we make sure we devote more health care resources to kidney failure than to plastic surgery? Do you think that the rich should contribute more to the financing of health care than the poor?

Further reading

- Mabry and Ulbrich, chapter 2
- Lipsey and Chrystal, chapter 1
- Sloman, chapter 1

CHAPTER 3
Markets

So far, we have noted that goods and services are scarce. Because of the scarcity problem they have to be rationed among competing users. Goods and services may be rationed in a number of different ways; for example, health care may be allocated to consumers on a first-come, first-served basis, or it may be auctioned off to the highest bidder, or even provided only to people with blue eyes and brown skin. It is the auctioning method that is used in markets. This means that those people who are prepared to offer the highest price (bid the most) are indicating that they are more willing than other people to sacrifice some other goods in order to purchase health care.

In this chapter, we continue to use the example of health care to look at how the price mechanism operates to ration scarce goods and services. We outline what economists mean by a market and we illustrate why clearly defined property rights are essential if markets are to work effectively. The chapter also examines how the forces of supply and demand serve to establish 'normal' prices in markets. Finally, we show how the equilibrium of supply and demand in a market maximizes the total benefits received by buyers and sellers.

What is a market?

One way in which the problem of scarcity in health care can be overcome is to let people buy the health care they want. To some extent this is what happens with cosmetic surgery. Men can have a facelift for about £2,500, a nose correction for just over £2,000, and their eyes tightened for about £3,000. Such treatments (and many more) are available if you are willing and able to pay for them. Health care of this kind is sold just like any consumer good. People buy the treatment because they gain satisfaction from it, just as they would by purchasing a new car or a new television. The market for cosmetic surgery shows that it is possible to buy and sell health care. To understand how a market in health care might work as a resource allocation system, we need to develop a theoretical analysis of how markets operate.

The idea of a market for many people is one of back-to-back stalls in a town centre selling anything from fruit and vegetables to designer jeans. But, for economists, the term **market** has a much wider meaning. It is used to describe any process of exchange between buyers and sellers. Formally, a market can be defined as any set of arrangements that allows buyers and sellers to communicate and thus arrange exchange of goods, services, or resources. So, there are markets for the buying and selling of houses (the housing market), for the buying and selling of shares (the stock market), and for the buying and selling of footballers (the player transfer market). A free market is where such exchange occurs without any government intervention. Information is a vital ingredient for any market; both buyers and sellers need to have access to sufficient information if they are to make rational decisions. Thus, a buyer of a house is likely to have a structural survey undertaken before going ahead with the purchase, and a football manager will have a player watched closely before deciding whether or not to buy him.

One of the most striking features of a free market economy is that no-one issues commands or provides directions. Instead, markets act in the following ways: (i) they allocate resources to the production of different goods and services, (ii) they determine what resource mix to employ, and (iii) they distribute the goods and services among households. According to Adam Smith in his book *Wealth of Nations* (1776), it is the invisible hand of self-interest that acts as the guiding force in the market. This force is self-interested, maximizing behaviour with people responding to incentives. These incentives appear in the form of changes in prices, wages, and profits. But, for markets to work effectively there must be clearly defined property rights.

The role of property rights[1]

Property rights define the ownership of goods, services, and resources and set limits on their transfer and use. But why are property rights necessary for the proper functioning of markets? Isn't it sufficient simply to think of goods being physically traded and of possession? After all, when you buy a car the seller transfers possession of the physical object called a car to you in return for your transferring money to the seller. But this is not a complete picture of the transaction. As well as gaining possession of the car, you also gain a range of ownership rights; you take on a number of responsibilities for the car, and at the same time you become entitled to compensation if the car is damaged. The idea of ownership is more complicated than the idea of simple possession. This point is important because it is the idea of ownership that is relevant to most cases of trade. Typically, we do not trade all of our ownership rights; for example, when you rent a video recorder from an electrical shop, the shop trades some of its rights in the product (the right to record and play tapes) but not others (the right to sell the video recorder).

It is actually quite difficult to discuss ownership without reference to property rights. Your ownership of any particular item conveys a whole set of different rights, each of which may be traded separately. Where a system of property rights is in place, a wide range of deals (such as the video rental deal) can be done that could not be done if trade were restricted to goods and services that can be simply possessed. This is one of the major advantages of a system of property rights.

Is it possible to trade without property rights? Imagine a simple society in which there are no property rights. In this kind of society no-one can own anything, although individuals can still possess things. For example, if you pick a pear from a tree you possess that pear, but you would not own it in the sense of having any rights to the pear. If someone else took the pear from you, they would then possess it and you would have no real case for claiming it back. In such a society, provided possessions can be defended, trade can take place on the basis of possession but not on the basis of ownership. In other words, to keep what you possess you need to be able to fight anyone attempting to take the pear. In this case, anyone wishing to gain possession of a pear has three choices: find their own pear, fight you for this pear, or trade something they possess for the pear. But trade based upon simple possession and the threat of fighting is clearly inefficient since a scarce resource (labour) is being wasted. Instead of everyone spending time and effort defending their possessions, they could be doing something useful.

Even though property rights are important, it is not obvious why individuals should respect property rights. As long as other people fail to guard their possessions because they think you will respect their property, it will be easier (less costly) for you to take their possessions. One way of explaining respect for property rights is to assume a universal sense of moral duty; a second approach is to assume the existence of an agency enforcing property rights; a third possibility is that everyone recognizes the mutual benefits of respect for property rights and therefore does not infringe such rights, in which case there is no need for an over-riding sense of morality or for an enforcement agency.

Where an enforcement agency is needed the costs of defending property rights are shifted from the individual to the enforcement agency (part of the government, perhaps). The costs of maintaining and enforcing a system of property rights are the disadvantages of having such a system. Many of the costs associated with the legal system, the police force, and the criminal justice system are incurred in establishing a degree of security of property rights. When we look at it in this way, the institution of private property is a costly institution, but it does enable a wider range of markets to operate at lower costs.

The demand for health care

Both buyers and sellers need to be involved for a market to work. It is the forces of consumer demand and producer supply that operate in markets to determine prices. We will find it easier to understand the price mechanism if we separate the two sides of the market and study them individually. We begin with the demand side of the story.

Before focusing on the demand for health care, we need to ask, 'who are the buyers and who are the sellers in the health care market?' We all want to be healthy and so almost all of us would be prepared, if necessary, to buy medical treatment to cure an illness. This suggests that all of us are potential buyers (or consumers) of health care. More precisely, at any point in time, buyers are those who are ill, or those who want preventative treatment (such as a vaccination), or those who want guidance about their health. The sellers in the health care market are those people who can provide medical and health care services, such as doctors, nurses, dentists, and physiotherapists.

To illustrate the idea of a market we use osteopathy as our example. Until 1993 anyone in the UK could establish an osteopathy practice. Osteopaths operated outside the National Health Service, selling their services directly to consumers. Osteopaths worked either in small practices or as individuals and all of them sold a very similar service. This meant that the market for osteopathy corresponded quite closely to the economist's notion of a market. Since 1993 the market for osteopathy has been subject to tighter government regulation, so that today it is less like a free market.

Analysing the behaviour of buyers

What determines how much osteopathy people are willing to buy at any particular moment in time? The most important factor is the price of the treatment. *Ceteris paribus*, the more expensive it is to buy osteopathy, the less we will be prepared to buy and vice versa. This behaviour represents the **law of demand**. The law of demand says that at higher prices buyers demand smaller amounts, while at lower prices they demand larger amounts, everything else remaining constant. Why is this?

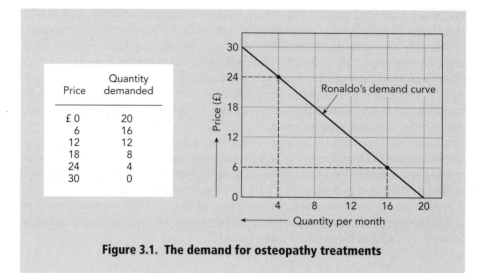

Price	Quantity demanded
£ 0	20
6	16
12	12
18	8
24	4
30	0

Figure 3.1. The demand for osteopathy treatments

When the price of osteopathy rises two things happen. First of all, relative prices change, and, second, our real income changes. We take both of these changes into account when we react to the price increase. The change in relative prices means osteopathy is now more expensive in relation to other goods and services. How do we deal with this? Since we try to get as much satisfaction as possible from our consumption of goods and services (we are maximizers), we react to the fact that the good is now relatively more expensive by choosing to buy less of it (this is called the **substitution effect** of a price change).

The increase in the price of osteopathy also reduces our real income. This means we can now buy less than before with our money income. For example, if you have a money income of £100 and the price of a treatment is £10, you can buy 10 treatments. But, if the price of a treatment rises to £20 with no change in your money income, you can now only buy 5 treatments. The way in which we react to a change in our real income depends on the nature of the good or service. Osteopathy, like most goods, is a **normal good**. That is, an increase in income leads to an increase in demand and vice versa. So, a fall in our real income further reduces the amount of treatment we wish to buy (this is called the **income effect** of a price change). When you see people living with their ailments rather than buying treatment as the price goes up, you are witnessing the law of demand in action.

This predictable relationship between price and quantity demanded allows us to develop a formal definition of demand. **Demand** refers to the quantity of a good or service that buyers are willing and able to buy at every conceivable price during a particular period of time. The **demand curve** in Figure 3.1 shows this relationship graphically. The curve represents Ronaldo's demand for osteopathy. At a price of £24 per treatment, he buys 4 treatments per month. At the lower price of £6 he purchases 16 treatments per month. We see that Ronaldo's quantity demanded increases with lower prices and falls with higher prices (it follows the law of demand). Note that a change in price leads to a *movement along* the demand curve.

It is also helpful to distinguish between individual and market demand. The **market demand** for a good or service is simply the sum of the demands of all consumers in a market at each conceivable price. Figure 3.2 shows a market demand curve for osteopathy, obtained

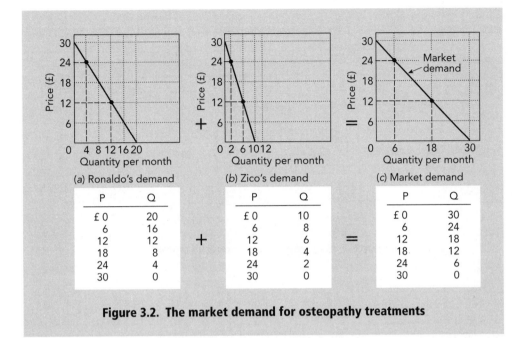

Figure 3.2. The market demand for osteopathy treatments

by summing two individual demand curves horizontally (for a two-person market). Each person's quantity demanded at each price is added. For example, at a price of £12 Ronaldo's quantity demanded is 12 treatments, while Zico's is 6, hence the total market demand is 18 treatments. If the price of a treatment was £24, their respective quantities demanded would be 4 and 2, making the total demand in the market equal to 6 treatments per month. Part (*c*) of Figure 3.2 is therefore the sum of parts (*a*) and (*b*).

The supply of health care

Demand is only part of the story of how market prices are determined. The way in which quantities supplied by osteopaths relate to price is the other component. We assume that the sellers of treatment (the osteopaths) wish to maximize their **profits**. We discuss the idea of profit more fully in later chapters, but for now it is sufficient to look at it in this way. Osteopaths earn money (revenue) by selling their services (treating joint problems). Out of this revenue they have to pay for the resources (or factors of production) they use to produce the treatment (costs). For example, costs are incurred in paying the rent on the property, in paying for staff, and in paying for new equipment. Profit is simply the excess of revenue over costs.

Because osteopaths seek to maximize profits they each want to sell more treatment at higher prices. There is, therefore, a predictable positive relationship between price and quantity supplied. Formally, **supply** is defined as the quantity of a good or service that sellers are willing and able to sell at every conceivable price during a particular period of time. This positive relationship is shown graphically as the supply curve in Figure 3.3. The **supply curve** reflects the law of supply. The **law of supply** says that the quantity offered for sale is positively related

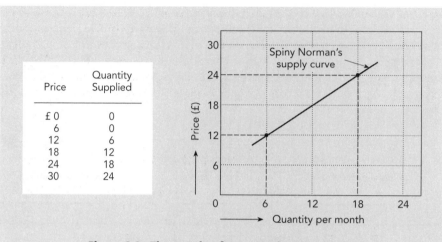

Figure 3.3. The supply of osteopathy treatments

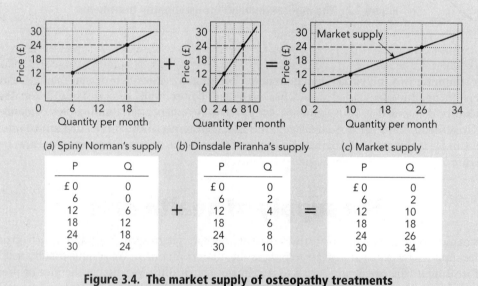

Figure 3.4. The market supply of osteopathy treatments

to the price; larger amounts are offered for sale at higher prices and smaller amounts are offered at lower prices, everything else remaining constant. If the price alters there is a *movement along* the supply curve. We can see this in Figure 3.3, which represents Spiny Norman's supply of treatments at each possible price. At a price of £12 he offers 6 treatments per month. At the higher price of £24 he is prepared to offer 18 treatments. Spiny Norman's quantity supplied increases with higher prices and falls with lower prices (it follows the law of supply).

As with demand, it is helpful to distinguish between individual and market supply. **Market supply** is the horizontal sum of the individual supply curves of osteopaths. Figure 3.4 shows a market supply curve, derived by adding the amounts supplied at each price by two osteopaths, Spiny Norman and Dinsdale Piranha. For example, at a price of £12 per treatment Spiny Norman is willing to supply 6 treatments, and Dinsdale Piranha is willing to supply 4 treatments. So, at this price the market supply is 10 treatments per month. If the price rose to £24, their respective quantities supplied would be 18 and 8 treatments per month, making a total supply in the market of 26 treatments. Part (*c*) of Figure 3.4 is therefore the sum of parts (*a*) and (*b*).

Market equilibrium

We can now put the two sides of the market together to get a picture of the market for osteopathy. This is shown in Figure 3.5. Notice that there is only one price at which the quantity of treatments people want to buy is the same as the quantity that osteopaths want to sell. This is called the **equilibrium price** and it occurs at the point of intersection of the supply curve (S_{market}) and the demand curve (D_{market}). **Equilibrium** means a state of rest where there is no pressure for change. In Figure 3.5, the equilibrium price (P_e) is £15 and the equilibrium quantity (Q_e) is 15 treatments. At any other price either buyers or sellers are dissatisfied and act to change the price.

We need to consider in a little more detail the establishment of the equilibrium price and quantity. The adjustment towards equilibrium can be shown with an example. Table 3.1 combines the information from our previous examples, using the market demand and supply schedules derived earlier. It is only at the equilibrium price of £15 that the quantity supplied (15) equals the quantity demanded (15). At the equilibrium price the market is said to clear. At prices below the equilibrium, such as £6, the quantity of treatments demanded by consumers is more than osteopaths are able and willing to supply, hence a temporary shortage of 22 treatments per month is created (24 treatments are demanded but only 2 are supplied). In this situation, consumers bid the price up to try to get a few more treatments whenever

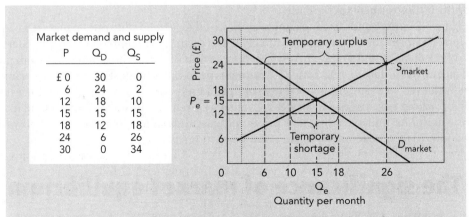

Market demand and supply		
P	Q_D	Q_S
£ 0	30	0
6	24	2
12	18	10
15	15	15
18	12	18
24	6	26
30	0	34

Figure 3.5. The market for osteopathy treatments: the market is in equilibrium at P_e and Q_e

Table 3.1. Equilibrium in the osteopathy market

Price (£)	Quantity demanded per month	Quantity supplied per month	Temporary shortage (−) or surplus (+)
0	30	0	−30
6	24	2	−22
12	18	10	−8
15	15	15	0
18	12	18	+6
24	6	26	+20
30	0	34	+34

there are some available. As prices rise, some consumers drop out of the market and some osteopaths increase their supply. Prices rise to the £15 equilibrium price, at which the temporary shortage is wiped out. At this higher price, consumers want fewer treatments (15 instead of 24) and osteopaths supply more (15 instead of 2). Thus, the actions of both buyers and sellers serve to eliminate the temporary shortage and establish an equilibrium quantity that allows the market to clear.

At prices above the equilibrium level, the number of treatments osteopaths wish to supply is greater than the quantity consumers wish to buy in the market, hence a temporary surplus is created. Again, the problem is eliminated over time by buyers (consumers) and sellers (osteopaths) pursuing their own self-interest. At the price of £24 per treatment, osteopaths want to sell 26 treatments each month, but consumers will only buy 6. The temporary surplus is equal to the difference between the quantity supplied and the quantity demanded, or 20 treatments per month. Osteopaths will act to reduce the price, causing them to supply less and consumers to buy more. Actions on both sides of the market eliminate the temporary surplus as the price falls, ultimately establishing the equilibrium price of £15 and the equilibrium quantity of 15 treatments per month.

Figure 3.5 corresponds to the example given in Table 3.1 and illustrates a market in equilibrium. As noted above, the equilibrium price and quantity are represented by the intersection of the demand and supply curves. This intersection occurs at the same equilibrium price and quantity as in Table 3.1: £15 and 15 treatments per month. In most markets equilibrium is rarely achieved for very long, because demand and supply curves are prone to alter their position for various reasons (as we will see in Chapter 4). Even so, this supply and demand model is very useful for understanding how prices and quantities adjust in a market and how they move toward their equilibrium values at any given moment.

The significance of market equilibrium

Figure 3.5 shows that the equilibrium price (£15) is determined by the forces of supply and demand. We can use this diagram to understand a little more the idea of **allocative efficiency** (introduced in Chapter 2 in the context of the production possibilities frontier). When a market

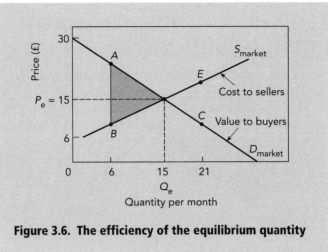

Figure 3.6. The efficiency of the equilibrium quantity

is in equilibrium, the price determines which buyers and sellers participate in the market. Anyone who values a treatment more than the market price will buy a treatment, while anyone who values a treatment below the market price will not purchase a treatment. In this sense, the demand curve represents consumers' willingness to pay (it is a 'willingness-to-pay curve'). Similarly, those osteopaths whose costs are below the market price choose to supply treatments, while those osteopaths whose costs are above the market price will not supply any treatments. Thus, the supply curve represents the osteopaths' (or suppliers') minimum supply price. So, in equilibrium (where supply equals demand) the valuation of the marginal consumer—the consumer who is just willing to pay for the extra cost involved in producing the treatment—is the same as the extra cost of supplying the product. In this sense, the equilibrium price is a 'fair' price since those people who would like the price to be lower and to buy more than Q_e are not prepared to pay the extra costs involved.

Also, for any given quantity of treatment, if the value to buyers (willingness to pay) exceeds the cost to osteopaths (minimum supply price) there is always an increase in society's net valuation of the output. Figure 3.6 shows this important result. At a quantity of 6 treatments per month, the value to buyers (measured by point A on the demand curve) exceeds the cost to osteopaths (shown by point B on the supply curve). In fact, at up to 15 treatments per month the value of the output to buyers is greater than the cost to the osteopaths, hence, within the shaded region, an increase in the quantity of treatments raises the net valuation of the output. On the other hand, at a quantity of 21 treatments per month the value to buyers (point C on the demand curve) is less than the cost to osteopaths (point E on the supply curve), so producing more than the equilibrium amount reduces the net valuation. Thus, the equilibrium quantity is the one that maximizes society's net valuation of the product. In the free market equilibrium, therefore, we have an efficient allocation of resources, or allocative efficiency.

An alternative way to look at the efficiency of a market equilibrium is in terms of consumer surplus and producer surplus. Since the demand curve measures peoples' willingness to pay, it enables us to infer the value they place on what they consume. Any surplus of this value over and above what consumers actually pay is called consumer surplus. So, **consumer surplus** is

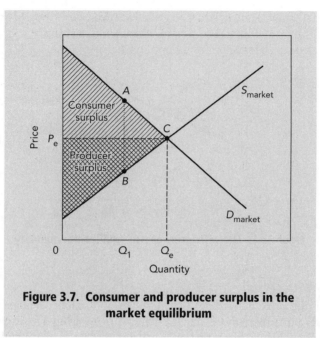

Figure 3.7. Consumer and producer surplus in the market equilibrium

the excess of what consumers would be willing to pay over what they actually pay. It can be computed by finding the area below the demand curve and above the price. Since the supply curve represents suppliers' minimum supply price, we can infer the benefit sellers get from participating in a market. If the amount received for selling a good is above the minimum amount sellers are willing to accept for the good, there is a surplus to producers. So, **producer surplus** is the amount sellers receive for their goods minus the minimum amount they are willing to accept. It can be computed by finding the area below the price and above the supply curve. These concepts are shown in Figure 3.7.

One way to measure the benefit to society of a free market outcome is to sum consumer and producer surplus. This measure is known as the **total surplus** (or **net valuation**) in a market. It is the total value to buyers of the goods minus the costs to sellers of providing those goods. In a free market the 'correct' quantity of goods is produced in the sense that the total surplus (the sum of consumer and producer surplus) is maximized. In Figure 3.7, if the quantity is below the equilibrium level (say at Q_1) the total surplus is not at a maximum; it can be increased in size by the area of the triangle ABC by raising output to the equilibrium level (Q_e). Producing more than the equilibrium level of output would lower the total surplus. Only at the equilibrium quantity is society's net valuation of the product (total surplus) at a maximum, hence we have an efficient allocation of resources.

Summary

1. A market describes any set of arrangements that allows buyers and sellers to communicate and thus arrange exchange of goods, services, or resources.

2. Property rights define the ownership of goods, services, and resources and set limits on their transfer and use. A central body (government) provides a framework of property rights and enforcement that enables a market system to work.

3. The substitution effect of a price change is the incentive for the consumer to substitute a particular good for others when that good's price falls or to substitute other goods when its price rises, because the opportunity cost of the good changes when its price changes. The income effect means that a lower price enables consumers to buy more of a good with the extra spending power of their income that results from the price cut. A price increase lowers the income available, so quantity demanded falls.

4. The forces of supply and demand set prices in markets. Market prices reflect the relative scarcity of goods, serve as a rationing mechanism, and provide signals to guide production and exchange.

5. Demand is a schedule showing the quantities consumers are willing and able to buy at every conceivable price during a specified time period. Demand curves slope downward to the right because of the law of demand. This says that at higher prices buyers demand smaller amounts, while at lower prices they demand larger amounts, everything else remaining constant.

6. Supply is a schedule showing the quantities producers are willing and able to sell at every conceivable price over a specified time period. Supply curves slope upward to the right because of the law of supply. This says that the quantity offered for sale is positively related to the price; larger amounts are offered for sale at higher prices and smaller amounts are offered at lower prices, *ceteris paribus*.

7. Equilibrium exists at the price at which quantity demanded just equals quantity supplied. There are no forces at work to change price or quantity. It is shown graphically by the intersection of the supply curve and the demand curve.

8. If the market price is above (below) the equilibrium price a temporary surplus (shortage) exists. The actions of buyers and sellers pursuing their own self-interest work to restore the equilibrium.

9. Consumer surplus is the excess of what consumers would be willing to pay for a good over what they actually pay. It can be computed by finding the area below the demand curve and above the price. Producer surplus is the amount sellers receive for their goods minus the minimum amount they are willing to accept. It can be computed by finding the area below the price and above the supply curve.

10. The equilibrium of supply and demand maximizes the total surplus (the sum of consumer and producer surplus) in a market. An allocation of resources that maximizes the total surplus is said to be efficient.

Key terms

allocative efficiency	market supply
consumer surplus	net valuation
demand	normal good
demand curve	producer surplus
equilibrium	profits
equilibrium price	property rights
income effect	substitution effect
law of demand	supply
law of supply	supply curve
market	total surplus
market demand	

Review questions

1. What property rights does the owner of a house enjoy? What restrictions does government place on the owner's property rights?

2. Imagine a town where there is no free health service. The information below shows a hypothetical demand schedule for doctors' services.

Price of consultations (£)	Quantity of consultations demanded per month
0	600
5	400
10	150
15	100
20	90

   (i) Draw a demand curve for doctors' services using this information.
  (ii) If the price of each consultation is £5, what is the total amount people will spend on consultations?

(iii) If the price of a consultation rose from £10 to £20, what would happen to the quantity demanded?

3. Imagine a town where there is no free health service. The information below shows a hypothetical supply schedule for doctors' services.

Price of consultations (£)	Quantity of consultations supplied per month
0	0
5	40
10	80
15	100
20	150

(i) Draw a supply curve for doctors' services using this information.
(ii) If the price of consultations rose from £5 to £15, what would happen to the quantity of consultations doctors are prepared to supply?

4. Use your answers to part (i) of Questions 2 and 3 to draw a market diagram for doctors' services.

(i) What is the equilibrium price and quantity?
(ii) How much revenue are doctors receiving?

5. Define the terms *demand*, *supply*, and *market equilibrium*.

6. Suppose the equilibrium price is £4 and the equilibrium quantity is 1,500 in the market for luminous socks. Sellers tell you they could sell 2,000 pairs of socks if they cut the price to £3; however, at £3 they would be willing to supply only 1,000 pairs. Assuming both the supply curve and the demand curve are straight lines, draw the market situation described by this information.

7. Use a supply and demand diagram to show consumer and producer surplus when a market is in equilibrium. In what sense is this an efficient outcome?

Note

1. This is adapted from Alan Hamlin, 'Private Property', *Economic Review*, 11. 1 (Sept. 1993), 7–9.

Further reading

- Mabry and Ulbrich, chapter 4
- Lipsey and Chrystal, chapter 3
- Sloman, chapter 2

Markets: some extensions

In Chapter 3, we showed how the demand for and supply of osteopathy treatment determines equilibrium prices and quantities in that market. The same principles of supply and demand operate in all markets. We also said that equilibrium in markets is often temporary because demand and supply curves frequently shift their position. Here, we consider what other factors affect the positions of supply and demand curves.

We also extend the analysis by applying the supply and demand model to the idea of disequilibrium in markets. What happens when market prices cannot adjust upward or downward? Why are markets sometimes characterized by persistent shortages or surpluses? These effects are illustrated with reference to price controls in the market for private rented accommodation (rent controls) and in the market for European agriculture (the Common Agricultural Policy).

Changes in the demand for and supply of health care

Price is the main factor affecting how much osteopathy consumers buy and how much osteopaths produce. But it is not the only factor. Demand and supply curves reflect the relationship between price and quantity demanded or price and quantity supplied, holding everything else constant (*ceteris paribus*). What other factors affect the positions of demand and supply curves? What happens to either curve if not everything else is constant?

Market demand

Changes in a number of factors can cause demand to increase or decrease *independently* of price. These factors include income, preferences, and the price of other goods, and are known as the **determinants of demand**. Because osteopathy is a normal good, a rise in income means we will buy more treatment at each price; if income falls we will buy less at each price. If preferences change in favour of (against) osteopathy we will buy more (less) at each price. Finally, the prices of related services will affect our demand for osteopathy. An obvious example is the price of physiotherapy, which is an alternative treatment for many of the conditions treated by osteopaths. For example, if the price of physiotherapy falls then some people are likely to switch from osteopathy to physiotherapy, so the demand for osteopathy would fall.

Whenever there is a change in income, preferences, or the price of a related good or service, the demand curve shifts, as shown in Figure 4.1. The original demand curve is D_0. If income

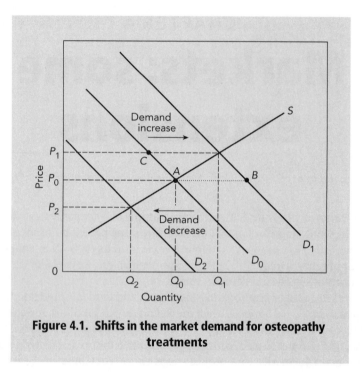

Figure 4.1. Shifts in the market demand for osteopathy treatments

rises, or preferences change in favour of osteopathy, or the price of physiotherapy rises, the demand curve shifts to D_1. The shift of the demand curve to the right represents an increase in demand. Demand will fall (the demand curve will shift from D_0 to D_2) if income falls, or preferences change against osteopathy, or if the price of physiotherapy falls.

Changes in demand and quantity demanded

The distinction between changes in demand and changes in quantity demanded is one of the most important aspects of demand analysis. Demand is a schedule of price–quantity combinations. Thus, a **change in demand** means all the quantities in the schedule change for each price; that is, the demand curve *shifts* such that different quantities correspond to each possible price. This change in demand must be due to a change in one or more of the factors listed in relation to Figure 4.1. So, in Figure 4.1, the shift in the demand curve (from either D_0 to D_1 or D_0 to D_2) shows a change in demand. To illustrate this idea, we locate the price P_0 and the point A on the original demand curve D_0. When the demand curve shifts to D_1, we move to point B for the same price P_0. The move from A to B is thus an increase in demand; at the price of P_0 demand is higher at point B than it is at point A. When the demand curve shifts to the right we have an increase in demand at each possible price. So, a change in demand results in the entire demand curve shifting its position.

A **change in quantity demanded**, however, only occurs when the price of a good (in this case osteopathy) changes. Changes in quantity demanded involve *movements along* the same demand curve from one price–quantity combination to another (as we saw in Chapter 3). These movements are always the result of a change in price. In Figure 4.1, an increase in price

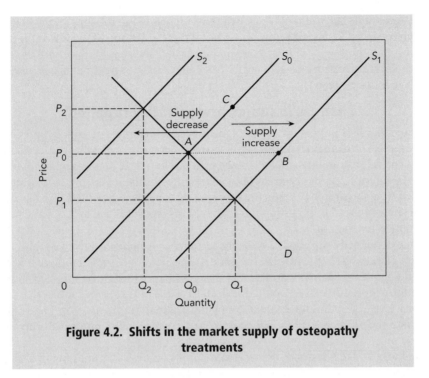

Figure 4.2. Shifts in the market supply of osteopathy treatments

from P_0 to P_1 produces a change in quantity demanded: the fall in quantity demanded along demand curve D_0 is shown by the move from A to C. Notice that the demand curve after the price change is the same as before the price change; only quantity demanded changes, and not demand.

Market supply

Price is the primary influence on quantity supplied as well as quantity demanded. The supply curve shows the relationship between price and quantities supplied, holding all other influences constant. Among the other factors which affect quantities of osteopathy treatment supplied, independent of price, are the number of sellers of osteopathy, and the prices of the factors of production. These other influences are called the **determinants of supply**.

The number of osteopaths supplying a service in a market affects the market supply. This is because market supply is the sum of the supply curves of individual osteopaths. When additional osteopaths enter a market, larger quantities of that service are available at all possible prices, shifting the market supply curve to the right. Similarly, supply falls when osteopaths leave the profession, shifting the supply curve to the left. We can see this in Figure 4.2. An increase in supply is shown by the shift of the supply curve from S_0 to S_1, while a fall in supply is represented by the supply curve shifting from S_0 to S_2.

When there is an increase in the prices of factors of production (such as land or labour), the supply of osteopathy treatments decreases; that is, the entire supply schedule shifts to the left (from S_0 to S_2 in Figure 4.2). So, if the wages of nurses increase or if there is a rise in land rents, the supply of the service falls for any given price. If, on the other hand, the wages of nurses go down or if land rents fall, the supply of treatments increases and the supply curve shifts to the right (from S_0 to S_1 in Figure 4.2). To summarize, if there are more osteopaths in the market or factor prices fall, the supply of treatments increases and the supply curve shifts to the right. If there are fewer osteopaths or factor prices rise, the supply of treatments decreases and the supply curve shifts to the left.

Changes in supply and quantity supplied

As with demand, it is important to distinguish between changes in supply and changes in quantity supplied. A **change in supply** results from a change in one of the factors which causes the entire schedule of amounts offered at each price to change. It is shown by a shift in the supply curve. In Figure 4.2, a change in supply is represented by the *shifts* from S_0 to S_1 and S_0 to S_2. At a price of P_0, along supply curve S_0, the supply of osteopathy is at point A. For the same price P_0, and the new supply curve S_1, supply is represented by point B. So, for the same price of P_0, supply is larger than before.

A **change in quantity supplied** always refers to a *movement along* a given supply curve, and is the result of a change in the price of the good or service. For instance, if there is an increase in the market price of osteopathy treatments, a larger quantity would be supplied at the higher price, but the supply curve itself would not shift. In terms of Figure 4.2, if the price rises from P_0 to P_2 we move from point A to point C along the original supply curve S_0. The price change does not alter the position of the supply curve; price changes cause movements up and down the curve.

Having looked at the basics of demand and supply analysis, we are now in a position to examine the supply and demand model in greater detail, and apply the analysis to a variety of interesting economic questions.

Market disequilibrium

So far we have seen how the forces of supply and demand determine equilibrium prices and quantities in markets. We have also seen that markets are self-correcting in the sense that when there are temporary shortages or surpluses, market forces act to correct the problem and restore equilibrium. But this is not the complete story; some markets do not achieve equilibrium even when the forces of supply and demand have had time to adjust. The blocking of the price adjustment mechanism is often due to the law or other government action. Blocking the price mechanism may sometimes be desirable and justifiable, but it always results in **market disequilibrium**. Whatever the reason for government intervention, market disequilibrium takes the form of either a persistent shortage or a persistent surplus.

Persistent shortages

When the market price is below the equilibrium level and it is not allowed to adjust upward to the equilibrium price, market forces cannot eliminate excess quantity demanded. This excess quantity demanded is a **persistent shortage**. Suppose a law was passed which held down the price of osteopathy treatments to a maximum of £10. Such a law establishes a **price ceiling** or a legal maximum price. What would be the result of setting a ceiling price of £10? In Figure 4.3, the ceiling price of £10 would create an excess quantity demanded of 8 treatments per month (the quantity demanded is 18 treatments but the quantity supplied is only 10). If the price

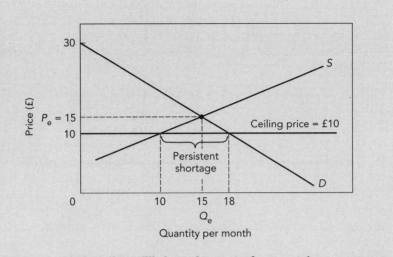

Figure 4.3. Market disequilibrium: shortage of osteopathy treatments

could be bid up, the number of treatments demanded by consumers would fall as the price rose and the number supplied by osteopaths would rise, eliminating the temporary shortage. Graphically, as the price goes above £10, we move up the supply curve in a north-easterly direction (increasing the quantity supplied) and up the demand curve in a north-westerly direction (reducing the quantity demanded) until we reach the point where the two curves intersect.

However, government action now makes it illegal for osteopaths to raise the price above the ceiling level. As a result, the market cannot reach equilibrium. A persistent shortage of 8 treatments will remain until the law is changed, until the legal maximum price is raised to or above the equilibrium price, or until the supply and demand curves shift in response to other factors. For example, a fall in consumer incomes might shift the demand curve far enough to the left so that it crosses the supply curve at a price of £10. If that were to happen, the shortage would be wiped out. Note that a price ceiling is only effective when it is set below the equilibrium price.

Although this example is hypothetical, ceiling prices that result in persistent shortages do exist. A good example is the use of **rent controls** in private sector housing markets. In the UK, rent controls were introduced as a temporary measure in 1915, and they still exist in a very limited form today. Rent controls in other countries go back as far as the early nineteenth century, and they continue to play a significant role in housing markets. Rent controls were designed to help low-income tenants who could not afford to pay the market rent. But because there is a persistent shortage of rent-controlled accommodation, landlords are able to discriminate among renters. Renters often have to 'know someone' in order to obtain rent-controlled accommodation, or they may pay 'key money' (effectively, the payment of a higher rent) in order to jump the queue. Also, because it is illegal for landlords to raise rents (although many do) they have little incentive to fix faults and make general repairs. As a result, much of the accommodation in the rent-controlled sector is allowed to deteriorate over time.

Most economists oppose laws that mandate ceiling prices, because such laws prevent the price mechanism from carrying out its rationing function. If there is a housing shortage,

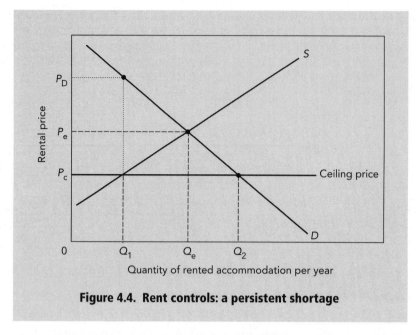

Figure 4.4. Rent controls: a persistent shortage

controlling rents will not create new housing. Rent controls simply alter the way scarce accommodation is rationed among competing users. Instead of rationing based on price, the rationing method may be 'first-come, first-served'. Those who actually get accommodation at rents below the equilibrium level come out ahead. Other groups, however, lose from rent controls. To see who gains and who loses, consider the rental price ceiling in Figure 4.4.

Without rent controls, the equilibrium price would be P_e and the equilibrium quantity would be Q_e. At the controlled price of P_c, however, only Q_1 amount of accommodation is supplied and occupied. Thus, Q_1 to Q_e is the amount of accommodation lost due to rent control, and the people who would have occupied this accommodation lose. Furthermore, Q_e to Q_2 is the amount of extra accommodation (beyond the equilibrium amount) that people want at the artificially low controlled price. Also, note that at the amount of accommodation available, Q_1, some people are willing to pay landlords as much as P_D (reading from the demand curve) to secure the rent-controlled accommodation. This represents the payment of 'key money'.

So, because rent controls prevent the price system from carrying out its rationing function, the amount of accommodation available at the rent-controlled price is insufficient to satisfy the demand. There is a persistent shortage of accommodation because rents cannot be bid upwards to clear the market. This kind of analysis helps explain why the previous Conservative government all but phased out this particular price ceiling. The current Labour government's attitude to rent controls is not very different. In the main, rents will be allowed to adjust to their market clearing level. If this adversely affects low-income groups in the housing market, then alternative schemes need to be developed to provide enough affordable housing. So, what might be done? The following extracts from the *Guardian* newspaper suggest that the solution is new house-building; they also illustrate how the housing market provides a good example of economics in action:

There is good reason to be concerned about the housing market . . . We are not building nearly enough new homes, so if demand takes off again . . . there could be another bout of price inflation. Instead of using subsidies to build cheap, affordable houses for purchase or rent, the government is spending £8.6 million (and rising fast) on income support for those who cannot afford their rents—which are higher than they ought to be, given the shortage of accommodation caused by houses not being built. Landlords and subsidised tenants have a vested interest in higher rents if the tab is picked up by the taxpayer. Why on earth shouldn't most of this money be used to build more affordable homes, especially for the low-paid? (21 August 1995)

[T]he total of new houses started last year—199,000—is still 21 per cent below 1988 and 43 per cent below the Macmillan peak (1954). There is no shortage of people wanting homes. An authoritative report for the Joseph Rowntree Foundation . . . forecasts that during the two decades to 2011 there will be demand for about 250,000 new dwellings annually for sale or rent in England alone. This is well above the current rate of housebuilding . . . But where will the new houses come from? Housing associations . . . do a good job, but they haven't risen to the magnitude of the task in hand. Owner occupation . . . is near saturation point . . . All this points to the need to rehabilitate the council house . . . Local councils must now be allowed to use the proceeds of their asset sales to build affordable homes. The government's policy of switching subsidies from bricks and mortar to people is now counter-productive. Rents have been raised so much that any further rises will only be offset by matching increases in housing and other benefits . . . (30 October 1995)

Persistent surpluses

Just as governments can be persuaded to keep prices from rising to their equilibrium levels for certain goods, they are often persuaded to set price floors. A **price floor** is where a legal minimum price is set so as to favour certain firms or groups. Price floors prevent prices from falling to their market clearing (or equilibrium) levels. Thus, effective price floors create a **persistent surplus**, or chronic excess quantity supplied. If a price floor is to have any effect it must be set above the equilibrium price. A good example of a price floor is found in the **Common Agricultural Policy** (CAP) operated by the European Union (EU). A simple illustration of the CAP is shown in Figure 4.5.

Figure 4.5 represents the market for cereals. Without any intervention the free market price is £15 per tonne and the equilibrium quantity is 15 tonnes. But the floor price is set above £15, at £20 per tonne of wheat. This creates a surplus in the market of 20 tonnes (the quantity demanded is 6 tonnes and the quantity supplied is 26 tonnes). In a free market, the price adjustment mechanism would operate to wipe out the surplus. The price would be bid down to the equilibrium level. A lower price would raise quantity demanded (we move down the demand curve in a south-easterly direction) and decrease quantity supplied (we move down the supply curve in a south-westerly direction) until the equilibrium price of £15 is restored. But the CAP does not allow this to happen. For equilibrium to be established, we require either a change in policy or a shift in the demand curve or the supply curve.

The CAP results in minimum prices being set for many agricultural products, from milk to wheat. These price floors are designed to help (transfer income to) poor farmers. But the CAP keeps prices unnecessarily high for consumers and results in surpluses (wine lakes, butter mountains, and so on) that cause headaches for the EU. In many cases, these surplus commodities are bought by the EU (all taxpayers) to distribute as school lunches, store for a 'rainy day', or distribute to needy people in non-EU countries (they become EU exports). So, like a price ceiling, a price floor prevents price from carrying out its rationing function. Whenever price is not allowed to adjust freely, scarce goods will be allocated among competing users in other ways.

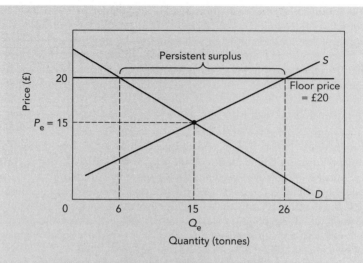

Figure 4.5. Market disequilibrium: surplus of cereals

Summary

1. Changes in the determinants of demand—consumer incomes, the price of related goods, and consumer preferences—cause demand curves to shift. A shift in the demand curve represents a change in demand. A movement along a demand curve is caused by a change in price and indicates a change in quantity demanded.

2. Changes in the determinants of supply—the number of producers, and the prices of factors of production—shift supply curves. A shift in the supply curve represents a change in supply. A movement along a supply curve is caused by a price change and indicates a change in quantity supplied.

3. Persistent shortages or persistent surpluses mean that a market is in disequilibrium. Price ceilings (such as rent controls) result in persistent shortages; prices cannot be bid upwards to eliminate the excess demand. Price floors (such as the CAP) create persistent surpluses; prices are prevented from being bid downwards to wipe out the excess supply.

Key terms

change in demand

change in quantity demanded

change in quantity supplied

change in supply

Common Agricultural Policy (CAP)

determinants of demand

determinants of supply

market disequilibrium

persistent shortage

persistent surplus

price ceiling

price floor

rent controls

Review questions

1. Imagine a town in which there is no free health service. The information below describes the demand and supply schedule for doctors' services. Use the information to draw a market diagram for doctors' services.

Price of consultations (£)	Quantity of consultations demanded per month	Quantity of consultations supplied per month
0	600	0
5	400	40
10	150	80
15	100	100
20	90	150

(i) A fall in costs causes supply to increase by 70 consultations per month at every price. Illustrate this on your diagram.

(ii) What is the new equilibrium price and quantity?

(iii) Describe how the market reaches its new equilibrium position.

(iv) An increase in income now causes demand to increase by 70 consultations per month at every price. Illustrate this on the same diagram.

(v) What is the new equilibrium price and quantity?

(vi) Describe how the market reaches its new equilibrium position.

2. 'Barbers in Leicester raised their regular haircut prices by £1 this week, and demand decreased immediately.' What is wrong with this statement?

3. The following extract is from the *Guardian* newspaper of 26 March 1996:

The price of poultry shot up by 12 per cent over the weekend and is expected to rise by almost as much again as the BSE scare hits sales of beef . . . All the large supermarket groups are understood to have recorded heavy falls in beef sales at the weekend—put at between 30 and 50 per cent by industry observers—and most were reimbursing customers who bought meat before the disclosure of the risk to human health.

Use supply and demand diagrams to illustrate the short-term effects of the BSE scare on the markets for beef and poultry. Why might you expect the prices of beef and poultry to return to their original levels in the longer term?

4. The following extract is from the *Guardian* newspaper of 6 June 1991:

In the quest for glamour and good looks, more and more youngsters are asking plastic surgeons to give nature a helping hand. Plastic surgery is gaining popularity among the young. At the Pountney Clinic, the average age for a nose job (rhinoplasty) is now just 22, down from 31 in 1985. The average for ear correction is 21. It is not yet as common in Britain as in America, where 640,000 operations were performed last year and where TV programmes like *Beverley Hills 90210* suggest you're not allowed to graduate from a Californian high school unless you've got a liposuctioned bum. A 20-year-old waiting for a breast enlargement operation at the West Hampstead Clinic, when asked why now, replied 'We've just got the money. My husband got a big quarterly bonus.'

   (i)   Why are more young people demanding plastic surgery?
  (ii)   What would you expect to happen to the price of plastic surgery as demand grows?
 (iii)   Draw a simple supply and demand diagram to analyse this information.
  (iv)   How would you expect suppliers to react to the increase in demand?
   (v)   Market theory assumes that the consumers are able to make rational buying decisions. Do you think that this applies to cosmetic surgery?

5. During the winter of 1777–8 the Pennsylvania state legislature introduced price controls on those commodities (for example, grain) most used by George Washington's army. The theory was that this policy would reduce the expense of supplying the army. Use supply and demand analysis to explain why price controls almost resulted in Washington's army starving to death. (The price controls were ended by the Continental Congress on 4 June 1778.)

6. With the aid of diagrams, show why a surplus of cereals will develop if the EU regulates the price of cereals above the market clearing level.

Further reading

- Mabry and Ulbrich, chapter 5

- Lipsey and Chrystal, chapter 3
- Sloman, chapter 3

CHAPTER 5

Applications of market analysis

In Chapters 3 and 4, we outlined the basics of the supply and demand model and demonstrated how it could be used to examine the idea of market disequilibrium. In particular, we looked at how government intervention in markets prevents the price mechanism from rationing scarce goods among competing users. In this chapter, we extend the analysis of supply and demand, to show you how the model can be applied to a number of real-world issues facing consumers, business, and government; namely, the demand for water, ticket touting, and the second-hand car market.

The demand for water[1]

Since the privatization of the UK water industry in 1989, water has been supplied to households by private water companies. The performance of these companies is monitored by a regulatory body called OFWAT, which is mainly concerned with water charges. We are not specifically concerned with this here; our interest is the **demand** for water, and how we can apply the economic concepts we have covered so far.

We have seen that economics is the study of the allocation of scarce resources. Most of us probably think that water is not particularly scarce, especially when you think how much it seems to rain in the UK. But remember that the economist's idea of scarcity does not simply mean physical abundance or the lack of it. Scarcity is defined in relation to human wants. People want water that is fit to drink, and which they can use to wash their clothes, their car, and (sometimes) themselves! So, when we talk of water, we are referring to water in the form that satisfies these kinds of human wants. Since this type of water is scarce (it is not available in unlimited quantities relative to the uses that people have for it) it is a subject fit for the attention of economists. Many questions can be asked about the appropriate way of producing and distributing water to those who want it. For example, should water continue to be provided by private companies or should it be produced by publicly owned 'authorities' (as was the case before privatization)? What is a fair or efficient price? Should water be available to everyone as a right? How do we guarantee that water is safe to drink?

These sorts of questions can be answered using microeconomics, especially the concept of demand. In particular, we are concerned with what demand theory suggests about the consequences of replacing water rates by water charges based on metering. Making water available free of charge may be what consumers would like, but is this generally desirable? We can use one of the most basic pieces of economic analysis to look at the appropriate way of charging for water.

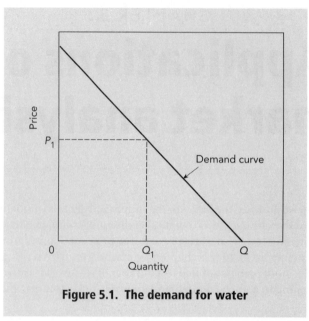

Figure 5.1. The demand for water

It is human wants that are important in defining scarcity. In economics we can replace the word 'wants' with 'demand'. As we have seen, one of the most important influences on the demand for a good is its price, and we have illustrated the relationship between quantity demanded and price by drawing a demand curve. So, how are people in the UK charged for the water they use? For over 90 per cent of customers in 1997 the charge was based on water rates; these are charged irrespective of how much water a household actually consumes. Under this system, the price of water is zero; using an additional litre of water costs the consumer nothing. Thus, when we talk about the price, it is the cost of an additional unit (litre) that we are referring to.

In terms of Figure 5.1, a system of water rates implies that the quantity demanded is determined where the demand curve meets the horizontal (quantity) axis (at point Q). But notice that Figure 5.1 does not mean that the charge made for water via water rates has no influence on the quantity of water that is demanded. It is still possible that an increase in water rates might affect the demand for water because consumers have less money to spend on all other goods (their real income falls). A fall in the demand for water (some people give up washing) will shift the demand curve to the left, although the effect is likely to be small. If water rates were lowered or abolished and water metered instead, then, at a price of P_1 per litre, we might expect the demand for water to fall from Q to Q_1 in Figure 5.1.

Whether or not to meter?

How do we tell whether it is appropriate to charge for water via water meters? In part, the answer depends on the attitude of the water companies. The 'bottom line' is whether they get more **revenue** from water rates than from charging a price of, say, P_1 (in Figure 5.1), and whether the fall in the quantity of water demanded results in lower costs for the water suppliers. To help clarify matters we make a simplifying (though not realistic) assumption:

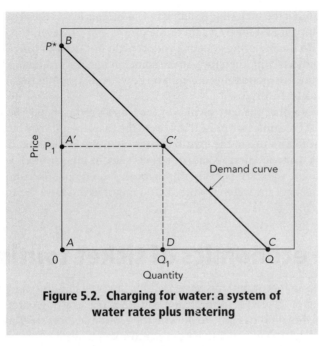

Figure 5.2. Charging for water: a system of water rates plus metering

suppose that when meters are introduced, water rates are maintained at the same level. The private water companies will definitely be better off charging customers twice (once through the rates and once through meters) and providing less water (an amount Q_1 compared to Q). Consumers will, of course, be worse off. In order to judge whether the change to water rates plus metering is a good thing or not, we have to make a comparison between the loss to consumers and the gain to the water companies. The reason the concept of demand is so useful in this context is that it allows us precisely to evaluate the loss to consumers. We do this in monetary units, because this is something people can understand.

In terms of Figure 5.2, since the demand curve measures peoples' **willingness to pay** for water, it enables us to infer the value they place on the water they consume. Any surplus of this value over and above what consumers actually pay is called **consumer surplus** (see Chapter 3 for more discussion of this idea). So, consumer surplus is the excess of what consumers would be willing to pay over what they actually pay. In terms of Figure 5.1, with a system of water metering some people are willing to pay more than P_1 but they do not have to, so they receive a surplus. The first litre of water produced is very valuable. With the demand curve in Figure 5.2, we can conclude that someone would be willing to pay P^* for this first unit (litre) of water. Subsequent litres are less and less valuable as we move down the demand curve. If water is only charged via water rates (zero price), then total consumer surplus is given by the area of the triangle ABC minus the total water rates paid by consumers. If water is metered and charged at a price of P_1, consumer surplus falls to $A'BC'$ minus the amount of rates still payable. The difference in consumer surplus is the area $A'C'CA$.

We interpret this area as a measure of the cost to consumers of having water meters and being charged a price of P_1 per litre. The water companies, however, are beneficiaries. In addition to the rates, they receive a revenue which is also shown in Figure 5.2. The amount consumers pay through the metering system is $A'C'DA$. This leaves the area $C'CD$ as a loss to consumers not compensated for by a gain to the producers. However, this does not account for the fact that with the metering system, producers do not need to provide so much water as before. The producers will, therefore, make some savings by producing less. On balance, whether metered water is a good thing depends on how the cost savings to companies compare with the loss in consumer surplus.

It might be the case that the cost savings of the water producers will be sufficiently large to outweigh the lost consumer surplus. If this were the case, then it may be beneficial to set a positive price for water on top of the existing water rates. But notice that this discussion has only made use of a demand curve. Many questions remain unanswered. For instance, what is the correct price for water? What ought to happen if some people cannot afford to pay? What about the quality of the water produced? You might like to raise these questions in class discussions.

The economics of ticket touting[2]

One area in which microeconomics is very useful is in understanding the problem of ticket touting. The selling of tickets for Wimbledon (or other big sporting/entertainment events) may look to you as though it has little to do with the economics you are studying. Even if you could be persuaded that it has, you might be even more sceptical if you were told that this subject also sheds light on the problems which faced the former Soviet Union (and other command economies) in the **distribution** of food. In this example, we illustrate how the problem of ticket touts highlights a fundamental question that all societies face and a question to which microeconomics is directed.

Who goes to the tennis finals?

Most definitions of economics concentrate on scarcity. Because of the scarcity problem, hard choices have to be made. As we have already seen, these choices are mostly resolved by a market mechanism whereby people get goods or services according to their willingness to pay. In the case of tickets for Wimbledon, it is possible to imagine lots of potential buyers, some of whom will be prepared to pay a good deal of money, some moderate amounts, and some very little. We can represent the willingness to pay of these potential purchasers in the form of a demand curve. In Figure 5.3, if tickets were to be made available at a price of P_1, then everyone who is prepared to pay at least this amount will wish to buy tickets. The lower the price, the greater will be the quantity of tickets demanded.

In a free market, scarce finals tickets will be allocated on the basis of willingness (and ability) to pay. The price adjustment mechanism will operate to ensure that the supply of tickets is equal to the demand for tickets, and the market will clear. In the case of Wimbledon, there is a fixed number of tickets available. Since it would seem reasonable to suppose that the tickets will be made available regardless of price, we should expect demand and supply curves as in Figure 5.4. The supply curve is vertical because of the fixed supply of tickets; the **supply** (number of tickets available) does not alter with changes in the price. The market equilibrium price is P_e. At this price, only individuals who are prepared to pay a price of P_e or more will get tickets, and there will be no-one who wants a ticket at price P_e who will go without. Note also that at prices above P_e everyone who wants a ticket will get one, because there is a temporary

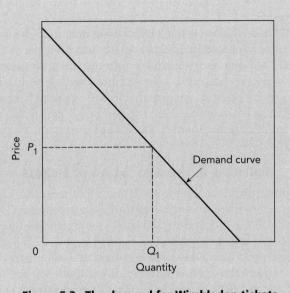

Figure 5.3. The demand for Wimbledon tickets

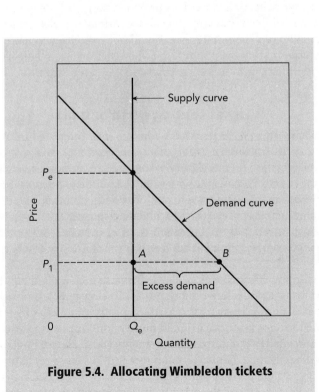

Figure 5.4. Allocating Wimbledon tickets

surplus (excess supply). Market forces will then operate to bid down the price, so wiping out the temporary surplus.

But this is not the way in which tickets are allocated in practice. What happens is that ticket prices are set low relative to people's willingness to pay, at a price like P_1 in Figure 5.4. At this price, there are lots more people who would like tickets than there are tickets available. We have a temporary shortage (or excess demand) of tickets measured by the distance A to B. A system of rationing is therefore introduced. The way that this is supposed to work is that the names of people who apply for tickets are placed in a ballot. The winners of the ballot are then given tickets. Why does the All England Tennis Club adopt this system, and what problems does it cause?

Fairness in the allocation of tickets

The All England Tennis Club does not try to get as much for finals tickets as it could. Why does it sell tickets for a price of P_1, when it could sell all the tickets it wants for P_e? As noted above, the market-based solution allocates tickets on the basis of willingness to pay. This is where the problem lies. What we are willing to pay for something depends not only on how much we want the good, but also upon our ability to pay. Many tennis supporters cannot afford to pay the price P_e. While it is true that the people buying tickets are willing to pay P_e, this may be more a reflection of how little money means to them rather than how much tennis means to them. So, in an attempt to be fair to all tennis fans, tickets are made available at the lower price of P_1.

It is the attempt to be fair, however, that makes ticket touting possible. To see this, think how the ballot works. People will apply for tickets provided they are prepared to pay P_1. But then some people who are willing to pay only just above P_1 may win tickets, whereas some people who are prepared to pay even more than P_e will not win tickets. Ticket touts exploit this discrepancy by offering to buy tickets for somewhere between P_1 (their face value) and the amount that disappointed supporters are prepared to pay to see the finals. The tickets are then offered to these fans at high prices.

Is ticket touting good or bad?

Ticket touts are usually attacked as profiteers who are only interested in making money for themselves at the expense of the true sports fan. The economic analysis, however, places a rather different interpretation on the activity of touts. To an economist, a ticket tout provides a way of reallocating tickets from people who value them little to people who value them a lot (where valuation is in terms of willingness to pay). To put this another way, if the ballot winner is someone who values a finals ticket close to P_1 and if he/she comes across a rich tennis fan, we would expect them to strike a deal. There are what economists call potential **gains from exchange**. For a range of prices both parties feel as if they have struck a bargain. Is there any profiteering here?

Ticket touts are simply acting as intermediaries between such individuals. It is also true that they make a profit from their dealings, but they are allowing gains from exchange to be realized. If you look at it this way, you might regard the profits of touts as their just reward. The problem is that the touts frustrate the original motivation for placing a low price on tickets. The low price was intended to be fair to the poorer tennis fans. The All England Club therefore dislikes touting and has introduced stricter monitoring of tickets to try to prevent it. But from the perspective of an outsider there appears to be a trade-off. On the one hand, it seems reasonable to be fair to tennis fans, but, on the other hand, it seems fair to allow gains from exchange.

Finals tickets and command economies

The trade-off described above is one that societies generally face when it comes to allocating goods and services. In a market system, gains from exchange will be realized but there may be some people who cannot afford the basic necessities of life. This problem is often dealt with in market economies by trying to ensure that everyone has sufficient spending power to afford necessities. An alternative approach is to use something other than the market mechanism for determining who gets what.

In command economies (like the former Soviet Union) prices for basic goods are often set artificially low; as with Wimbledon tickets, the price is set below the market clearing level. Goods are then rationed, not by using a ballot, but by a queuing system. You have probably seen pictures of the enormous queues that used to build up outside shops selling essential foodstuffs. Intermediaries in this system are not called touts but rather capitalists, profiteers, or even social criminals. But things have changed somewhat in the past few years, maybe for obvious reasons. Resource allocation based on the price mechanism has tended to accompany political reform. So, we can see an insight into economic reform in Eastern Europe in an analysis of Wimbledon finals tickets.

The economics of 'clocked' cars[3]

There is believed to be widespread 'clocking' of second-hand cars. Car clocking involves tampering with the odometer of a car so that it understates the true mileage. *Which?* magazine claims that this practice 'costs' consumers in the UK over £10 million a year. At first sight this figure would appear to be just a transfer of money from consumers to either unscrupulous individuals or unscrupulous car dealers (depending on who does the 'clocking'). But if we think about this a little more it begins to look as if the existence of clocked cars has implications for those people who want to sell a genuine second-hand car. A simple economic model can help us to identify who gains and who loses from clocking.

Economists are careful to distinguish between things that are 'true' costs (resources are used up) as opposed to simple transfers of money between people in the economic system. In other words, the situation we have described so far appears to be one of distribution (a transfer of money only) rather than **efficiency** (a use of resources). However, there might be a real resource cost to the practice of clocking (an efficiency dimension) once we consider the role played by odometer readings in informing consumers about the value of a car. So, as well as condemning clocking because it unfairly reduces consumer welfare to the benefit of others, we can also condemn it for leading to a real waste of resources. We can use the tools of supply and demand analysis to examine who wins and who loses from clocking, and why the clocking of cars might be wasteful from society's point of view.

As usual in economics we need to make some simplifying assumptions. Imagine we live in a world with only two types of car: good-quality cars (because they have a low mileage) and 'clapped-out' cars (because they have covered more miles than the *Red Dwarf*). Clapped-out cars have some value to consumers, but obviously not as much as good-quality cars. It is also useful here to think of two different types of consumer. One type of consumer wants a car for reliable long-distance travelling and is interested in buying a good car, while the other type wants a car for 'local' journeys and is happy with a clapped-out car. To simplify things further,

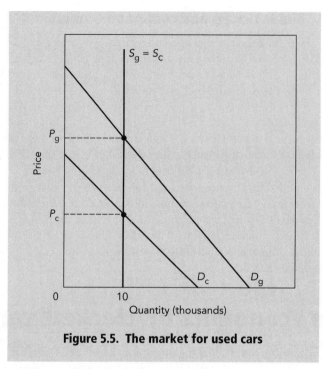

Figure 5.5. The market for used cars

suppose that there are 10,000 of both types of car available for sale and that the owners of these cars will sell them, whatever the price. (This is a fairly good description of the second-hand market for company cars.) In Figure 5.5, we have drawn demand and supply curves for the two types of car on the same diagram.

To illustrate the idea that good-quality cars are more valuable as far as consumers are concerned, we have drawn the demand curve for good cars, D_g, such that it lies everywhere above the demand curve for clapped-out cars, D_c. The supply curve for good cars, S_g, is the same as the supply curve for clapped out cars, S_c (there are 10,000 of each type available), and the demand and supply curves intersect to determine equilibrium prices of P_g for good cars and P_c for clapped-out cars.

Car clocking and confused consumers

Figure 5.5 is drawn on the assumption that consumers can identify which cars are good quality and which ones are clapped out, simply from observing the odometer readings (that is, consumers can tell which is which). But what happens if all cars are clocked so that consumers cannot distinguish between the two different types of car? In this case, since there are now 20,000 'identical' cars for sale, the supply curve in Figure 5.5 shifts to the right. What about demand? One possibility is that consumers think they have a 50 : 50 chance of buying a clapped-out car or a good car (based on the fact that 10,000 of each were being sold when consumers could distinguish between them). Some consumers might be prepared to take a chance in the market, and their valuation of the cars available will be somewhere between the value of

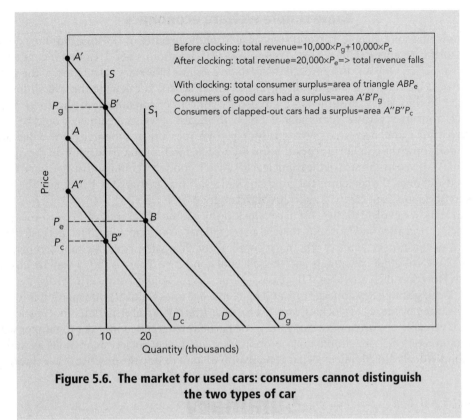

Figure 5.6. The market for used cars: consumers cannot distinguish the two types of car

a good car and the value of a clapped-out one. There is also the likelihood that many consumers will not be prepared to buy at any price, preferring instead to buy a new car—these people are then lost to the second-hand market. At the very worst, demand might correspond to D_c in Figure 5.5; at best it will lie somewhere below D_g. The result of this is that a new equilibrium is established in which all cars are sold at a price somewhere between P_g and P_c—shown as price P_e in Figure 5.6. The demand curve D indicates the new demand for cars when consumers cannot distinguish between types of car (that is, they cannot rely on the recorded mileage).

Figure 5.6 makes clear one consequence of clocking that is not obvious. Before clocking took place, the total revenue from car sales was $(10,000 \times P_g) + (10,000 \times P_c)$, but with the advent of car clocking total revenue from sales is $20,000 \times P_e$. Figure 5.6 shows clearly that total revenue has fallen (compare the size of the respective rectangles in the figure). So, the clocking of cars potentially hurts the car industry as well as consumers, half of whom end up with a clapped-out car for which they have paid more than P_c. But those people who now end up with a good car at the bargain price of P_e are better off. From society's point of view we have now identified those who gain—consumers who have bought a good car, and the car 'clockers'—and those who lose—the sellers of good cars, and those who end up with clapped-out cars. But what is important is how the gains and the losses balance out.

Some simple welfare economics

We know that some people gain and some lose from the practice of clocking, but how do we calculate the net effect? If the net effect is negative, we have another good reason for condemning the practice. One way to approach this is to do a simple monetary calculation of the gains and losses. We can easily add up the revenues of car sellers to calculate the overall loss of revenue. In the case of consumers, we can use the concept of **consumer surplus** to measure benefit. Consumer surplus, remember, is simply the excess of what consumers would be willing to pay for a good over what they actually do pay. We measure it as the area below a demand curve and above the equilibrium price. So, in Figure 5.6, total consumer surplus (in the case of clocking) is given by the area of the triangle ABP_e. When good cars could be distinguished from clapped-out ones, the consumers of good cars had a surplus of (triangle) $A'B'P_g$, and the consumers of clapped-out cars had a surplus of (triangle) $A''B''P_c$.

We can now calculate the net cost of car clocking by adding up revenues and consumer surplus before and after. In Figure 5.6, there is an overall net cost to clocking. The increase in the surplus of consumers (some of whom get good cars at a bargain price) does not compensate for the losses of other consumers and the sellers of good cars. There is thus a **welfare cost** to society. How does this come about? Because clocking cars prevents consumers from distinguishing between genuine low-mileage cars and high-mileage ones, valuable information is lost to the consumer by the act of clocking cars. Even worse, destroying information is not costless: it uses up valuable resources since cars have to be partially dismantled in order to tamper with their odometers. So, our simple microeconomics suggests that society as a whole, as well as those individuals directly affected, has good reason to want to stop the practice of car clocking.

Summary

1. The economist's model of supply and demand can be applied to a large range of real-world issues. In this chapter, we have applied the model to a number of specific topics. We have seen that a little knowledge of basic microeconomic theory can take us quite a long way in understanding the nature of these problems and in evaluating the 'best' outcome for society as a whole.

2. Economics offers an insight into the welfare cost to society as a whole of some particular action (ticket touting, car clocking, and so on). Typically, this is done by establishing the monetary gains and losses to the affected parties. For consumers, this involves an estimate of consumer surplus, while for firms we calculate the effect on revenues. The net cost to society is found by adding up revenues and consumer surplus, before and after the change.

Key terms

consumer surplus

demand

distribution

efficiency

gains from exchange

revenue

supply

welfare cost

willingness to pay

Review questions

1. What do you suppose would be the reaction of consumers to the introduction of water metering in addition to water rates? How would you try to convince consumers that the move is worthwhile? What might be done in order to make consumers support the move to water metering?

2. What is the effect of ticket touting (at Wimbledon or other major sporting/entertainment events) on economic efficiency?

3. How do we calculate the net welfare cost to society of car clocking?

Notes

1. This is adapted from Martin Chalkley, 'Water: A Question of Demand?', *Economic Review*, 7.1 (Sept. 1989), 13–14.

2. This is adapted from Martin Chalkley, 'Anyone for Tennis?', *Economic Review*, 9.1 (Sept. 1991), 16–17.

3. This is adapted from Martin Chalkley, 'The Simple Economics of "Clocked" Cars', *Economic Review*, 12.3 (Feb. 1995), 24–5.

CHAPTER 6

Elasticity of demand

Up until now, we have argued that when the price of a good changes it will cause a change in the quantity demanded (supplied) of that good. This is represented by a movement along a demand (supply) curve. The supply and demand model has also been applied to a number of different real-world problems.

In this chapter, we consider another application: the concept of elasticity of demand. This helps explain why the responses of consumers to price changes vary for different goods. If the average price of admission at football grounds was to rise by 10 per cent, will attendances (ticket sales) decrease by a little or a lot, *ceteris paribus*? Would the extent of consumer response differ, if instead of football attendance, we considered how sales of CDs, petrol, beer, or kebabs respond to a change in price? We also use the idea of elasticity of demand to examine who bears the burden of taxation, and to understand the price of coffee.

The concept of price elasticity of demand

Producers know of the inverse relationship between price and quantity demanded. In other words, they are aware that, on average, the quantity demanded of a good or service will fall when its price rises and it will rise when the price falls. However, they would also like to know by *how much* the quantity demanded will change. For example, if Nissan lowers the price of its Micra cars by 5 per cent, it wants to know whether its sales will increase by 5 per cent, by more than 5 per cent, or by less than 5 per cent. Knowing the answer to this question is important to Nissan because it determines whether its **total revenue** increases, decreases, or remains the same after the price cut.

The measure of the responsiveness of quantity demanded to a change in price is called the **price elasticity of demand**. Price elasticity of demand (*PED*) is normally defined as the ratio of the percentage change in quantity demanded to the percentage change in price, i.e.

$$PED = \frac{\text{percentage change in quantity demanded}}{\text{percentage change in price}}.$$

Suppose Sgt Pepper's record shop increases the price of its Beatles CDs by 10 per cent and finds that it sells 20 per cent fewer CDs each week. What is the price elasticity of demand for Beatles CDs? The answer is:

$$PED \text{ for Beatles CDs} = \frac{-20\%}{+10\%} = -2.$$

The price elasticity coefficient is −2, or just 2 (omitting the minus sign is normal practice). This says that the change in quantity demanded is twice the size of the percentage change in price.

Table 6.1. Some price elasticities in the UK

Product	Price elasticity of demand
Cheese	1.20
Carcass meats	1.37
Fresh potatoes	0.21
Bread	0.09
Frozen peas	1.12
Fruit juices	0.80

Source: Figures adapted from K. A. Crystal and R. G. Lipsey, *Economics for Business and Management* (Oxford: Oxford University Press, 1997), 105.

Therefore, Sgt Pepper's record shop can expect the number of Beatles CDs it sells to fall by 10 per cent if it raises the price by 5 per cent, or to rise by 20 per cent if it lowers the price by 10 per cent.

When the percentage change in quantity demanded is larger than the percentage change in price, the *PED* is greater than 1, and we say demand is **price-elastic**. This means quantities demanded of these goods are highly sensitive to price changes. On the other hand, when the change in quantity demanded is small relative to the change in price, the *PED* is less than 1, and we say demand is **price-inelastic**. The demand for these goods is price-insensitive; prices can vary without causing people to change the quantity bought very much. Finally, if the change in quantity demanded exactly matches the change in price, the *PED* is equal to 1, and we say demand exhibits **unitary elasticity** in that price range. A few examples of price elasticities in the UK are shown in Table 6.1.

Price elasticity and total revenue

Knowledge of the price elasticity of demand for particular goods and services can be very useful to producers. Suppose Sgt Pepper's record shop is thinking of increasing the price of its CDs. The shop knows it is likely to sell fewer CDs at a higher price (it is aware of the law of demand), but it is unsure as to how much its sales will fall. If the number of CDs sold each day falls only slightly, the shop will earn more money because the effect of the higher price will more than offset the effect of selling fewer CDs. On the other hand, the shop will make less money if the fall in CD sales more than offsets any benefit from the higher price. So, because there is a close link between revenue and elasticity, knowing the price elasticity of demand for CDs will help the shop come to the right decision.

Any firm's total revenue (*TR*) is simply price (*P*) times quantity sold (*Q*), or $TR = P \times Q$. A higher price tends to raise total revenue because each unit sold fetches a higher price. But at the same time, a higher price tends to reduce revenue because of the reduction in quantity sold. The opposite is true for a price cut. So, the net effect of a price change on total revenue depends on whether the change in *Q* is proportionately greater or smaller than the change in *P*. Changes in total revenue that result from price changes depend on the price elasticity of demand.

Suppose Sgt Pepper's record shop raises the price of its CDs from £12 to £14.40 (a 20 per cent increase). If the quantity sold each week falls from 200 to 100 (a 50 per cent drop), then

Table 6.2. Price changes, elasticity, and total revenue

Price change	Elasticity	Change in total revenue
Increase	Elastic ($PED > 1$)	Decrease
Decrease	Elastic ($PED > 1$)	Increase
Increase	Inelastic ($PED < 1$)	Increase
Decrease	Inelastic ($PED < 1$)	Decrease
Increase	Unitary ($PED = 1$)	No change
Decrease	Unitary ($PED = 1$)	No change

demand is price-elastic (the percentage change in quantity demanded—50—is greater than the percentage change in price—20), and the shop's total revenue will fall. Selling 200 CDs at the old price of £12 brings in £2,400, while selling only 100 discs at £14.40 yields a total revenue of £1,440. Thus, when demand is price-elastic, total revenue falls with a price increase. Similarly, when demand is price-elastic, total revenue rises with a price cut.

Now suppose that when the price increases by 20 per cent (from £12 to £14.40) quantity demanded falls by only 10 per cent, from 200 to 180 CDs per week. In this case, demand is price-inelastic (the percentage change in quantity demanded is smaller than the percentage change in price). Total revenue increases from £2,400 (£12 × 200) to £2,592 (£14.40 × 180). Thus, when demand is price-inelastic, total revenue rises with a price increase and, similarly, it falls with a price cut.

When there is unitary price elasticity ($PED = 1$), total revenue remains the same when there is a price change. In the unitary elasticity case, the extra revenue from a price increase is exactly offset by the drop in revenue from selling fewer units. A 20 per cent price increase matched by a 20 per cent fall in the amount sold yields the same total revenue as before. The relationship between price changes, elasticity, and total revenue is summarized in Table 6.2.

Most demand curves are made up of both elastic and inelastic portions. Even so, we can describe any demand curve as relatively more elastic (or inelastic) than another. In Figure 6.1, since the two demand curves cross each other, they have one common point. However, the curve labelled D_A is relatively more elastic than the one labelled D_B. If we compare the same percentage price increase, from P_1 to P_2, there is a relatively larger change in quantity demanded along D_A (quantity falls from Q_1 to Q_A) than along D_B (quantity falls from Q_1 to Q_B).

A word of caution. One problem with the practice of calculating elasticities by expressing changes in quantity and price as a percentage of the **starting value** (as we have done here) is that it leads to inconsistencies. In the previous example, a 20 per cent increase in the price (from £12 to £14.40) which is matched by a 20 per cent fall in the amount sold (from 200 to 160) produces an elasticity value of 1 (unitary elasticity) and total revenue should therefore remain unchanged. But instead of total revenue staying the same, it falls from £2,400 (£12 × 200) to £2,304 (£14.40 × 160). Why is this? The discrepancy occurs because when elasticity of demand is calculated between two points on a demand curve the value varies according to whether we begin with the starting value or the final value. A price increase from £12 to £14.40 represents a 20 per cent change, as does a fall in quantity demanded from 200 to 160. The elasticity of demand is therefore equal to 1 (20/20). But if we move in the opposite direction we find something different. A price cut from £14.40 to £12 represents a fall of 16.7 per cent, while an increase in quantity demanded from 160 to 200 is a 25 per cent change. In this

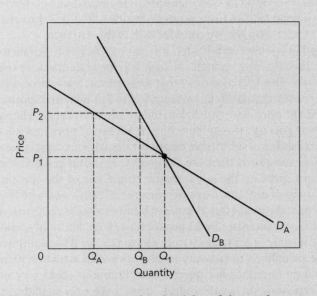

Figure 6.1. Comparing the elasticity of demand curves

case the elasticity of demand is 1.5 (25/16.7). The elasticity of demand is different depending on whether we begin with the starting value or the final value.

One way to avoid this problem is to calculate elasticity using percentages of the average or **midpoint values**. This method computes a percentage change by dividing the change by the midpoint of the starting and final values. For instance, £13.20 is the midpoint of £12 and £14.40. So, according to this method, a change from £12 to £14.40 is considered a rise of 18.2 per cent (because [(14.40 − 12)/13.20] × 100 = 18.2). Similarly, a change from £14.40 to £12 is considered a fall of 18.2 per cent. So, the midpoint method gives the same answer regardless of the direction of the price change. For quantity demanded the midpoint value is 180. In this case, if the quantity increases from 160 to 200 (or falls from 200 to 160) we consider it a change of 22.2 per cent (because [(200 − 160)/180] × 100 = 22.2). So, using this method, the price elasticity of demand equals 1.22 (22.2/18.2).

In this book we are not especially interested in how elasticity is calculated; it is more important that you understand it as the responsiveness of quantity demanded to price. Even so, this example illustrates that if you need to calculate elasticity it is better done using percentages of the average or midpoint value.

Determinants of price elasticity of demand

As Table 6.1 shows, the demand for some goods is relatively price-elastic (*PED* > 1) and the demand for others is relatively price-inelastic (*PED* < 1). Why is this the case? The three main determinants of the price elasticity of demand are (i) the availability of substitutes, (ii) the total amount spent on a good relative to consumers' incomes, and (iii) the time available to consumers to adjust to price changes. We consider each of these in turn.

If a good has only a few close substitutes, it is more difficult for people to respond to price changes in either direction. For example, in Table 6.1, the price elasticity coefficient for bread is close to zero at 0.09. This reflects the fact that there are not many close substitutes for bread; consumers cannot easily change their consumption of this item in response to price changes. On the other hand, the price elasticity of demand for carcass meats is relatively high at 1.37. If the price of red meat goes up you can buy chicken, turkey, or pork instead, or even become a vegetarian. The availability of substitutes means the demand for carcass meats is price-elastic. Thus, the more close substitutes there are, the greater will be the price elasticity of demand.

The total amount spent on the good relative to the size of the consumer's income also influences the elasticity of demand. Consider the case of Jenny Cool, who likes wearing luminous socks. At £5 a pair, she might buy 10 pairs of luminous socks each year, spending a total of £50. If the price of socks increases by 25 per cent, to £6.25, her total spending on luminous socks will increase by only £12.50 a year (from £50 to £62.50) if she continues to buy 10 pairs. Since most people are unlikely to take very much notice of an extra £12.50 over the course of a year, Jenny is unlikely to reduce her purchases of luminous socks very much. Thus, price increases (and decreases) for 'small budget' items have only a slight effect on quantity demanded, making the demand for this sort of item relatively price-inelastic.

However, where consumers spend a large fraction of their income on 'big' items (such as cars) the story is likely to be different. If the monthly repayments for a typical car increase by 25 per cent, payments may rise from £500 per month to £625. This would increase car spending from £6,000 to £7,500 a year, not an insignificant sum for many people. Consumers are likely to respond to this 25 per cent price increase with a large fall in quantity demanded, *ceteris paribus*, making the demand for cars price-elastic. Thus, the larger the fraction of a consumer's budget spent on a particular good, the more likely that good is to be price-elastic, *ceteris paribus*.

The third determinant of price elasticity of demand is the amount of time available to consumers to adjust to price changes. For most goods, people require time to find alternatives and change their consumption behaviour. As a result, price elasticity will be lower (more inelastic) in the short run than in the long run. For example, if the price of heating fuel rises significantly, there is not much consumers can do in the short run other than pay the higher prices and attempt to cut down on their use of heating. This makes the short-run demand for heating fuel price-inelastic. But in the long run the story is different, because consumers have time to respond to the price increase; they will, for example, install loft insulation to cut down on their consumption of heating. In the long run, the price elasticity for heating fuel is more elastic. In short, the longer the time period involved, the more price-elastic is demand.

Using elasticity of demand

The concept of price elasticity of demand has many applications in economics. Here we look at two in particular: (i) who actually pays taxes on goods—consumers or producers, and (ii) the price of coffee.

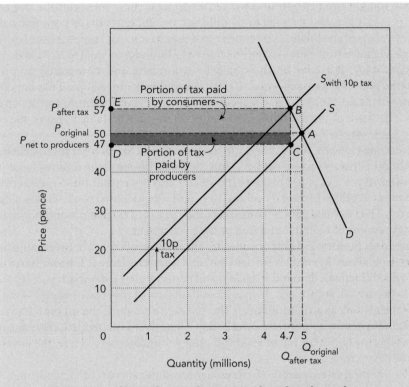

Figure 6.2. Effect of an excise tax on chocolate bar prices

Who pays taxes?

Taxes are often levied by governments according to the following two criteria: which taxes might raise the most revenue and which ones are 'fair'. To judge whether or not a particular tax is fair, the government needs to know who actually ends up paying the tax. Consider the example of an **excise tax**. Excise taxes (or excise duties) are levied on particular products, such as petrol and alcohol, made for sale in their home markets. What we want to know is: how much of the excise tax falls on the consumers of the product in the form of higher prices, and how much falls on the sellers of the product in the form of reduced revenue (and profits)?

Suppose the government is informed by its Chief Medical Officer that people who eat too much chocolate increase their chance of having a heart attack. The government's response is to place an excise tax on each bar of chocolate produced in order to reduce chocolate consumption and, at the same time, raise revenue. Figure 6.2 illustrates the effects of an excise tax of 10p per chocolate bar. The pre-tax equilibrium price is 50p, and the equilibrium quantity sold (quantity demanded and supplied) is 5 million bars per year. The 10p excise tax per bar shifts the supply curve upward (to the left) by the amount of the tax. For chocolate producers, the excise tax works like an increase in the cost of production, since it now costs them 10p more to produce each bar (they must send this amount of tax to the government for each bar of chocolate sold).

The new equilibrium price (found where the demand curve intersects the shifted supply curve, $S_{\text{with 10p tax}}$) is 57p, and sales fall to 4.7 million bars. The effect of the tax is that consumers now eat fewer bars of chocolate (as intended), and they have to pay more for each bar. The total tax revenue is shown by the area of the rectangle *BCDE*, and it is equal to £470,000 (10p × 4.7 million bars sold). But how much is paid by consumers and how much by producers? Although the price of a bar of chocolate has increased (from 50p to 57p), it has not done so by the amount of the tax (10p). So, in effect consumers do not pay the entire 10p tax on each bar they buy. The share of the tax bill for consumers is the lightly shaded area of the rectangle *BCDE*, or £329,000 (7p × 4.7 million bars).

Producers must send the 10p excise tax to the government for each bar sold, so they can only keep 47p of the 57p they receive per bar. Thus, the price they actually receive is now 3p lower than the original price of 50p. Therefore, producers also pay part of the excise tax: their contribution totals £141,000 (3p × 4.7 million bars), and is represented by the darker shaded area in Figure 6.2. The £329,000 paid by consumers and the £141,000 that producers pay add up to the total tax revenue of £470,000 received by the government.

So, where does the idea of elasticity come in? The division of the tax between consumers and producers depends on the elasticity of demand (and supply). Figure 6.3 shows the two extreme cases of perfectly **inelastic demand** (part (*a*)) and perfectly **elastic demand** (part (*b*)) for chocolate bars. In part (*a*), consumers demand 5 million bars of chocolate regardless of the price (these are the nation's chocolate junkies). The 10p excise tax shifts the supply curve to the left (upward), and raises the equilibrium price to 60p. Since there is no reduction in consumption, consumers pay the entire tax bill of £500,000 (10p × 5 million bars). Here, the government's tax revenue has increased.

The other limiting case, perfectly elastic demand, is shown in part (*b*) of Figure 6.3. After the supply curve shifts upward by 10p, there is a reduction in the number of chocolate bars sold. The equilibrium price is unchanged. The tax is absorbed entirely by producers, who receive only 40p per bar after paying the 10p tax out of the 50p price they still receive. They cut back their quantity sold to 4 million bars, while consumers (presumably) switch to other sweet products. The government's tax revenue falls to £400,000 (10p per bar × 4 million bars). Thus, the more elastic is the demand (the flatter the demand curve), the lower the tax revenue to the government. This explains why governments tend to levy excise taxes on goods with relatively inelastic demand, such as alcohol and petrol. Typically, the proportions of the excise tax paid by consumers and producers lie somewhere between the two extreme cases shown here.

Understanding the price of coffee[1]

In July 1994 severe frosts in Brazil caused coffee prices to increase dramatically. Immediately following this, there was an increase in the price of instant coffee in the UK. The initial price increase was modest in relation to the new price of coffee beans. However, it still prompted complaints in the newspapers that when the price of coffee beans falls we do not see a cut in the price of instant coffee, but when coffee prices rise we do get an increase in the price of instant coffee. The makers of instant coffee are frequently suspected of colluding to keep prices high. But a report in 1992 by the Monopolies and Mergers Commission cleared the companies of collusion. In fact, contrary to popular belief, the evidence shows that instant coffee prices do respond downwards to lower coffee bean prices. In other words, the more modest movement in the price of instant coffee reflects greater price stability for this product compared with the

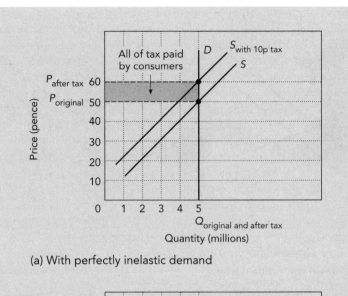

(a) With perfectly inelastic demand

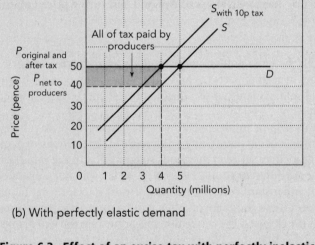

(b) With perfectly elastic demand

**Figure 6.3. Effect of an excise tax with perfectly inelastic
demand and perfectly elastic demand**

price of coffee beans. But, how can this be the case if coffee beans are the main ingredient of instant coffee? Our explanation lies with the concept of price elasticity of demand.

Because coffee production is highly susceptible to changes in climate, the supply of coffee in one year may be very different from that in another year, simply because of the weather. The extent to which price and quantity respond to these supply changes can easily be understood by referring to a supply and demand diagram, as shown in Figure 6.4. Part (a) of Figure 6.4 shows the case of a relatively elastic demand curve. Here, a shift in the supply curve (from S_1 to S_2) results in only a small increase in price, from P_1 to P_2. When demand is relatively inelastic,

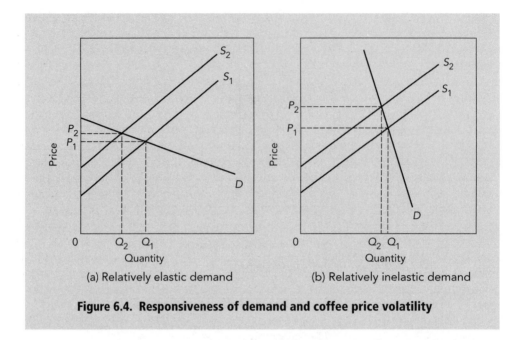

(a) Relatively elastic demand   (b) Relatively inelastic demand

Figure 6.4. Responsiveness of demand and coffee price volatility

as in part (*b*), exactly the same shift in supply results in a large increase in price. Corresponding to the price changes in each of parts (*a*) and (*b*) are the changes in the quantity of coffee that will be bought and sold. As you can see, the quantity change is largest when demand is relatively more elastic.

But how does this help us to understand why instant coffee prices change less than coffee bean prices? The answer lies in there being a difference in the elasticity of demand for these two goods. Different elasticities between the goods suggests that in the minds of consumers 'real' and 'instant' coffee are different goods. How could we tell whether consumers actually distinguish between real and instant coffee? One way forward is to see what happens when exactly the same quantities of these goods are on offer at different prices. If consumers always choose whichever drink is the cheapest, we can reasonably argue that the two drinks are equivalent.

But we can go further than this. What we are saying is that if we start from a position of equal prices for the two drinks, consumers will switch between real and instant coffee in response to a small change in their relative prices. In other words, a small reduction in the price of instant coffee should result in consumers switching to it, so decreasing the consumption of real coffee. We have here another elasticity of demand: in this case, it is the **cross-price elasticity of demand** between real and instant coffee. This is defined as:

$$\text{cross-}PED = \frac{\text{precentage change in the quantity demanded of good } X}{\text{percentage change in the price of good } Y}.$$

If we have two goods for which the cross-price elasticity of demand is positive (the price of one rises and the quantity demanded of the other increases), the goods in question are known as **substitutes**. So, goods which are seen by consumers as good substitutes for each other (for example, Coke and Pepsi) should have a large positive value for the cross-price elasticity of demand. But how do we relate cross-price elasticity of demand to the elasticity of the demand curves that might explain the relative volatility of real and instant coffee prices?

A good which has many close substitutes is expected to have an elastic (relatively flat) demand curve, simply because, as its price rises, those substitutes become relatively cheap. So, if it is the case that for most consumers there are more close substitutes for instant coffee than for real coffee, we can explain real coffee price volatility in terms of price elasticity of demand. The existence of alternative drinks, like tea or drinking chocolate, might explain the apparently greater elasticity of demand for instant coffee. Thus, if most consumers regard tea as a close substitute for instant coffee but a poor substitute for real coffee, we ought to find that instant coffee has a more elastic demand.

To summarize, the apparent paradox of the price of coffee beans being more volatile than the price of instant coffee can be understood with reference to elasticities of demand. The demand for instant coffee is price-elastic; hence its price should be less volatile. Or, to put this another way, because the demand for real coffee is more price-inelastic than the demand for instant coffee, real coffee prices ought to be more volatile (look at the gradients of the demand curves in Figure 6.4). Appreciating why the price elasticity of demand might be high or low draws upon an understanding of another elasticity concept—the cross-price elasticity of demand. Any product which has a close substitute will have a large (and positive) cross-price elasticity of demand. It is precisely such goods which ought to have elastic (relatively flat) demand curves.

Summary

1. Price elasticity of demand measures the responsiveness of quantity demanded to changes in price. Elasticity determines whether a firm's total revenue increases, decreases, or stays the same when price changes. When demand is price-inelastic, total revenue and price change in the same direction. When demand is price-elastic, they change in opposite directions.

2. The three main determinants of the price elasticity of demand are the availability of substitutes, the total amount spent on a good relative to consumers' incomes, and the time available to consumers to adjust to price changes.

3. Who bears the burden of an excise tax (consumers or producers) depends on the price elasticity of demand. If demand is perfectly inelastic, consumers bear the full burden of the tax, and government maximizes its revenue. Producers bear the full burden of the tax if demand is perfectly elastic.

4. To identify how closely goods are related we use the concept of cross-price elasticity of demand. This measures the responsiveness of quantity demanded of one good to changes in the price of another good. Goods which have a close substitute should have a large and positive cross-price elasticity.

Key terms

cross-price elasticity of demand

elastic demand

excise tax

inelastic demand

midpoint value

starting value

price-elastic

price elasticity of demand

price-inelastic

substitutes

total revenue

unitary elasticity

Review questions

1. When Steely Dan's record shop cut the price of its CDs from £15 to £12, sales increased from 100 to 150 CDs per day. Using the total revenue test, say whether demand for these CDs is price-elastic, price-inelastic, or unitary elastic.

2. If one of the aims of the Chancellor of the Exchequer is to raise revenue for the government, why does it make sense to levy an excise tax on goods that are price-inelastic?

3. Complete the following table:

Price (£)	Quantity	Total revenue	Elasticity value
10	200	2,000	—
9	240	2,160	2.0 (20% ÷ 10%)
8	280	2,240	1.5 (16.7% ÷ 11.1%)
7	320		
6	360		
5	400		
4	440		

What happens to the elasticity value as price continues to decline?

4. Goods which are substitutes for one another have a positive cross-price elasticity of demand. Why is the cross-price elasticity of demand for some goods (such as tennis balls and tennis rackets, or cars and tyres) negative?

Note

1. This is adapted from Alan Hamlin, 'Understanding the Price of Coffee', *Economic Review*, 12.2 (Nov. 1994), 21–2.

Further reading

- Mabry and Ulbrich, chapter 5
- Lipsey and Chrystal, chapter 4
- Sloman, chapter 2

CHAPTER 7

Production and costs

In Chapter 2, we mentioned that one of the fundamental questions any society has to face is 'how to produce' the goods and services that individuals wish to consume. Because firms have certain advantages over households with respect to specialized or large-scale production, much of the output consumed by individuals is produced by firms. When making goods and services, firms combine resources so as to minimize total production costs.

When deciding how much to produce, firms compare expected revenues against expected costs, and they select the output that maximizes profit. Changes in the market price will affect expected revenues, so firms tend to set a different profit-maximizing output level for each possible market price. Tracing out these price–quantity combinations determines the supply curve of a firm.

The production function and production efficiency

When consumers want certain goods and services they rely on firms to supply them. Firms make goods and services by combining factors of production (resources) in a particular way. A **production function** describes the various combinations of factor inputs needed to produce a particular product. For example, suppose you plan to set up in business making computer games. To produce the games you need land, buildings, labour, micro-processors, machinery, and other raw materials. A production function for computer games tells you how many of each of these inputs is needed to produce given amounts of output (games).

Imagine you have a target output of 100 games per day. Your production function might say that 100 games can be produced by using two units of labour (workers), one unit of capital (a machine), and three micro-processors. However, other combinations of these factors may also be used to produce the same 100 games. For instance, it may be possible to substitute units of capital for a worker. The substitution of some of one input for a little of another characterizes the production of most goods. Recently, robots have taken over welding and painting duties in most car factories, and laser scanners have changed the nature of many supermarket check-outs. Both are cases of firms substituting capital for labour.

Efficiency in production

Because of the substitution possibilities in production functions, firms have the chance to maximize output for a given level of cost, or minimize cost for a target level of output. They do this by responding to input prices. Because each input has a different price, the total cost of a given output level depends on the combination of inputs chosen to produce it. So, when producing

Table 7.1. Least-cost input combination to repair 100 televisions per week

Input	Units of labour	Units of capital	Total cost
A	12	1	£5,120
B	8	3	£4,160
C	6	6	£4,320

Weekly cost of labour @ £10 per hour = £400 per unit.
Weekly cost of capital equipment @ £8 per hour = £320 per unit.

a given level of output, firms aim to select the combination of inputs with the lowest cost. If firms can achieve the least-cost combination of inputs, they are **efficient in production**.

The production function and the relative prices of the different types of inputs determine the choice of inputs used in production. Given the various possible combinations of inputs, the most efficient (or least costly) combination depends on relative input prices. For example, the information in Table 7.1 can be used to show that the television repair shop will use the least costly combination of inputs in order to repair 100 television sets per week. At a wage of £10 per hour, each unit of labour (worker) costs £400 per week. At a price of £8 per hour, each unit of capital equipment costs £320 per week. Input combination A uses 12 service engineers and only 1 unit of equipment. Combination C uses 6 units of each to repair the same number of televisions each week. The least costly input combination is combination B, which uses 8 units of labour (£3,200) and 3 units of capital (£960) for a total cost of £4,160 per week.

Since relative prices determine which combination of inputs is most efficient, the actual resource mix used to make a particular good or service will change as input prices change. If the price of one of the inputs increases relative to another, firms will substitute more of the relatively cheaper input for less of the relatively expensive one. When the price of an input falls, more of it is used at the margin in place of some other input. For example, in many high street banks cash machines have replaced some bank tellers (as well as floor space). This is because, since the early 1990s, the prices of computer hardware and software have fallen quickly relative to the prices of skilled bank staff and floor space.

Economic costs

Economists assume that people who run businesses are motivated by a desire to maximize profit—the difference between total revenue and total cost. We looked at how to calculate total revenue in Chapter 6; here, we consider how firms measure their costs.

The **economic cost** of a good always equals the full opportunity cost of that good. This means that the true cost of producing any good is the value of what must be given up to obtain it. One aspect of economic cost is the money payments for using productive resources; these are called **accounting costs**. Accounting costs are the usual costs recorded by accountants in the firm's books: wages paid to labour, payments for raw materials, interest paid on debt, and other money outlays for resources.

A second kind of economic cost (and just as important) is the value of alternatives forgone in the production of a good, irrespective of whether money payments are made. These sorts of *implicit costs* include benefits given up and for which no direct money payments are made. Although these kinds of costs involve no monetary payments, they are still important because they often affect decisions. For example, an implicit cost for a grocer who runs a corner shop is his/her building's rental value. Although the owner does not have to pay rent, the shop could be rented to others. This forgone rent is an implicit cost of running the business. If the owner could rent out the building for more than the shop's monthly **accounting profit**, the owner would maximize income by renting out the shop, and ceasing to trade. So, the rental value of a building is a true (implicit) opportunity cost. It should be added to the **explicit costs** (money outlays) to arrive at the total economic cost.

A second type of implicit cost is the income that could be earned by an entrepreneur in his or her next best alternative job. The payments an entrepreneur receives for doing the job (being an innovator, taking risks, and so on) must be included as costs. Consider an individual who has just set up her own business, and who could expect to earn up to £20,000 per year working for someone else. As a self-employed person, she needs to make £20,000 per year, otherwise she will take a salaried job. So, her maximum expectable salary of £20,000 is the implicit cost of her self-employment. In effect, in order to remain in this line of business she requires a rate of return at least as large as her maximum expectable salary. This level of return for her business is called a **normal profit**. Since she must receive at least a normal profit to prevent her taking a salaried job, that amount of profit is an opportunity cost and must be counted as an implicit cost.

Economic profit

For the production of a given level of output, **economic profit** is the difference between total revenue and total economic cost. If a firm's total revenue and total economic cost are the same, the firm makes a normal (or zero economic) profit. If total revenue exceeds total economic cost, the firm earns an economic profit; if total revenue is less than total economic cost, the firm makes an economic loss. The idea of economic profit is important because it determines whether a firm will join or leave an industry in the long run. When there are economic profits in an industry we expect to see firms entering that industry; economic losses will prompt exit from the industry. If a normal profit is being made (zero economic profit) we expect to see neither entry nor exit. We consider these ideas in more detail in the next few chapters.

Production in the short run and the long run

To minimize production costs and respond to changes in factor prices, firms must be able to adjust the number of inputs they use. In the **short run**, firms can change some inputs but not all of them. In fact, the short run is defined as the time period during which at least one of the firm's inputs (usually land or capital) is in fixed supply.

In the short run, then, firms operate with both fixed inputs and variable inputs. A **fixed input** is one which cannot be adjusted (upward or downward) to change output in the short run. Quite often, the planning and building of new manufacturing plants takes a number of years. The amount of a **variable input**, on the other hand, can be changed (increased or decreased) in the short run. Typically, variable inputs include labour and materials. For example, your local fish-and-chip shop can increase its daily 'food' output by taking on more workers (labour) and purchasing more potatoes, baps, fish, pies, and vinegar (materials). On the other hand, it can reduce output by laying off workers and cancelling orders for supplies. The shop's fixed inputs are its buildings, counter space, cash registers, and cooking equipment.

It is only in the **long run** that firms can adjust all of their factor inputs. The long run is a planning period of sufficient length that all the firm's inputs are variable. If Microsoft decides it wants to increase its output of computer software, it can do so in the short run only by employing more workers and using more materials. But in the long run, the company also has the option of building a larger factory and using more machines, as well as using more workers and materials. Note that the short run and the long run are analytical concepts that we use to explain how firms make decisions about levels of output and costs; they are not specific periods of time. The length of the short run varies from industry to industry.

Short-run costs

In the short run, because some factor inputs are fixed (capital) and some are variable (labour), firms operate with both fixed costs and variable costs. **Fixed costs** (*FC*) do not vary with increases or decreases in the level of a firm's output. Examples of these kinds of costs include fire insurance on buildings, lease contracts for equipment, and property taxes (the uniform business rate). Fixed costs have to be paid in the short run whether the firm produces 10 units, 1,000 units, or nothing at all. Firms cannot escape these fixed costs in the short run even by closing down.

Variable costs (*VC*) include expenses that increase and decrease with changes in the level of a firm's output. Wage payments, expenses for raw materials, and the cost of electricity and fuel are examples of variable costs; they vary with different output levels as more or fewer units are produced. Raising output increases variable costs, while lowering output reduces variable costs. If production ceases altogether, variable costs become zero.

Total cost (*TC*) for a given level of output in the short run is the sum of all fixed and variable costs, whether those expenses are explicit or implicit. In symbols we write:

$$TC = FC + VC.$$

Fixed, variable, and total costs for Bill and Ben's Flowerpot Company are shown in Table 7.2.

Various output levels (pots per day) are given in column (1). Columns (2), (3), and (4) show the associated costs. Fixed cost is constant at £20 for all output levels in the short run. Variable cost increases at an increasing rate after the first few pots are made. Total cost is the sum of fixed and variable cost.

The law of increasing cost

The variable costs in column (3) of Table 7.2 change according to the **law of increasing cost**. This law states that beyond some level of output in the short run, variable costs (and therefore total costs) increase by progressively larger amounts as output increases. When output is quite low (before the law of increasing cost starts to work) variable costs may increase by constant amounts or increase at a decreasing rate as output expands. But eventually the law of increasing cost sets in. Because firms have some fixed inputs in the short run, adding more of a variable input (say, labour) to a fixed amount of another input (say, capital) adds smaller and

Table 7.2. Short-run costs for Bill & Ben's Flowerpot Company (£)

Total output (1)	Fixed cost (2)	Variable cost (3)	Total cost (4)	Average FC (5)	Average VC (6)	Average TC (7)	Marginal cost (8)
0	20	0	20	—	—	—	
							6
1	20	6	26	20	6	26	
							2
2	20	8	28	10	4	14	
							4
3	20	12	32	6.66	4	10.66	
							8
4	20	20	40	5	5	10	
							12
5	20	32	52	4	6.4	10.4	
							16
6	20	48	68	3.33	8	11.33	

smaller amounts to total output. These extra units cost more and more to make because each extra unit produced requires ever larger quantities of the variable input.

The law of increasing cost is an example of a more general principle called the **law of diminishing returns**. This says that the return from adding more of a variable input to a given quantity of a fixed input diminishes as the ratio of variable to fixed inputs gets larger and larger. Consider the case of Bill and Ben's Flowerpot Company; it decides to employ more workers in order to produce more flowerpots. When output is low the firm needs only one or two extra workers to produce an extra pot. However, as output increases, production of the same extra output requires ever larger increases in the number of staff, so pushing up the costs of production. Eventually, lots more extra workers are needed to produce one more pot, making the production costs relatively high. It is even possible for output to go down if workers get in each other's way. In this situation, the cost of producing an extra pot may be extremely expensive.

The variable costs in Table 7.2 reflect the law of increasing cost. The first flowerpot can be made for a variable cost of £6, but the variable cost for two pots is only £8. The second pot can be made for only £2 more instead of the £6 the first one costs. After two pots, however, variable cost begins to increase by ever larger amounts with each increase in output.

Average and marginal cost

Columns (5) to (8) of Table 7.2 show average fixed cost, average variable cost, average total cost, and marginal cost for Bill and Ben's business. Each of these concepts helps Bill and Ben decide how many flowerpots to supply at various prices.

Average fixed cost (*AFC*) is total fixed cost divided by the number of units produced:

$$AFC = \frac{FC}{Q}.$$

Average fixed cost continually falls as output levels increase, because a constant amount of fixed cost is divided by larger levels of output (Q). Average fixed cost declines from £20 at a production level of one flowerpot per day to £3.33 for six pots per day. As the output level increases, the fixed-cost component of each unit's average cost is reduced.

Average variable cost (*AVC*) is the total variable cost divided by the number of units produced:

$$AVC = \frac{VC}{Q}.$$

Average variable cost may decline, remain constant, or rise for the first few units of output, but it eventually increases in the short run because of the law of increasing cost.

Average total cost (*AC*) is total cost divided by total output. It is also the sum of average fixed cost and average variable cost for any given output level:

$$AC = \frac{TC}{Q}$$

$$= AFC + AVC.$$

At low levels of output, average total cost may decline because the effect of falling average fixed cost outweighs the weak effect of increasing average variable cost. But once output goes beyond a certain level, average total cost increases because average variable cost rises by more than enough to offset the reduction in average fixed cost. This pattern for average total cost is shown in column (7) of Table 7.2. Average cost declines up to the first four flowerpots produced per day but rises for output levels of five and six pots.

Marginal cost (*MC*) is the extra cost per additional unit of output produced. Marginal cost is calculated by dividing the change in total cost by the change in output:

$$MC = \frac{\text{change in } TC}{\text{change in } Q} \left(\text{or in symbols,} \ \frac{\Delta TC}{\Delta Q} \right),$$

where Δ is the Greek letter capital delta, meaning 'change in'. In Table 7.2, the marginal cost of the first flowerpot produced is £6; for the second flowerpot it falls to £2. After two flowerpots have been produced, however, marginal cost rises for each additional unit of output, once again reflecting the law of increasing cost.

Average and marginal cost curves

The average and marginal cost curves corresponding to the short-run costs for Bill and Ben's Flowerpot Company are drawn (not to scale) in Figure 7.1. These are typical-looking curves for any business. The average fixed cost (*AFC*) curve declines over the entire range of output, since a constant number (fixed cost) is divided by larger and larger levels of output. The average variable cost (*AVC*) curve declines at first, and then increases because of the law of increasing cost. In most cases, the *AVC* curve is U-shaped.

The average total cost (*AC*) curve is also U-shaped, but it reaches its minimum point farther to the right. Average total cost declines and then rises, but, because of the effect of falling average fixed cost, it does not have exactly the same shape as the average variable cost curve. The *AC* curve is the vertical sum of the *AFC* and *AVC* curves (*AC* = *AFC* + *AVC*). This means that at any output level, the vertical distance between the *AC* and *AVC* curves is a measure of *AFC*. The quantity that minimizes average total cost is called the **efficient scale** of the firm. For Bill and Ben's business, the efficient scale is four flowerpots. If the business produces more or less than this number, the average total cost rises above the minimum of £10.

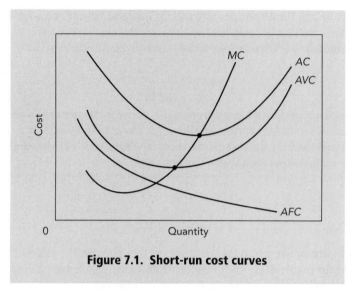

Figure 7.1. Short-run cost curves

Because of the key role played by 'the margin' in economic decision-making, economists take a special interest in the marginal cost (*MC*) curve. As we see in Figure 7.1, the *MC* curve intersects both the *AVC* and *AC* curves at their minimum points. To see why this is so, think about the relationship between the margin and the average of anything, for example, a cricketer's batting average. Imagine that after 10 completed innings, David Gower's batting average is 46.7 (he has scored 467 runs in 10 innings). In his next (or marginal) innings he scores 88. He has now scored a total of 555 runs in 11 innings, and his average rises to 50.45 (555 ÷ 11). So, if his marginal (next) score is bigger than his average score, it pulls his average up; similarly, when his marginal score is below his average score, it pulls his batting average down. When his marginal score is the same as his average, his batting average is unchanged. (You may also be able to think of other suitable examples, such as the average height of students in a classroom, or your average examination marks.)

Thus, when average variable cost is falling the value of marginal cost must be below average variable cost in order to pull down the average value; if *AVC* is rising, *MC* must be above the average value in order to pull up the average value. As the *AVC* curve is U-shaped, *MC* must lie below its falling portion and above its rising portion. Where the value of *AVC* is neither rising nor falling (at its minimum point), *MC* must be equal to *AVC* at this point. Hence, the *MC* curve will always cross the *AVC* curve at the minimum point of the *AVC* curve. The same relationship holds for marginal cost and average total cost.

The profit-maximizing rule

Because firms aim to maximize economic profit, they try to reduce costs and increase revenue whenever possible. Here, we look at how a firm determines which level of output is the one that maximizes profit for each possible price.

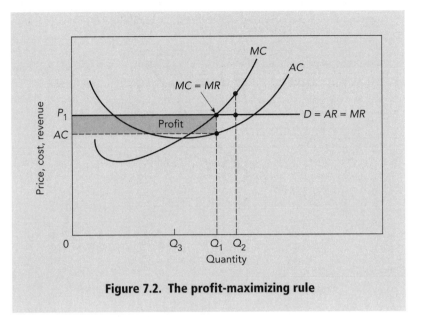

Figure 7.2. The profit-maximizing rule

Firms choose their level of output on the basis of both costs and demand. They use the profit-maximizing rule in order to get the largest possible profit from their available resources. This rule says that, in the short run, a firm will maximize profit by producing that output level at which marginal revenue equals marginal cost ($MR = MC$). **Marginal revenue** (MR) is defined as the extra revenue gained from selling one more unit of output. For present purposes, we assume that marginal revenue is equal to price. In essence, the profit-maximizing rule says that it is only worth producing extra output if it adds at least as much to total revenue as it does to total cost. In other words, the extra unit is worth producing and selling only if $MR \geq MC$.

When output is above the profit-maximizing level, marginal cost is greater than marginal revenue ($MC > MR$). In this situation, the firm should lower output because the last unit produced adds more to cost than it adds to revenue. When output is below the profit-maximizing level, marginal cost is less than marginal revenue ($MC < MR$); the last unit produced adds less to total cost than it adds to total revenue. Here, the profit-maximizing firm should increase output. So, firms will maximize profit by increasing output to the level at which marginal cost equals marginal revenue.

Figure 7.2 illustrates the profit-maximizing rule using a horizontal demand curve (the nature of which we will examine more closely in Chapter 8). The firm chooses output level Q_1 to maximize profit, as this is the output where the marginal cost curve crosses the marginal revenue curve ($MC = MR$). Producing more than Q_1, such as Q_2, would mean $MC > MR$. Here, the marginal unit would add more to total cost than to total revenue, so profit would fall. At an output such as Q_3, the firm would add more to its revenue than to its costs ($MR > MC$), so profit would increase. Therefore, Q_1 (where $MC = MR$) is the profit-maximizing level of output. Any other output level (larger or smaller) would result in a lower profit for the firm.

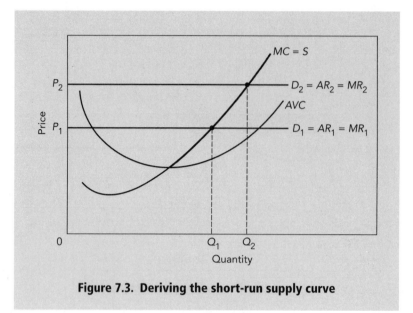

Figure 7.3. Deriving the short-run supply curve

Short-run supply

Figure 7.3 shows how the marginal and average cost curves for a typical firm can be used to find the short-run supply curve. If we assume that the firm can sell all it wants to at the prices P_1 and P_2, then price equals marginal revenue. The firm chooses the profit-maximizing output by equating MC to MR (which equals price). When the price is P_1, profit is maximized at an output of Q_1, and when price is P_2 the profit-maximizing output is Q_2. We see that the firm supplies a larger quantity when the price is higher—a result we saw in Chapter 3. These two price–quantity combinations on the marginal cost curve are also two points on the firm's short-run supply curve. The supply curve shows the quantities the firm is willing to offer for sale at each possible price; so, the profit-maximizing rule proves that the marginal cost curve determines those output levels.

This firm's supply curve is the part of the marginal cost curve which lies above the AVC curve (shown by the thicker part of the MC curve in Figure 7.3). Notice that the firm will produce nothing at all when the MC curve lies below the AVC curve; this is because the price received is not high enough to cover AVC. The law of increasing cost plays a key role here; it determines that short-run marginal cost curves slope upwards, and, therefore, that short-run supply curves also slope upwards.

Price elasticity of supply

We know that price and quantity supplied form a positive relationship: both rise and fall together. But we do not know by how much quantity supplied will respond to a price change without more information. This is where price elasticity of supply comes in. **Price elasticity of**

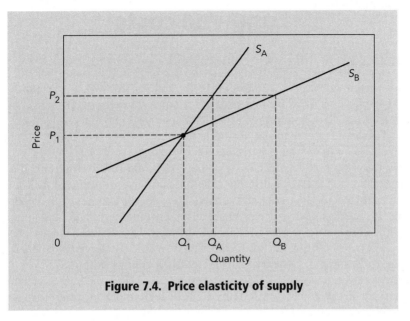

Figure 7.4. Price elasticity of supply

supply (*PES*) measures the responsiveness of quantity supplied to changes in price. The price elasticity of supply between the old and the new price is the ratio of the percentage change in quantity supplied to the percentage change in price:

$$PES = \frac{\text{percentage change in quantity supplied}}{\text{percentage change in price}}.$$

It is quite useful to have some knowledge of supply elasticities. Suppose the market price of North Sea oil falls by 20 per cent. By how much will the oil companies cut their production? If oil companies respond by reducing output by only 5 per cent, the price elasticity of supply for oil is less than 1:

$$PES = \frac{-5\%}{-20\%} = 0.25.$$

Supply is price-elastic if a 1 per cent change in price causes a greater than 1 per cent change in quantity supplied, or *PES* > 1. Supply is price-inelastic if a 1 per cent change in price causes a less than 1 per cent change in quantity supplied, or *PES* < 1. Finally, supply is unitary-elastic if the percentage change in quantity supplied equals the percentage change in price, or *PES* = 1.

In Figure 7.4, we illustrate the idea of relative price elasticity of supply. Supply curve S_B is relatively more elastic than supply curve S_A. A price increase from P_1 to P_2 causes the quantity supplied to increase from Q_1 to Q_B along supply curve S_B. But the same price increase causes a smaller increase in quantity supplied along S_A, from Q_1 to only Q_A. So, because of different supply elasticities, the same price change can lead to very different responses in quantity supplied.

Long-run costs

The long run is considered to be a planning period for firms because they have no fixed inputs in the long run. In the long run, firms plan for the size of plant that yields the efficient scale of operation. Long-run average cost curves normally slope downward at first and then upward (they are U-shaped). As firm size increases in the small to medium-size range, average cost often declines because of **economies of scale**. These are long-run production efficiencies encountered as firms increase in size, enabling them to lower cost by using more specialized inputs (skilled labour or more efficient capital equipment).

However, once the firm has reached a certain size, long-run average and marginal cost increase with firm size, reflecting diseconomies of scale. **Diseconomies of scale** are long-run production inefficiencies, encountered as firms increase beyond some size in the long run, that cause long-run average cost to rise. Where firms become very large and bureaucratic it becomes difficult to control the firm. There may be many layers of management and factories located in many parts of the world. So, as companies become ever larger and increasingly complex, average and marginal costs eventually increase with higher output.

We have now examined a number of cost concepts, as well as the idea of demand. We can now begin to put all this together by looking at the behaviour of consumers and firms operating in particular kinds of markets.

Summary

1. A production function describes the various combinations of factor inputs needed to produce a particular product. A production function also illustrates how inputs can be substituted for one another in the production process.

2. Production efficiency occurs when firms produce any given level of output at the lowest possible cost. It is, therefore, the prices of the factors which determine the actual mix of resources used in the production process.

3. In the short run, firms have fixed inputs; these cannot be varied with changes in the level of output. In the long run, all inputs are variable.

4. Economic cost is the sum of implicit and explicit costs; it includes all the opportunity costs of production. Economic profit is the difference between total revenue and total economic cost. Economic cost includes a normal return to the owner of a business, hence making a zero economic profit is the same as a normal profit.

5. Short-run production is subject to the law of increasing cost. Marginal cost rises as output increases beyond some level. Short-run supply curves reflect the law of increasing cost.

6. To maximize profit, firms choose an output level where marginal cost equals marginal revenue. This is the profit-maximizing rule.

7. Price elasticity of supply measures the responsiveness of quantity supplied to changes in product price. If quantity supplied changes proportionately more (less) than the change in price, supply is elastic (inelastic).

8. Long-run average cost curves are normally U-shaped. They slope downward at first because of economies of scale (production efficiencies encountered as firms increase in size) and then upward due to diseconomies of scale (production inefficiencies encountered in the long run as firms increase beyond some size).

Key terms

accounting costs	implicit costs
accounting profit	law of diminishing returns
average fixed cost	law of increasing cost
average total cost	long run
average variable cost	marginal cost
diseconomies of scale	marginal revenue
economic cost	normal profit
economic profit	price elasticity of supply
economies of scale	production function
efficient in production	short run
efficient scale	total cost
explicit costs	variable costs
fixed costs	variable input
fixed input	

Review questions

1. Dinsdale Piranha is self-employed. Last year he made an operating surplus of £25,000 but he could have earned £30,000 by working for his brother Douglas. What is his economic profit?

2. Explain why increasing the level of output produced in the short run is likely to require a higher product price than if the same increase in output takes place in the long run.

3. A firm making spacehoppers estimates that whenever it doubles labour, capital, and any other inputs in the long run, its output also doubles. Assuming input prices do not change as the firm expands, draw the firm's average cost curve.

4. Firms maximize profit where marginal cost equals marginal revenue ($MC = MR$). Using a diagram, explain why this is the case.

5. An oil company responds to a 10 per cent increase in the price of North Sea oil by raising its production by half. Is supply price-elastic or price-inelastic? Why?

Further reading

- Mabry and Ulbrich, chapter 6
- Lipsey and Chrystal, chapter 8
- Sloman, chapter 5

The competitive market model

Markets for different goods and services—CDs, wheat, footballers, cars, houses, yoghurt, haircuts, rock concerts—differ a lot in terms of their competitiveness. Markets such as wheat consist of thousands of producers, whereas others, such as cars and laser disc players, are controlled by a small number of firms. Many markets operate without any outside intervention from government, while in others, regulatory agencies exist to monitor firms' performance (for example, in water, gas, and telecommunications).

The competitive structure of an industry (lots of small firms, or a few large producers) is crucial in determining how firms behave in response to changes in demand, supply, or other economic conditions. In the next few chapters, we will examine some of the basic models developed by economists to try to understand the behaviour of firms in markets. We begin with the simplest **market model**: perfect competition. In subsequent chapters, we consider markets where the degree of competition is less than perfect.

Assumptions of perfect competition

The model of **perfect competition** helps us to understand a number of aspects of firms' behaviour in highly competitive markets; most notably, how firms determine the price to charge and the amount to produce. The model of perfect competition applies to markets with:

A large number of buyers and sellers. In a competitive market, each buyer and each firm are very small relative to the total number of buyers and sellers. This means that the action of one firm or consumer goes almost unnoticed by all other firms and consumers. All firms and consumers are minor players in the market.

A homogeneous product. Competitive firms produce a **homogeneous product**; in other words, the goods made by each firm in the industry are identical. Examples of these types of goods include class 1 tomatoes, light wool, and copper wire. Buyers are not concerned with which firm supplies the goods they want, since all firms in a perfectly competitive market produce exactly the same thing.

Free entry and exit. In perfect competition, individuals are free to set up a business and enter any industry they want to; they are also free to leave the industry whenever they feel like it. Because of free entry and exit, all kinds of resources are freely mobile. Resources, such as labour, can be bought or sold or moved from one place to another without restriction.

Perfect knowledge of prices and technology. Perfect knowledge means that consumers and firms are fully aware of the prices of all resources and products in the market. In perfectly competitive markets, consumers always know where they can get the product at the lowest price. Firms know of the latest production techniques and they know the prices of substitute factors. This ensures they produce with the least-cost combination of inputs.

As a result of these assumptions, firms in perfectly competitive markets have no **market power**. That is, they cannot affect the market price by producing more or less. Small firms that raise the price of a good will lose out as consumers switch to an identical (cheaper) product made by rival firms. Similarly, individual consumers cannot affect price because each one buys too small a fraction of the total output. So, in competitive markets both consumers and firms are **price takers**; they take the market price as given since they have no control over it. The model of perfect competition does not exactly fit many (or even any) industries. But, it comes close to describing the behaviour of firms in a number of important industries, notably farming, building contracting, and financial services.

Short-run decision-making in perfect competition

In perfect competition, firms need both cost and revenue information in order to choose their best (profit-maximizing) output. We saw in Chapter 6 that firms calculate total revenue (TR) as price multiplied by quantity sold ($TR = P \times Q$). But, there are two other revenue concepts (average revenue and marginal revenue) that are also relevant for decision-making. These ideas are similar to those we discussed in relation to costs in Chapter 7.

(i) **Average revenue** (AR): this is the total revenue per unit sold, or TR/Q. The average revenue curve and the demand curve are one and the same, because price and average revenue are always the same at each output level. If a firm sells 10 shirts at a price of £10 each, its total revenue is £100; average revenue is £100/10, or £10, which is the same as price.

(ii) **Marginal revenue** (MR): this is the change in total revenue resulting from selling one more unit of output. Thus, marginal revenue is the amount added to total revenue for selling an extra unit (or in symbols, $MR = \Delta TR/\Delta Q$, where Δ is the Greek letter capital delta, meaning 'change in').

Remember that firms in this type of market are price takers; they can sell all they want to at the market price. Therefore, average revenue and marginal revenue are equal to the equilibrium price in the market. To see this, suppose a firm can sell 10 shirts at £10 each for a total revenue of £100. If it can sell all it wants to at the market price, then it can sell 11 shirts at £10 each; this gives the firm a total revenue of £110. The sale of the eleventh shirt adds £10 (its price) to the firm's total revenue (new £110 revenue − old £100 revenue). Thus, the marginal revenue associated with producing and selling the eleventh shirt is the same as its price. This is also the same as the average revenue from the sale of the eleventh shirt (£110 ÷ 11). Because $MR = AR = P$, individual competitive *firms* face a horizontal price line, or demand curve.

Market demand curves in perfect competition slope downwards, as shown in part (*a*) of Figure 8.1. The price facing any competitive firm is the equilibrium price set by the intersection

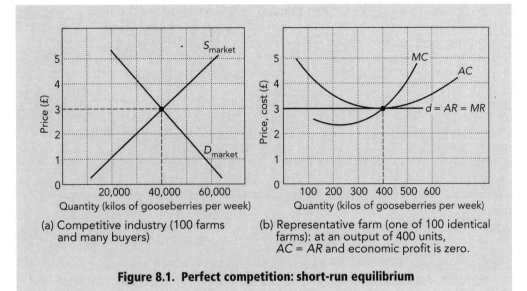

Figure 8.1. Perfect competition: short-run equilibrium

of the market supply and demand curves (S_{market} and D_{market}, respectively). Since each firm faces the same market price of £3, each **representative firm** faces a horizontal demand curve (price line), such as d in part (b) of Figure 8.1.

In this case, the representative firm is one of 100 gooseberry farmers, each of whom can sell 100, 300, or even 600 kilos of gooseberries per week at the market price of £3 per kilo. Thus, the farm faces a horizontal demand curve, d, where $AR = MR = £3$. This gooseberry farm is only one of 100 identical farms in the industry; all of them are selling their output at the going market price of £3. Each farmer adopts the profit-maximizing rule to maximize profit, so selecting that particular quantity of output for which marginal cost equals marginal revenue ($MC = MR$).

Maximizing short-run profits

As shown in part (b) of Figure 8.1, by choosing an output where $MC = MR$, the representative gooseberry farmer produces and sells 400 kilos of gooseberries per week at £3. Since every other farmer in the market is identical to this one, those other 99 farmers also produce 400 kilos per week. Total industry production is 40,000 kilos, shown as the market quantity in part (a). In this situation, each farmer is doing the best she can. If a farmer were to raise output above 400 kilos (say, to 500 kilos) per week, marginal cost would exceed marginal revenue, and profit would be lowered. On the other hand, if output were set below 400 kilos (say, at 300 kilos) per week, marginal revenue would exceed marginal cost, so potential sales (and profits) would be lost. Part (b) of Figure 8.1 shows our representative farmer is making a normal profit (zero economic profit) when output is 400 kilos, because average cost equals average revenue, or $AC = AR = £3$. The farm's revenue per unit is just covering total cost per unit, including a normal return to the owner.

Figure 8.2 shows what happens if market conditions change. Suppose the demand for gooseberries increases, so shifting the market demand curve to the right (from D_1 to D_2). As

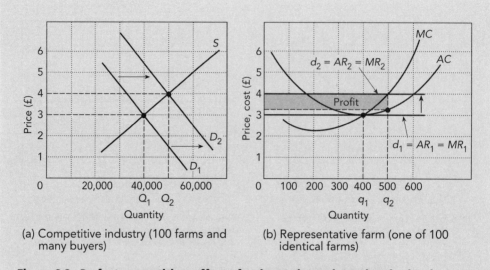

Figure 8.2. Perfect competition: effect of a change in market prices in the short-run

shown in part (*a*), this results in a higher equilibrium market price for gooseberries of £4 (where the demand curve D_2 intersects the supply curve). What is of interest is how competitive farms respond to this higher market price. At the higher market price, the representative gooseberry farmer's demand curve (in part (*b*)) rises to d_2, where $d_2 = AR_2 = MR_2 = £4$. Given that this price must be taken, all the farmer can do in the short run is to increase her use of variable inputs (labour and materials) to raise output until MR again equals MC. Profit is now being maximized at 500 kilos per week.

Total profit is shown by the shaded rectangle in part (*b*) of Figure 8.2. The total amount of profit is £400, calculated as total revenue (£4 × 500 = £2,000) minus total cost (£3.20 × 500 = £1,600). In terms of profit per unit, if average cost is £3.20 and average revenue is £4, then profit per unit sold is £0.80. Total profit is then £0.80 × 500 = £400. Every farmer in the industry makes the same profit. If the market price had fallen (due to a fall in demand), the representative farmer, in the short run, would have suffered a reduction in output and economic losses. Try to illustrate this effect for yourself.

The competitive supply curve in the short run

In Chapter 7, we mentioned that the short-run supply curve for an individual competitive firm consists of its marginal cost curve. The reason for this is that the representative firm produces an output level for which $MC = MR$. Since price and marginal revenue are equal in perfect competition, the profit-maximizing output is always derived from the marginal cost curve where price equals marginal cost. In Figure 8.3, the combinations of price and quantity which

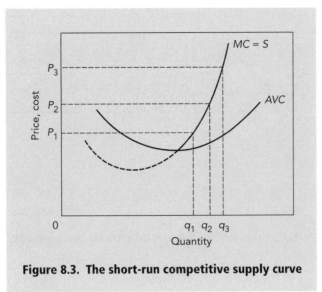

Figure 8.3. The short-run competitive supply curve

maximize profits for the competitive firm are found along the *MC* curve; hence, it is equivalent to the firm's supply curve.

It is only the marginal cost curve above the average variable cost curve that represents the firm's supply curve. Below the minimum point of the *AVC* curve, price is not high enough to cover average variable cost; that is, the firm cannot cover its variable costs on each unit produced. In this situation, the firm is better off producing nothing, or even closing down, in the short run. If it continues to produce, it will lose money on each unit produced in addition to what it loses by paying its fixed costs. Thus, because the fixed costs are less than the losses from operating, the firm would do better (lose less money) if it closed down.

Perfect competition in the long run

In the short run, competitive firms select an output level where $MC = MR$. Frequently, this output will deliver economic profits, although it is possible for economic losses to be made. Short-run profits or losses do not affect the situation in the industry as a whole because firms have insufficient time to join or leave the industry. But in the long run, because the number of firms in the industry is not constant, the picture will change. The number of firms changes in response to economic profits (new firms enter) or economic losses (existing firms leave).

We can see how this works using the example of the gooseberry farm. In part (*a*) of Figure 8.4, the representative farm sells gooseberries at a price P_1; it takes the price set by the intersection of the market demand curve D_1 and the market supply curve S_1. In part (*b*), the representative farm chooses an output q_1 and makes a normal profit ($AR = AC$). Suppose we not let market demand increase to D_2 in Figure 8.4a. How do the gooseberry farmers respond to a higher market price? Initially, the market price rises to P_2 (where D_2 intersects S_1), with a corresponding increase (shift) in the farm's demand curve to $d_2 = AR_2 = MR_2 = P_2$.

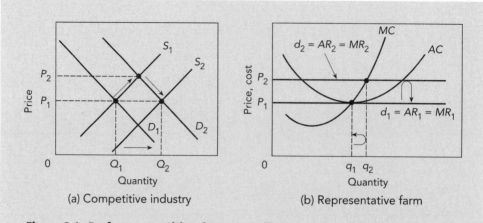

Figure 8.4. Perfect competition: long-run adjustment to an increase in demand

The farmer continues to follow the profit-maximizing rule, and so raises output to q_2, where marginal cost again equals marginal revenue ($MC = MR_2$). Now, the representative farm makes an economic profit since average revenue (AR_2) is above average cost (AC) at the new output level (q_2). The output of the industry has increased because each farm is supplying more at the higher price. As we saw earlier, this marks the end of the story in the short run.

But, in the long run rival farmers are attracted to the industry by the economic profit that is being made. Other farmers decide to enter the gooseberry business. The entry of several new farms into the industry will have a noticeable effect on supply and market price. (Remember, if one farm were to enter the industry there would be no noticeable effect on supply or market price). The entry of several new farms shifts the industry supply curve to the right from S_1 to S_2. (We saw in Chapter 4 that the number of sellers was one of the factors affecting market supply.)

As supply in the industry increases, the market price starts to fall, as does each farmer's horizontal demand curve (it shifts downwards). Each farmer responds to the lower price by reducing output, and each sees a fall in the amount of short-run economic profit. Because economic profit is still positive, new farmers continue to join the industry, so industry supply increases further (the supply curve shifts farther to the right), and the market price continues to fall. Individual farms continue to reduce their output until all their economic profit is wiped out. The adjustment process finally comes to an end when supply has increased enough (the supply curve has shifted far enough to the right) for the new market price to equal the minimum average cost. This is where farmers make a normal profit, and there is no incentive for other farmers to enter the industry or for existing ones to leave.

In Figure 8.4, equilibrium in the industry is restored when supply has increased to S_2 and price has returned to the original level of P_1 (where S_2 intersects D_2). At P_1, each farm is again making zero economic profit. So, after the market adjustment is complete, each gooseberry farmer makes only a normal profit; each supplies the same output as before (q_1) at the original market price. The output of the industry, however, is larger (Q_2) because more farms are operating in the market.

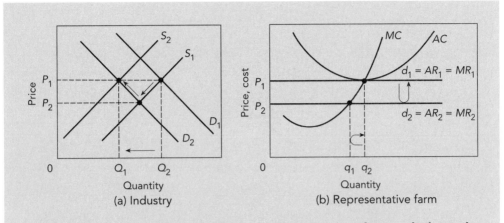

Figure 8.5. Perfect competition: long-run adjustment to a decrease in demand

When demand decreases, there is a similar long-run adjustment to a lower market price. In part (*a*) of Figure 8.5, the market demand curve shifts to the left to D_2. At the lower price of P_2, the representative farm cuts its output to where $MC = MR_2$, but the best it can do is minimize its loss by producing q_1 ($AC > AR_2$). Since individual farms are making losses, some decide to leave the industry in the long run. Market supply falls (the supply curve shifts to the left), so raising the price. Farms continue to leave the industry until the supply curve has shifted to S_2 and the price returns to P_1 (where S_2 intersects D_2). In the long run, farms make a normal profit, and industry output is lower because fewer farms are left in the industry.

Our representative farm will also make long-run adjustments to changes in its costs of production. Try to work out for yourself the initial and long-run effects of an increase (and decrease) in costs.

Evaluating perfect competition

In the long run, perfect competition yields the desirable results of production efficiency and allocative efficiency. We met both these ideas earlier in the book. Production efficiency was discussed in Chapter 7 in the context of the organization of production and firm costs. The idea of allocative efficiency was examined in Chapters 2 (in the context of the production possibilities frontier) and 3 (in terms of the significance of the free market equilibrium). We now consider these ideas in a little more detail in the context of the competitive market model.

Firms in competitive markets produce efficiently. This means competitive firms produce and sell their output at the lowest possible long-run cost; that is, price equals minimum average total cost ($P = AC_{min}$). So, in perfect competition goods are produced as cheaply as possible and consumers pay a price equal to this lowest possible cost. Figure 8.6 illustrates this important result. The firm's demand curve, d_e, is just tangent to the minimum point on both the short-run and long-run average cost curves, AC_{min}. By producing at q_e, the long-run profit-maximizing level of output for this firm occurs where average cost is minimized. Recall from Chapter 7 that this output is known as the efficient scale of the firm.

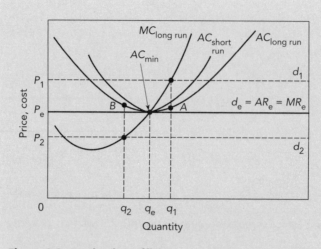

Figure 8.6. Production efficiency in competitive markets

If price is above the equilibrium level, at P_1, the firm produces at a higher average cost in the long run (see point A). Economic profits are being made ($P > AC$). These profits attract other firms to the industry in the long run. As a result, market supply increases and price is driven back to $P_e = AC_{min}$, wiping out the economic profit. On the other hand, if price is below P_e, such as at P_2, output will fall (to q_2). The representative firm will have higher average costs (at point B) and will incur an economic loss ($AC > AR$). Economic losses ensure that some firms leave the industry in the long run. The consequence of firms leaving is a reduction in supply, and an increase in price to P_e; average cost is lowered to AC_{min}. Charging consumers a price equal to the lowest possible production costs (**production efficiency**) is a major benefit of the perfectly competitive market model.

The model of perfect competition also provides **allocative efficiency** in the long run. In Chapter 3 we showed that the free market equilibrium leads to an allocation of resources that maximizes the total surplus (consumer surplus plus producer surplus), or economic well-being, of society. More formally, allocative efficiency exists when price is equal to marginal cost ($P = MC$). This means that resources are used in a way that reflects consumer preferences: consumers get the goods they demand without having to sacrifice other goods of greater value. Figure 8.7 illustrates how this works. The marginal cost of producing a good represents the value of alternative goods not produced with those resources (opportunity cost). When $P_e = MC$, consumers get the good for exactly what it is worth in terms of other goods forgone. If price is above marginal cost, not enough resources are being devoted to its production. In other words, the value placed on the output by consumers (at point A) is greater than the value of the resources used to make this good in their next best use (marginal cost—shown as point B). When this happens, society as a whole is better off if more resources are devoted to the production of this good. Output is raised (from Q_1) until the reduction in price (a move south-eastwards along the market demand curve) and the increase in marginal cost (a move north-eastwards along the market supply curve) make price equal to marginal cost ($P_e = MC$).

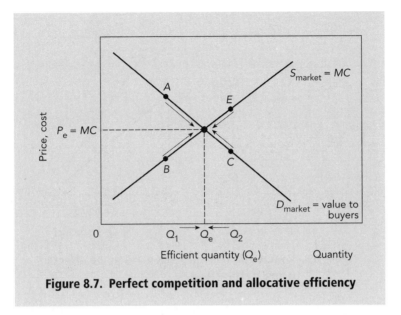

Figure 8.7. Perfect competition and allocative efficiency

On the other hand, when price is less than marginal cost too many resources are devoted to producing that good. The value of the resources in their next best use (marginal cost—shown as point E) is greater than the value of the good as measured by its price (at point C). Here, society would like resources to be allocated to the production of other goods. In Figure 8.7, as the output of this good is reduced (from Q_2), the price rises (a move north-westwards along the demand curve) and the marginal cost falls (a move south-westwards along the supply curve) until the two are equal ($P_e = MC$). So, in perfect competition all resources are allocated efficiently in the long run; they are put to their highest-valued use.

The competitive model serves as a useful benchmark for comparison with other less-competitive models (as we will see in Chapter 9). Despite a number of desirable results, however, perfect competition does have some drawbacks.

One problem with perfect competition is a lack of product variety. Since all firms in perfectly competitive markets produce an identical product, there is little variety to satisfy consumer preferences. The element of product variety is included by consumers when maximizing their satisfaction. This is why you can buy training shoes in many different colours and many different styles. In contrast, perfect competition gives you products sold in bulk, such as crushed rock, or sold in plain bags, like potatoes and carrots. Would you prefer your choice of training shoes to consist of one competitively produced, standardized shoe that comes only in black (like the Adidas All Black of the mid-1980s)? This point about variety and competition is further developed in the next section.

Perfect competition is also criticized on the grounds that the constant long-run adjustment to the number of firms in an industry wastes resources. With every brand new out-of-town shopping complex comes the need for extra nearby parking spaces, and new streets leading to the complex. At the same time, similar shops located in the high street close down, leaving buildings empty for months or years. Wherever you live you have almost certainly seen the rapid development of new retail centres and shop closures in the older parts of town; this is an example of competitive forces in action.

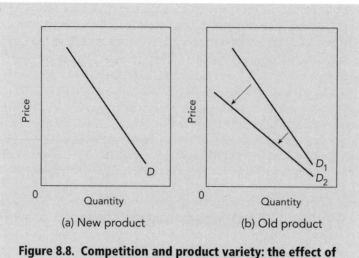

Figure 8.8. Competition and product variety: the effect of a new bottled beer

Variety and competition[1]

The model of perfect competition described above does not always fit well with our ideas about the **process of competition** between firms. There seems to be an emphasis on uniformity: identical firms making identical products that are sold at a single price. But, in practice, competition seems to be about variety, with lots of different firms producing different products at different prices. Earlier in the chapter, we discussed perfect competition in terms of price-taking behaviour. That is, competitive firms do not set prices but simply take the market price. But this seems to be at odds with our everyday experience. In the real world, we see firms not only setting prices, but also setting different prices. There does not appear to be the emergence of a single market price. Again, in the real world we see variety, but the competitive model indicates uniformity.

Here, we discuss **variety in competition** and link this back to the central idea of competition —the entry of new firms and products. To do this, we have to depart a little from the model of perfect competition introduced earlier. How do firms and products compete with each other? Most goods are slightly different from one another. In other words, the individual products or brands are not perfect substitutes for each other, but are close substitutes. Examples include cars, chocolate bars, and types of beer. We can see how competition works by considering the introduction of a new brand of bottled beer.

The new bottled beer faces a downward-sloping demand curve D, as illustrated in part (a) of Figure 8.8. But what is important is the way the introduction of this new product affects existing products in the market—that is, how the new competition works. This is shown in part (b) of Figure 8.8. The demand curve D_1 represents one of the established products in the market before the entry of the new brand of beer. The new brand has two effects on this demand curve:

(i) It shifts the curve to the left (to D_2) because the new product takes away some of the market from the old product. While the new brand of bottled beer may expand total beer sales to some extent, many of its sales are likely to come from people switching brands.

(ii) The shifted demand curve, D_2, will be more price-elastic than the old one (D_1). To understand this idea we need to remember that a demand curve shows the relationship between price and quantity demanded, holding everything else constant. One of the things held constant is the price of related products, including the new brand of beer. In the absence of any competition, consumers of the old brand of beer can either reduce their consumption or pay more when the price goes up. But with an alternative product on the market whose price is not rising, they have another alternative—to switch brands. So, the introduction of another (substitute) good makes the demand curve for the original brand more price-elastic.

Producers of the old brand of bottled beer respond to falling demand by cutting the price; as they now sell a smaller amount at a lower price, their profits are reduced. The introduction of the new product has thus widened consumer choice and put downward pressure on prices; at the same time, it has reduced the profits of the existing firm. New entry into the market is, therefore, crucial. Competition from new products reduces prices and profits, even if the new products are imperfect substitutes for the established products.

As the process of new entry continues indefinitely, the market for bottled beer becomes more and more crowded and the demand curve for each beer becomes more and more elastic. This results in each firm receiving only a normal profit, since each one now produces a smaller and smaller percentage of industry output. Thus, the textbook model of perfect competition is the logical outcome of the realistic process of competition between imperfect substitutes.

So far, we have assumed that each maker of bottled beer produces just one brand. But in reality we see firms producing a range of beers which appear to compete with each other. Tetley, Bass, and Heineken all produce a number of brands, each of which is slightly different. Why might they do this? Consider a company that is currently producing only one brand. It knows that the introduction of other bottled beers into the market will reduce its own sales and profits. But it also realizes that rival firms will only enter the market with a new product if they expect to make a profit. In a market with only one bottled beer, there are excellent opportunities for profitable entry. Faced with the inevitable launch of new products, the company may decide to introduce further products itself, partly as a way of keeping other firms out of the market. So, the threat of entry by new firms is crucial in providing an incentive for the existing firm to widen its product range. Further, the threat of entry also operates to reduce prices and profits.

A discussion of product variety also provides a key to understanding the prices we observe. There are two puzzles we need to resolve: the first relates to the idea of price-taking behaviour, and the second is concerned with price variation. For the idea of price-taking behaviour, we need to refer again to Figure 8.8. The introduction of the new brand of beer made the demand curve for the existing brand more and more elastic. This implies that the range over which prices can be set is reduced. The firm may still set prices, but its freedom of choice is constrained by the demand curve. With more and more competition in the market, this constraint becomes more binding until, in the extreme case of a horizontal demand curve, the firm has no discretion. In this way, market competition weakens the price-making power of the firm; the firm is forced to become a price taker.

Concerning the second puzzle, it seems fairly obvious that if the typical market is made up of a range of individual goods which are close but not perfect substitutes, we would expect differences in their prices, even in market equilibrium. This fits the market for bottled beer quite well, where the differences between beers clearly justifies some difference in their prices. But there are also rather more subtle price variations. Some shops consistently sell certain bottled beers at a lower price than other shops (compare prices in Tesco or Safeway with those at a corner shop or off-licence, for example). In this case it appears that the products are the same. But with more thought we can discover significant differences.

When you purchase any particular item you buy a range of associated factors, as well as the item itself. A good example is a cup of coffee. While the cup of coffee may be identical each time, it is very different to buy a coffee in different settings—after an expensive meal in a top-class restaurant, on a train, in a university coffee bar—and we might expect demand (and hence prices) to reflect these differences.

So, we might expect to find price differentials across goods that are almost identical, or across identical goods sold in slightly different situations. But the main point remains the following: the entry of new firms (or products) into a market is likely to exert downward pressure on prices, to the benefit of consumers and to the detriment of firms' profits. In this way, the key idea of competition becomes relevant to practical markets rather than just being confined to the abstract model of perfect competition.

To summarize, the key point is that competition is crucially linked to the actual (or potential) entry of firms or products into a market. The process of competition mainly revolves around entry and the reactions to entry by existing firms. We may find product variation, price setting by firms, and price variation between close substitutes. But increased competition, in the sense of **entry into a market**, can be expected to put downward pressure on prices and profits. Consumers benefit in the form of both increased choice and lower prices.

Summary

1. The model of perfect competition describes a market with many small firms in competition, all of whom have little or no control over the market price.

2. The perfectly competitive model is based on a number of assumptions: many buyers and sellers, a homogeneous product, free entry and exit, and perfect knowledge. These assumptions imply an absence of market power. Firms are price takers.

3. A firm's best output in perfect competition is that for which $MC = MR$. In the short run, this may produce economic profits or economic losses.

4. The firm's short-run supply curve is that part of its marginal cost curve which lies above the average variable cost curve.

5. Long-run equilibrium occurs where all firms make only normal profits. Short-run economic profits attract firms into the market, so increasing supply and driving price down until only normal profits are made. When short-run losses are made, firms leave the market, so decreasing supply and pushing up price until all firms make only normal profits.

6. In long-run equilibrium, perfect competition results in production efficiency ($P = AC_{min}$) and allocative efficiency ($P = MC$).

7. The model of perfect competition is frequently criticized. Two main criticisms are: there is a lack of product variety, and resources are wasted because of the constant adjustment to the number of firms in the long run.

8. The formal model of perfect competition does not always fit well with our ideas about the process of competition between firms. The model assumes identical firms, an identical product, and a single price set by the market. But, in reality competition thrives with different products and price setting by firms. The model of perfect competition can be reconciled with practical competition by emphasizing the key role played by the entry of new firms and products in the process of competition. If continued indefinitely, we would have a situation close to that described by the model of perfect competition.

Key terms

allocative efficiency	perfect competition
average revenue	perfect knowledge
entry into a market	price takers
homogeneous product	process of competition
marginal revenue	production efficiency
market model	representative firm
market power	variety in competition

Review questions

1. If demand curves slope downwards, how can it be that the individual firm in perfect competition faces a horizontal demand curve?

2. D. P. Gumby & Co. make sleeveless sweaters. Suppose the firm operates in a perfectly competitive market. It can produce the following quantities of sweaters per day at the following costs:

Quantity	Total cost	Average cost
0	40	—
1	44	44
2	48	24
3	54	18
4	64	16
5	80	16
6	108	18
7	152	21.8
8	216	27

   (i) What price will the firm charge in long-run competitive equilibrium? (Hint: you need to calculate marginal cost.)

  (ii) Draw the *AC* and *MC* curves for this firm and draw Gumby's demand curve.

 (iii) Explain the process by which the firm adjusts to an increase in market demand for sleeveless sweaters that raises the price to £28. What does Gumby & Co. immediately do in the short run? Describe the long-run adjustment for the sleeveless sweater industry and for Gumby & Co.

3. Dinsdale Piranha sells pinball machines in a perfectly competitive market. What happens to his price and output in the short run if: (i) more people want to play pinball; and (ii) labour costs increase? Now explain what happens in each case in the long run.

4. What are the essential features of a perfectly competitive market? Illustrate a firm making a short-run loss. Why is this situation unlikely to persist in the long run?

5. Why are resources allocated efficiently in perfect competition?

6. 'If we see the process of competition in terms of the entry of new firms into a market, it is possible to reconcile the practice of competition with the perfectly competitive model.' How might you justify this statement?

Note

1. This is adapted from Alan Hamlin, 'Variety and Competition', *Economic Review*, 10.1 (Sept. 1992), 2–4.

Further reading

- Mabry and Ulbrich, chapter 7

- Lipsey and Chrystal, chapter 9
- Sloman, chapter 6

CHAPTER 9

Imperfect competition

In the model of perfect competition, no single firm has any influence over the market price; all firms are price takers. In this chapter, we consider two other market models where firms possess some market power: monopoly and oligopoly. Monopoly describes a situation where the firm and the industry are one and the same; it is at the opposite extreme from perfect competition. Monopolists have the power to affect price and they may make economic profits in the long run. Oligopoly is a market model that lies between the two extremes of perfect competition and monopoly. In oligopolistic markets, there are only a few large firms. If market conditions allow, these firms may establish cartels to try to increase their market power.

By studying these two models of imperfect competition, economists are able to make predictions about the behaviour of firms in a number of different industries as market conditions change.

Assumptions of monopoly

Monopoly describes an industry that consists of a single firm producing a unique product. The economist's model of monopoly is based on three main assumptions:

(i) *There is a single firm in the market.* This monopoly firm produces the entire output of the industry. Consequently, the monopolist faces the market demand curve; in short, the firm and the industry are one and the same.

(ii) *A monopolist produces a unique product.* In other words, there are no close substitutes for the firm's output. For example, until the end of 1997 domestic gas users in the UK could only buy their gas from British Gas; for many years it was the only supplier of gas to domestic households.

(iii) *There are significant barriers to entry to protect monopolists from competition.* These **barriers to entry** serve to keep other firms out of the monopolist's industry and enable the firm to exercise **monopoly power**. Monopoly power allows a monopolist to keep output low, raise prices significantly above the competitive level, and earn long-run economic profits.

It is rare to find examples of pure monopoly in the real world. But utility industries, such as electricity, gas, water, and telecommunications, come quite close. Before looking at how monopolists select their best output, we consider, in a little more detail, the role of entry barriers.

Barriers to entry

Monopolies are protected from competition by barriers to entry. By restricting entry into an industry, these barriers create some degree of **imperfect competition**. Barriers to entry may be either natural or artificial. A natural barrier is where there exist large economies of scale. As we noted in Chapter 7, economies of scale result from production efficiencies, which allow a firm's average costs to fall as output increases. With large economies of scale, the size of factory that is needed for cost minimization may be so large that there is only room for one firm in the market. If a firm's average cost falls as output increases over the entire range of market demand, we have a **natural monopoly**. Electricity utilities, the telephone service, water, gas, and railways are classic examples of natural monopolies resulting from economies of scale.

Artificial barriers to entry are often created (or assisted) by government. One example is that of patents and copyrights. These are entry barriers erected by government to encourage innovation and invention. A patent gives an individual or firm sole access to superior technology or the right to supply a particular product for a specified number of years. Polaroid's patent monopoly in instant cameras was reaffirmed in the late 1980s when legal action forced Kodak to abandon its new instant camera. Intel owns the patent on microprocessor chips used in most IBM computers.

Price and output in monopoly

Since the monopolist is the only firm in the industry, it faces the market demand curve for its product. The monopolist must, therefore, lower its price to sell a larger amount (remember, the demand curve is downward-sloping). When lowering the price, the monopolist has to reduce the price on *all* units sold, not just the last unit. This means that the change in total revenue from selling an extra unit—marginal revenue (*MR*)—is lower than the price received for that extra unit. For example, a firm selling 10 shirts at £15 each has a total revenue of £150. If it sells an eleventh shirt at £14.50, its total revenue rises to £159.50 (11 × £14.50). The change in total revenue (*MR*) is £9.50, which is less than the price received (£14.50). In other words, marginal revenue is equal to the extra revenue from selling one more shirt (£14.50) minus the revenue lost on each of the other 10 shirts (50p × 10), which now have to be sold at the new, reduced price. So, when firms face a downward-sloping demand curve, marginal revenue is less than average revenue (or price); hence, the *MR* curve must lie below the *AR* (demand) curve. Marginal values must be below average values when those average values are falling. (Think back to the cricket example in Chapter 7. If a cricketer's batting average is falling, then his marginal (next) score must be lower than his average score.)

Figure 9.1 shows this relationship. There is also a table of numbers to help reinforce your understanding of why the marginal revenue curve must lie below the demand curve once output becomes positive. In order to sell one extra unit, the firm has to charge the same (lower) price on all units; it must, therefore, reduce its price from £8 to £6 to sell the second unit. Total revenue is affected in the following way: £6 is added to total revenue from selling the second unit. But the first unit now only delivers £6 worth of revenue instead of £8, so £2 less revenue is being received for the first unit. Thus, the sale of the second unit increases total revenue by only

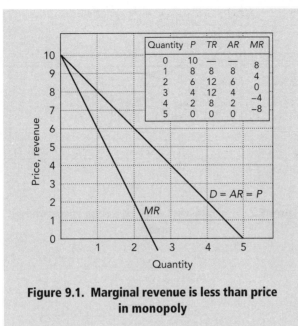

Quantity	P	TR	AR	MR
0	10	—	—	
				8
1	8	8	8	
				4
2	6	12	6	
				0
3	4	12	4	
				−4
4	2	8	2	
				−8
5	0	0	0	

Figure 9.1. Marginal revenue is less than price in monopoly

£4, not by the £6 received for the second unit. The *MR* curve must, therefore, lie below the downward-sloping demand (*AR*) curve.

In the short run, monopoly firms may make economic profits or economic losses, or may even close down. The primary difference between monopoly and perfect competition lies in the long run. Unlike firms in perfectly competitive markets, monopolies may make economic profits in the long run, mainly because the firm is protected from potential competition by barriers to entry. This persistent economic profit is called **monopoly profit**.

Like other firms, monopolies follow the profit-maximizing rule when choosing their output. In other words, maximum profit (or minimum loss) is made by producing an output level for which marginal cost equals marginal revenue (*MC* = *MR*). Figure 9.2 shows this output level as Q_1. The firm is making long-run monopoly profits (shown by the shaded area), because price (P_1) is above average cost (*AC*) at the profit-maximizing level of output (Q_1). Note that the monopolist firm first selects the profit-maximizing level of output, Q_1, and then (reading from the demand curve) it finds the price it can charge for that output.

Monopoly firms, however, are not guaranteed to make long-run monopoly profits. If the demand curve were lower (that is, each output level corresponded to a lower price) while costs remained the same, this firm might only make zero economic profit (a normal profit) in the long run. This is shown in part (*a*) of Figure 9.3; the profit-maximizing output, Q_1, corresponds to a price at which average revenue is equal to average cost. If the demand curve were even lower or costs were higher, as shown in part (*b*), the firm might suffer an economic loss (average revenue might be below average cost at the output level Q_1).

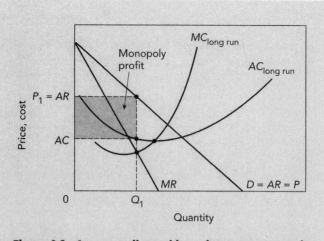

Figure 9.2. A monopolist making a long-run economic profit

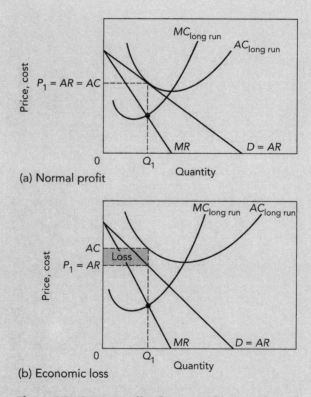

(a) Normal profit

(b) Economic loss

Figure 9.3. A monopolist does not always make an economic profit

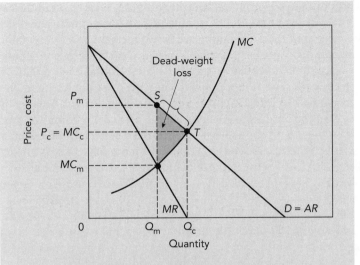

Figure 9.4. The inefficiency of monopoly

Evaluating the monopoly model

How does the model of pure monopoly compare with perfect competition? Monopolies are often subject to adverse criticism because they are said to overcharge consumers, make their owners very wealthy (the so-called 'fat cats' who run many of the private sector monopolies), and engage in 'dirty tricks' to protect themselves from competition. (You may recall the incident where British Airways were found guilty of conducting a 'dirty tricks campaign' against a rival airline, Virgin Atlantic, in a dispute over the allocation of landing slots at Heathrow Airport.) So, what, for economists, are the main problems with monopoly industries?

One way to look at this is to compare monopoly with the model of perfect competition. Because of the benefits the competitive model offers, it is often used as a standard for judging actual markets and comparing other, less competitive market models, such as monopoly. As we saw in Chapter 8, perfect competition in the long run offers production efficiency (firms produce at minimum average cost) and allocative efficiency (resources are allocated to maximize the total surplus in a market).

How does this compare with monopoly? In monopoly output is sold at a price above minimum average cost ($P > AC_{min}$), even when normal profits are made in the long run. In part (*a*) of Figure 9.3, the monopolist is making only a normal profit, but the firm does not produce an output that minimizes average cost. In this way, monopolies are productively inefficient. Another problem with monopoly is that it produces a smaller output and charges a higher price than the equivalent perfectly competitive industry. Suppose a monopoly industry were somehow organized as a competitive industry. Figure 9.4 compares the price and output results under the two models. In perfect competition, the intersection of the market supply and demand curves establishes the long-run price and quantity as P_c and Q_c, respectively. In the competitive equilibrium, output is sold at a price that equals marginal cost (a result we saw in

Figure 8.7). The monopolist's profit-maximizing output level is Q_m, found where $MC = MR$. This output, Q_m, is less than the output Q_c under perfect competition, and it sells for a higher price, P_m. High prices and restricted output are two of the main criticisms of monopoly.

Also, because monopoly price (P_m) is above marginal cost (MC_m), monopolies misallocate resources. There are some potential buyers of the good (in the range S to T on the demand curve) who value the product at more than its marginal cost but less than the monopolist's price. These people do not buy the good. This result is inefficient because the value these non-buyers place on the product is greater than the cost of providing the product to them. The shaded area in Figure 9.4 shows what is called the **deadweight loss**. Remember that the demand curve reflects the value to consumers and the marginal cost curve reflects the costs to the monopolist. So, the area between the demand curve and the marginal cost curve for output levels between Q_m and Q_c is equal to the total surplus lost because of monopoly pricing; this area is known as the deadweight loss triangle. Output ought to be expanded, which would cause price to fall and marginal cost to rise, until price equals marginal cost.

On the plus side, monopoly may be the only way to benefit from substantial scale economies in some markets, and the costs associated with entry and exit in competition are likely to be avoided with monopoly. It is also suggested that monopolies are more likely to develop new production methods and introduce new products because they are able to reap the benefits of research and development spending (R&D) for themselves. But, on the other hand, if there is no competition, there may be no incentive to spend money on R&D to stay ahead in the market.

Oligopoly and cartels

Oligopoly lies between the extremes of perfect competition and monopoly, but it is closer to the monopoly model. Almost every consumer durable you buy (cars, hi-fi systems, washing machines, and so on) is produced and sold in oligopoly markets. As usual we begin our analysis by outlining the main assumptions of oligopoly:

(i) *Oligopoly markets are dominated by a few (three or four) large firms.* In an oligopoly market, the largest firms in an industry produce most of the output.

(ii) *Oligopolies exist because barriers to entry (including economies of scale) protect them from competition.* Establishing brand names through advertising may act as an entry barrier for oligopolies. Few people are prepared to undertake the risk and expense of joining the breakfast cereal market against Kellogg's main brands.

(iii) *Oligopolies produce either homogeneous products or differentiated products.* Steel, aluminium, paper, and cement are examples of homogeneous goods. **Differentiated products** are ones that are very similar to each other but have certain distinctive characteristics that are important to consumers; for example, you may think that Heinz and Co-op baked beans are quite similar, but try convincing a baked-bean connoisseur (such as one of the authors) of that! The main reason firms attempt to differentiate their products is to make demand more inelastic.

Oligopoly price and output behaviour

In contrast to the other models we have looked at, there is no clear-cut theory of oligopoly behaviour. For this reason, we cannot predict exactly how oligopolists set price and output. However, one fact is clear: before changing price or output, oligopoly firms must consider the reactions of rivals. This **mutual interdependence** plays a key role in the determination of price and output.

Suppose Sony lowers the price of its video recorders (VCRs) by 10 per cent in an attempt to sell more VCRs. What do you think Panasonic and Philips will do? They are unlikely to let Sony get the extra sales and increase its market share. They are likely to match Sony's price cuts. If they do, Sony will sell very few additional VCRs. Since the managers at Sony are smart, they know this is likely to happen; therefore, they are not likely to lower prices without a very good reason (for example, the economy is in recession) that also applies to the other makers of VCRs. Oligopolists are very careful not to cut prices too often by themselves.

On the other hand, if Sony raises its VCR prices by 10 per cent to get more revenue, its rivals will probably let Sony price itself out of the market. Sony customers will switch to Panasonic, Toshiba, Philips, and so on. Since Sony is aware that the other firms are unlikely to match its price increases, it will not raise prices very often (unless there is a general cost increase that affects all firms in the industry simultaneously).

So, because of mutual interdependence, oligopolists tend to change their prices infrequently. Prices are regarded as 'sticky' in such markets, changing only at certain times of the year. In the case of cars, for example, prices change when new models are introduced in August of each year. One way for firms to deal with interdependence is to collude. The idea is that oligopoly firms are more likely to make long-run economic profits if they can overcome the uncertainty associated with how rival companies will react to price changes. Formal **collusion** among oligopoly firms in the setting of prices and in the allocation of quantities is known as a **cartel**. Cartels are illegal in the UK and in many other countries, including the US, where the monitoring of anti-competitive behaviour is especially vigilant. Interestingly, the one activity in the US where open collusion is allowed is major-league baseball. The league acts as a cartel by rigidly controlling entry into and exit from the league. Also, the teams openly co-operate with each other in order to provide a product (baseball games). Perhaps the most famous cartel in recent years is the Organisation of Petroleum Exporting Countries (OPEC). OPEC was able to raise oil prices from just over $2 per barrel in 1971 to $35 per barrel by 1982. In the mid-1980s the cartel fell into disarray, and the price began to fall. By the mid-1990s, OPEC oil was selling for between $15 and $20 per barrel.

A cartel in steel[1]

On 16 February 1994 the European Commission fined sixteen leading European steelmakers a total of £79 million. The largest individual fine was £24 million (about Ecu 32 million), imposed on British Steel. The companies had been found guilty of operating a cartel in the supply of steel beams to the construction industry. It is alleged that the steelmakers fixed prices, exchanged confidential information, and agreed to divide up the total market between the firms. Each of these activities contravenes European Union law.

Why might the firms risk such large fines in order to form the cartel? To answer this question, we need to examine the reasons for forming a cartel. Firms are interested in maximizing profits. To establish whether it is worthwhile to form a cartel we have to consider how much profit would be made within the cartel, and how much profit would be made if the firms were to act independently. Before doing this, however, it will help to identify the maximum level of

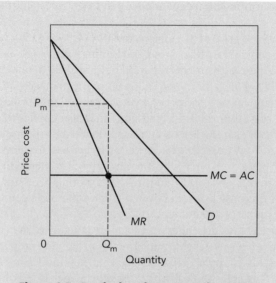

Figure 9.5. Producing the monopoly output

profits in an industry. We will then have a benchmark against which to measure the profits that firms might actually get in practice.

To keep things simple, suppose that the firms in a particular industry produce an identical product (say, a particular grade of steel), and they all operate with the same constant marginal cost (MC). This situation is shown in Figure 9.5. As a group, it is best for the firms to produce the monopoly output, Q_m, and sell the product for a price of P_m. Total industry profit is, therefore, maximized when the firms behave as if they were a single monopolist. One way of achieving this maximum level of profit would be for the parties to form an illegal cartel with binding agreements. But what if legally binding agreements are not possible? If the firms act independently, profits will typically fall short of the joint profit-maximizing level. This is because each firm is tempted to undercut the prices of its rivals. Consider the simplest possible case, an industry with two firms, Best & Co. and Marsh Ltd, who must choose their prices at the same time. Will each firm, acting independently, choose P_m?

The argument runs as follows. Suppose Best & Co. thinks that Marsh Ltd is going to choose P_m. What would be Best's optimal choice? If Best & Co. also opted for P_m, industry profit would be at the joint profit-maximizing level, and the firm would receive some proportion of the total. But Best & Co. can do better than this. If Best & Co. sets a price just below P_m, it will capture all the sales and so obtain the entire industry profit (slightly less than the joint profit-maximizing level of profit). This argument may be applied to any price that is above marginal cost. The incentive to undercut on price only ends if each firm expects the other to set price equal to marginal cost. So, in the absence of co-operation between firms, the theory predicts that price will be driven down to marginal cost; this may result in low profits, or even firm closure. Firms are, therefore, normally reluctant to engage in 'price wars'. So, while it is tempting to undercut a rival's price, the benefits of undercutting do not normally last for very long.

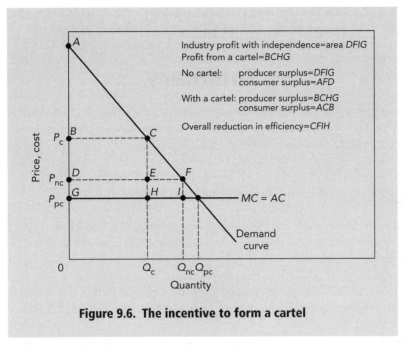

Figure 9.6. The incentive to form a cartel

The incentive to undercut explains why price will be below the joint profit-maximizing level. Now consider the effect of a cartel. The incentive to form a cartel is shown in Figure 9.6. The price in the absence of a cartel is denoted by P_{nc}. This is above marginal cost but below the cartel price, P_c. If firms act independently, industry profit is given by the area $DFIG$, whereas profit from a cartel is $BCHG$. The incentive to form the cartel is simply the difference between these two areas.

The rationale for the anti-cartel legislation in many countries is the argument that economic efficiency will be enhanced if there is more competition. As we explained in Chapter 3, efficiency can be measured using the concepts of **consumer surplus** and **producer surplus**. In Figure 9.6, in the absence of a cartel, producer surplus (profit) is the area $DFIG$, and consumer surplus is the area of the triangle AFD. With the cartel, producer surplus increases to $BCHG$, but consumer surplus falls to ACB. We measure the effect on efficiency by doing the following calculation: subtract the sum of producer and consumer surplus with the cartel from their sum without it. We find that there is a reduction in efficiency, given by the area $CFIH$: the cartel restricts output to Q_c despite the fact that the price (consumers' willingness to pay for additional output) is greater than the marginal cost to society of producing this output (compare points C and H).

Figure 9.6 also shows that, with or without a cartel, output will be lower and price higher in oligopoly than in perfect competition (compare prices P_c and P_{nc} with P_{pc}, and outputs Q_c and Q_{nc} with Q_{pc}). Thus, oligopolies, like monopolies, are allocatively inefficient ($P > MC$). The extent to which oligopoly price exceeds the competitive price depends on the strength of each individual oligopoly's barriers to entry. Where entry barriers are weak, firms cannot raise price much above the competitive level. In industries with strong barriers, and especially those that can collude successfully (form strong cartels), firms may be able to restrict output and raise price close to the pure monopoly level for a significant period of time.

Summary

1. A pure monopoly is where a unique product is sold by a single firm in an industry with high entry barriers. Because the firm is protected from competition, it has monopoly power: the power to raise price by restricting output.

2. There are both natural and artificial barriers to entry. The former may result from large economies of scale, while the latter may be due to patents.

3. Natural monopolies result from large-scale economies. In a natural monopoly, the market has room for only one firm, because when it reaches the lowest level of average costs it will supply the entire market demand.

4. Monopolies can make long-run economic profits, although economic profit is not guaranteed. Persistent economic profit (monopoly profit) is the result of monopoly power.

5. Monopolies are not productively efficient (because $P > AC_{min}$) and they misallocate resources (because $P > MC$). The level of output is below that which maximizes the sum of consumer and producer surplus (total surplus). As a result, monopoly causes a deadweight loss.

6. In oligopoly markets a few large firms dominate the production of a slightly differentiated product. The key feature is mutual interdependence, which leads to prices being stable. Generally, oligopolies can earn long-run economic profits through restricting output and raising price. Cartels are oligopolies that make formal arrangements to restrict group output and set a monopoly price. They often do not last very long.

Key terms

allocative efficiency

barriers to entry

cartel

collusion

consumer surplus

deadweight loss

differentiated products

imperfect competition

monopoly

monopoly power

monopoly profit

mutual interdependence

natural monopoly

oligopoly

producer surplus

production efficiency

Review questions

1. Why must marginal revenue be less than price for any firm that faces a downward-sloping demand curve for its product?

2. Stig O'Tracy is a monopoly supplier of spacehoppers. The table below shows his demand curve. Marginal cost is constant at £5. What is his profit-maximizing price–quantity combination? (Hint: you need to calculate marginal revenue.) What would be the equilibrium price and quantity for a perfectly competitive firm?

Price (£)	Quantity demanded
9	0
8	1
7	2
6	3
5	4
4	5
3	6
2	7
1	8
0	9

3. In what sense does monopoly lead to a misallocation of resources?

4. On 1 November 1997, competition in the supply of domestic gas formally began in Scotland and the north-east of England. By mid-1998 around 4 million consumers were able to choose their own gas supplier. The entry of competitive suppliers in the market is expected to cut around £10 a month off the average winter gas bill, according to Clare Spottiswoode, Director-General of Gas Supply. Why would you expect gas prices to fall? What might be the effect of competition on (allocative and productive) efficiency in the industry?

5. In 1995 the UK Restrictive Practices Court (RPC) found the ten largest UK suppliers of ready-mix concrete guilty of price fixing. What is the incentive for these firms to collude when setting prices? Why did the RPC object to this behaviour?

6. Why are most cartels doomed to failure in the long run if they use their cartel power?

Note

1. This is adapted from Geoff Stewart, 'Cartels', *Economic Review*, 12.1 (Sept. 1994), 25–6.

Further reading

- Mabry and Ulbrich, chapter 8

- Lipsey and Chrystal, chapters 10 and 11
- Sloman, chapters 6 and 7

CHAPTER 10

Imperfect competition in action

In the previous chapter, we discussed the market models of monopoly and oligopoly. We concentrated on an exposition of the underlying theory, without attempting (too often) to apply the ideas to cases of topical interest. Having covered the basic ideas we now focus on how they can be applied in practice. We look at three issues to illustrate the relevance of the monopoly model: the pricing of CDs, the profitability of British Telecom, and the relationship between the football industry and television.

Monopoly and the price of CDs[1]

If you read the broadsheet newspapers you will often see economic arguments presented by journalists. One example of this is discussed here. It shows you that the economics you have met so far can be useful in assessing the validity of the comments made. In the article, the journalist concerned appears to have accepted the views of a company executive without proper investigation. Using some simple economic concepts we can assess the validity of the comments made.

The issue concerns the price of CDs in Britain and the reactions to the strong condemnation of CD pricing by the National Heritage Select Committee in May 1993. This led to a Monopolies and Mergers Commission investigation of the industry. Consumer groups, as well as a number of newspapers, have run a campaign against the 'high' price of CDs for some time. A CD sold in Britain can cost 100 per cent more than the same CD sold in the US. The cost of producing a CD in its box is around £1 and yet it sells for about £14. While production costs have fallen from £2 when CDs were first introduced in 1983, there has been hardly any reduction in price. There is also considerable variation in CD prices between shops. A survey carried out in May 1993 into ten stores' prices showed that the difference between the price in the most expensive store and the price in the cheapest was around 50 per cent. The CD industry is also dominated by four producers. This would suggest that the firms possess **monopoly power** and that it is this monopoly power that explains the high prices.

Over the years, the CD industry has produced a series of arguments to justify CD prices. Jeremy Warner (an executive at Warner Brothers) said in May 1993 that the National Heritage Select Committee had failed to prove that a monopoly operates in the supply of music, or that there is anything wrong with the pricing of CDs. Moreover, he argued that the industry is charging appropriate prices. We now examine these arguments.

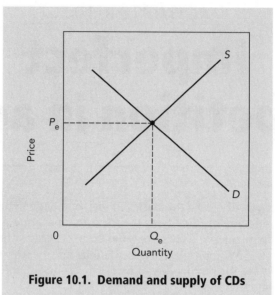

Figure 10.1. Demand and supply of CDs

Mr Warner says that he (like the Chairman of the Select Committee) would like to see lower prices; he adds that it would be just as nice if David Hockney could be persuaded to reduce the price of his paintings. To examine this point we have to explain what determines price. If we have a perfectly competitive market (as shown in Figure 10.1), the equilibrium price, P_e, is determined by the forces of supply and demand. We have said previously in the book that the demand curve can be interpreted as a 'willingness-to-pay curve', while the supply curve represents the 'marginal cost curve'. Figure 10.1 says that at a price of P_e, the marginal consumer is just willing to pay for the extra cost involved in the production of the CD (we have **allocative efficiency**). This means P_e is a 'fair' price, since those consumers who would like lower prices and would like to buy more than Q_e are not willing to pay the extra costs involved.

But, if Mr Warner's claim—that the current price of CDs is a competitive price—is correct, the price has to equal marginal cost. This, however, seems unlikely given that the retail price is over twelve times the production cost (even allowing for retail and distribution costs). If prices were (perfectly) competitive, they would be equal to marginal cost, but they are not. This suggests that the perfect-competition model is inappropriate, and that monopoly may be more relevant. How do David Hockney paintings fit into this? The main difference is that paintings are not mass-produced items—they are one-offs. An original painting exists in a fixed supply of one, hence the supply curve is vertical (not upward-sloping). There is still an equilibrium (market clearing) price, but we cannot give it our usual marginal cost interpretation. It is interpreted as a payment for scarcity; so, because the price is not related to production cost, CDs are not like original Hockney paintings in this respect.

Another comment made by Mr Warner is that CD prices in Britain reflect the fact that the music industry is a major player in the world market; if you make dealers set lower prices, companies will have to sell three times as many CDs in order to sustain their profit margins in the home market. There are two points to note here: (i) Mr Warner thinks current profit levels are

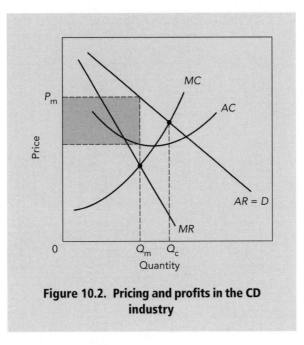

**Figure 10.2. Pricing and profits in the CD
industry**

about right, and (ii) as home profits affect exports, it is desirable to have high prices in the
home market in order to help boost exports.

Regarding the first point, we have to be able to say at what level profits should be. In our discussion of perfect competition, we said new firm entry into a market leads, in the long run, to
zero **economic profit**; normal profits induce firms to stay in business. In the case of monopoly,
economic profit is positive, as shown in Figure 10.2. Total profit is represented by the shaded
area. We can compare the competitive and monopolistic cases by regarding the monopolist's
marginal cost curve as equivalent to the supply curve for the competitive industry (we saw this
idea in Figure 9.4). From this, the monopolist earns positive economic profit by restricting
output to Q_m rather than producing the competitive output level, Q_c. So, if the CD industry is
a monopoly, the current level of profit will be too high. The fact that the proposed action of the
Select Committee (to cut prices) would serve to reduce profits seems to be a desirable outcome.

It is often said that monopoly is required to support exports. The idea of subsidizing
exporters to improve foreign currency reserves is known as 'mercantilism'. It was Adam Smith
in his book *Wealth of Nations* (1776) who pointed out that what makes economies wealthy is
not the extent of their gold reserves, or the amount of exports they can sell, but what they consume. Subsidizing monopoly will generally lead to a worsening of the performance of the
economy. Smith's legacy is that, if anti-competitive practices are to be allowed to boost exports,
they need to be explicitly justified. One justification for protecting exporters is to foster the
development of new small industries until they are large enough to compete on their own
terms in world markets. However, Mr Warner admits that the UK music industry is large in
world terms: UK sales are 10 per cent of the world total, while recordings account for 25 per
cent. In this situation, the industry ought to be competitive (and profitable) in world terms,
and not need subsidizing by the UK consumer.

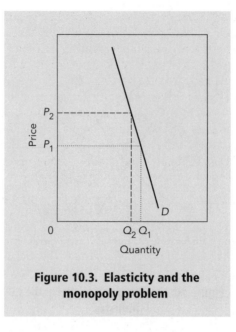

Figure 10.3. Elasticity and the monopoly problem

Mr Warner's next point is that he can see nothing wrong in setting a price according to what the market will bear, with the specific intention of maximizing profits. But this is precisely the problem of monopoly: it is the use of monopoly power to keep prices high and output low that monopoly policy is intended to control. In Figure 10.2, the monopolist chooses a price of P_m in order to maximize profit, whereas society would prefer a lower price and larger output (Q_c). A greater output would raise the size of the total surplus in the market to the benefit of society as a whole.

Mr Warner then explains how a firm's pricing policy works. He uses the example of a Madonna CD, produced by Warner Brothers. He says that if the company thought it could sell more Madonna CDs by cutting the price it would do so; but lowering the price by £2 will make no difference. This comment suggests that the demand curve for Madonna CDs is highly inelastic, as in Figure 10.3. But when the demand curve is of this type, price can be forced up without a large fall in quantity sold. In Figure 10.3, a small reduction in quantity sold from Q_1 to Q_2 leads to a large price increase from P_1 to P_2. Although there is not a major efficiency problem here (the size of the **deadweight loss** is small when demand is very inelastic), there may be a significant distributional question (the higher price increases the surplus of producers at the expense of consumers).

Earlier we mentioned the problem of substantial variations in the price of CDs across different retail outlets. We might find, then, that even if CD producers behaved competitively, retailers are acting as monopolists. In the 1993 survey of prices for a package of ten CDs, the total cost ranged from £114.90 in a shop in Portsmouth to £156.40 in Tower Records in London. The competitive model assumes that consumers have perfect knowledge; that is, they know the location of all the sellers and know all the prices. In this situation, one seller cannot charge more than another for the same product because, if it does, it will lose all its customers. In fact, for many people it is too much trouble to find out where cheap sellers might be and what their prices are (the costs of doing so outweigh the benefits of having the information). Lots of buyers of CDs probably buy on impulse and so do not expend effort in searching for the lowest price. So, some retailers probably maximize profits by charging high (monopoly) prices to those who buy on impulse or who do not know where cheap suppliers are. They will, of course, lose those customers who hunt for bargains.

In conclusion, there are two morals to this story. First, it probably pays to look around for cheap CDs and, if you buy a lot, buy them by mail order from the US. If this happened on a large enough scale, competitive forces would drive down prices in the UK. Secondly, beware of articles by journalists that appear to be nothing more than industry press releases. Make sure you examine the arguments in the light of your understanding of microeconomics.

Is British Telecom too profitable?[2]

If you have followed the news at all in the past few years, you will be aware that British Telecom, along with other privatized industries, makes substantial profits. Almost every time these profits are reported, consumer organizations complain. They claim that profits are too high and that prices could be even lower, whilst allowing reasonable profits to be made. British Telecom claims that it is making large profits because it is efficient; it is the efficiency that allows prices to fall. For the most part, key questions in the debate, like 'what is a reasonable amount of profit?' and 'must profitability and economic efficiency go hand in hand?', are hardly ever addressed.

In this example, we illustrate how microeconomics helps provide a way of addressing these questions. There are two fundamental ideas to consider: (i) the debate partly focuses on the distribution of economic welfare rather than on allocative efficiency, and (ii) even if we leave the distribution issue to one side, we need to understand the nature of the relationship between profits and economic performance if we are to give a sensible answer to the question about the efficiency of profitable firms.

The distribution of welfare and profitability

British Telecom is close to being a monopoly supplier of telecommunication services. There is some competition from Cable & Wireless and local cable operators, but British Telecom's share of the domestic market is around 80 per cent. Given this, it would seem sensible to use the monopoly model to carry out the analysis. The range of possible outputs and the consequent prices and costs of production can be illustrated in Figure 10.4.

The demand curve measures the demand for minutes or hours of telephone conversations. The average cost curve is shown by the curve AC. Because of the importance of fixed costs in the production of telephone services, British Telecom can initially provide more output ('telephone hours') for a lower unit cost. Eventually, we should expect average cost to rise due to frequent equipment breakdowns and the system becoming saturated with calls. A decision to produce Q_1 units of output will result in a price of P_1 and an average cost of AC_1. If output rises to Q_2, price will fall to P_2 and average cost will decline to AC_2.

Figure 10.4 enables us to see that some output decisions will favour British Telecom (it will make large profits) whilst others would benefit consumers (giving lower prices). It is straightforward to measure profits from Figure 10.4. If output is Q_1, total revenue is $P_1 \times Q_1$ and total costs are $AC_1 \times Q_1$. Profits are therefore measured by the area of the rectangle P_1AC_1AB. We can

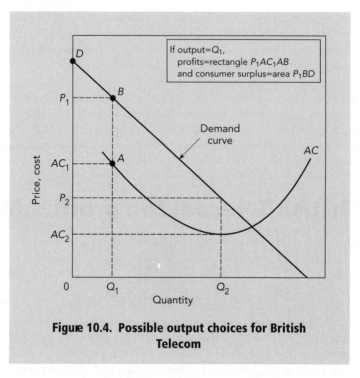

Figure 10.4. Possible output choices for British Telecom

use a concept we have met before to measure the benefits to consumers of an output Q_1 and a price per unit of P_1. Some consumers (located along the demand curve at prices above P_1) are willing to pay more than P_1 for their first few telephone conversations. The surplus of willingness to pay over their need to pay (**consumer surplus**) is measured by the area of the triangle P_1BD.

It is clear from Figure 10.4 that consumers are better off the more that is produced (the lower is the price). But, it is not so clear what happens to profits. Figure 10.5 attempts to clarify things by showing the relationships between profits (π) and output. An increase in output will generate higher profits along the profit curve (π). At some output level, profits reach a maximum. Eventually, as output becomes quite large profits begin to fall (the gap between total revenue and total cost gets smaller).

The shape of the profit curve in Figure 10.5 reflects the fact that the size of the profit rectangles in Figure 10.4 first increase, and then decrease, in size. This helps us to understand the friction between British Telecom's shareholders and its customers. Low prices (high output) produce a lot of consumer surplus but not much profit. So, a reduction in profits brought about by lower prices would be to the benefit of consumers. The distribution of the benefits of British Telecom services would shift towards consumers and away from British Telecom shareholders. If British Telecom maximizes its profits, it will choose an output of Q_m; at this output level consumer surplus is relatively low. Also, the sum of profits and consumer surplus is not constant for different levels of output. So, any given price may not correspond to the greatest total of benefits. It is this that economists focus on when considering the efficiency of a particular price and output combination.

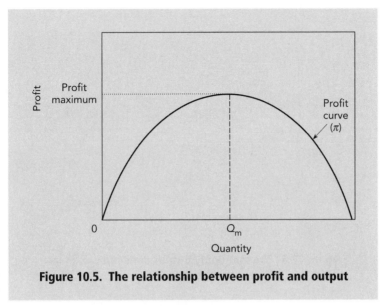

Figure 10.5. The relationship between profit and output

Efficiency and profits

The correct **distribution of welfare** is a matter of opinion. Because British Telecom's high profits are as good for shareholders as they are bad for consumers, you might legitimately hold the view that shareholders need high profits more than consumers need lots of consumer surplus. Because the issue is subjective, economists focus on **economic efficiency** rather than distribution in considering claims for intervention. We have argued previously that an efficient output is one where price equals marginal cost. This output level maximizes the sum of producer surplus (in this case, the profits to British Telecom plus the surplus enjoyed by the suppliers of British Telecom's inputs) and consumer surplus in a market. We can illustrate the idea of total surplus by way of a total welfare curve.

In Figure 10.6, the output level corresponding to the maximum point of the total welfare curve must lie to the right of Q_m, such as output level Q_1. This is because a small increase in output from Q_m will have a negligible effect on profits but a quite marked effect on consumer surplus. This simple picture provides strong support for the claim that British Telecom's profits are too high. If British Telecom produces at Q_m (to maximize profits), it will set a price that yields too little consumption, relative to that which maximizes the total surplus (or total welfare). In Chapter 9, we showed that monopoly is allocatively inefficient. Here, we have another demonstration of this feature of monopoly.

It is important to note that an increase in producer surplus does not necessarily reduce welfare. Comparing Figures 10.5 and 10.6, we see that over a range of outputs both profits and total welfare may increase as output is increased. The problem is that if a monopolist maximizes profits, it will not choose the output level that maximizes the total surplus (see Figure 9.4). It is in this sense that we may regard British Telecom's profits as too high.

This problem has been known for a long time, and it is one reason for the existence of the regulatory body Oftel. Oftel's objective is not in itself to reduce British Telecom's profits; it is to

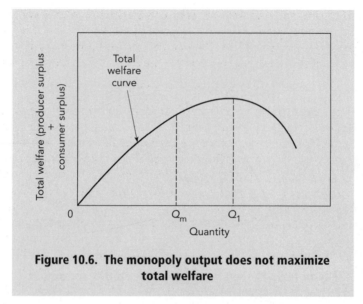

Figure 10.6. The monopoly output does not maximize total welfare

encourage the company to charge lower prices and so raise economic welfare. This is an important distinction, because we could always reduce profits by levying appropriate taxes. The Windfall Tax, recently levied on the profits of the privatized utilities, is an example. But this will not increase consumer welfare because the monopolist's output after the tax is unlikely to change in the short run (the profit tax lowers the firm's profits but it does not affect the profit-maximizing output choice).

Football, television, and monopoly[3]

In 1992 the satellite television company BSkyB, along with the BBC, struck a deal with the Premier League (now Premiership) for the following five years' broadcasting of football on television. This deal led to considerable comment and controversy in the media. Typical of the sentiments expressed by politicians (of all political parties) were those of Sebastian Coe (the newly elected MP for Falmouth), who said, 'I think it is wrong that only two million dish owners get access to major sporting events. It is bad for sport, bad for participation—and that means bad for everyone.' The National Federation of Football Supporters' Clubs issued a statement saying: 'The announcement of the new television deal confirms that it is once again the game's loyal fans who will suffer from decisions apparently geared to keeping supporters away from the game.' Although the contract between the Premiership and BSkyB was renewed for a further four years (and for a lot more money) in 1996, we will focus on the 1992 agreement, as this signalled a major change in the nature of the relationship between football and television. Prior to the 1992 deal, football earned relatively little money from the sale of its product to television.

Behind many of the comments made in 1992 was the suggestion that the Premier League 'fixed' the bidding process. Here, we use some simple arguments to consider these views, and to see to what extent they are valid. First of all, we ask if the bidding system was a fix, and whether another bidding system might have produced a different result. Second, we consider why the BBC joined forces with BSkyB. Then we ask whether the deal was in the interests of the Premier League; and finally, we examine whether the deal was best for society as a whole.

Was there a 'fix'?

We begin by considering the outcome that would result from an open-cry auction. An **open-cry auction** is one where every bidder attends the auction and bids openly in competition with everyone else. To keep things simple, we name the ITV companies as Party A and the BBC/BSkyB partnership as Party B. To understand the sort of bids that both parties might make, we need to anticipate the return to them from winning the auction. Both BSkyB and ITV are motivated by the profit that could be earned. The motivation of the BBC is more complex, but suppose there is some monetary gain to the BBC from showing highlights. The profits of the two parties may be denoted as π_A and π_B. Each party is prepared to bid up to the level of its profits to win the auction. This is because although each wants to pay as little as possible, neither is willing to let the other win at a price below its own **expected profit**. If we assume for the moment that π_A is less than π_B, then Party A will bid up to π_A, but no more; Party B will bid a little more than this and obtain a net profit of almost $\pi_B - \pi_A$. So, if the auction is open, the winner will be the bidder with the highest expected profit; the price paid will be just above the value of the second-highest expected profit level.

In the 1992 deal, the bidding method *actually* used was a **sealed-bid auction**. In this type of auction, each bidder is allowed just one bid, which is made privately to the auctioneer in a sealed envelope. The bids in a sealed-bid auction depend on the profits that each party might receive by winning the bid, and on what each bidder knows about the other. If each bidder has information on the expected profits of all bidders, the outcome will be the same as with an open auction. But if Party B does not know the value of π_A, then it has to make an educated guess as to what Party A might bid. It will then bid just above it, providing this is less than π_B. If Party B thinks π_A is larger than it is, then Party B will end up paying more than under an open auction. But it still remains the case that the party with the larger expected profits will win the auction. Of course, Party B, if it can, will attempt to discover what Party A has bid and then beat it. This is what happened in practice, hence the claim that the deal was 'fixed'. Again, the bidder with the higher expected profits will win the auction.

Is there any basis in this charge? The answer depends on each party's expected profits. The party with the higher expected profits will end up winning the auction under almost any bidding rules. For the ITV companies, the objective was the extra (advertising) revenue they would receive from showing televised football. The size of this revenue depends on the size and composition of the audience, as well as on the number of viewers who watch later programmes on the same channel. The retention rate is very important. If showing football leads to a whole evening's viewing on the same channel (and hence greater advertising revenues), ITV may find that it makes more profit by paying more for a programme than the programme itself earns in advertising revenue.

The BBC may be even more concerned with audience retention, since its main concern is its share of the viewing audience. BSkyB's incentives are more complex. It not only wants advertising revenues, but also has to consider the possibility of subscription channels, plus the problem of getting people to buy the equipment needed to watch its programmes. In a time of saturation television ownership, BSkyB not only has the problem of persuading people to switch on to a channel and stay with it, but also of persuading people to buy satellite dishes. If they do buy them to watch live football, then they might choose to receive all of BSkyB's programmes. (At the time, it was possible to subscribe to the sports channels only.) In this case, BSkyB will get an increase in advertising revenue equal to the increase in time that a new subscriber may spend watching BSkyB programmes. Because the effect of an extra viewer of live football on BSkyB may be to get additional viewing for the whole of the week, the marginal value of an extra viewer may be much greater to BSkyB than to ITV. For ITV, the effect of live football may be to get a family to watch ITV for the whole evening. Consequently, BSkyB would be expected to pay more to show live football.

To sum up, there are very good reasons why showing live football (and other leading sports) is worth more to BSkyB (and the BBC) than it is to ITV. In these circumstances, BSkyB would be expected to win any auction. The exact price paid by BSkyB in 1992 depended on how much it knew about the ITV bid.

Why did the BBC side with BSkyB?

At the time, a number of people indicated their surprise at the alliance between BSkyB and the BBC. The argument was based on a belief that the people buying satellite dishes were more likely to be transferees from the BBC than from ITV. So, if the BBC wished to prevent an increase in satellite dish ownership it ought to have sided with ITV. One main argument against this is that the additional revenue BSkyB would receive from showing live football would be more than the maximum value of any joint ITV–BBC bid. So, BSkyB would win the auction in any case; the BBC would simply lose viewers whatever it did. In this situation, it might as well drop out of the race and pick up those viewers who are happy to watch only highlights.

The interests of the Premier League

To this point the interests of the Premier League have been couched solely in terms of how much money it might make from selling its product (football) to the television companies. In fact, the calculation of the Premier League is not as simple as this, because clubs receive income from sources other than television, such as gate receipts (although this income source is not as important to the top clubs as it used to be). So, we ought to consider the interaction of the demand for football on television and football demand at a stadium. In Figure 10.7, we show two demand curves, one for live television matches, D_{TV}, and the other for match attendance, D_{M1}. Since the two goods are close substitutes, the demand for going to a match will depend on the price of live football on television, whilst the demand curve for football on television will depend on the price (or cost to the supporters) of going to a match.

Imagine for now that it is free to watch football on television, but clubs charge an admission price of P_2. In this situation, N_1 people will watch on television (at zero price), and N_2 attend matches at the ground. If live football is transferred to BSkyB it might charge a price of P_3 (either the cost of buying a dish, or the subscription fee to the sports channel). Now, N_3 people watch on television. The price increase involves a simple movement along the demand curve. But as the price of watching on television goes up, the demand curve for watching at a stadium will shift to the right, to (say) D_{M2}. Now, for the same admission charge of P_2, N_4 spectators go to games. If BSkyB is willing to pay more to the Premier League than ITV, and if BSkyB charges an amount P_3 (rather than nothing at all) to watch live football on television, then the Premier League must gain. It increases both its television revenue and its match receipts.

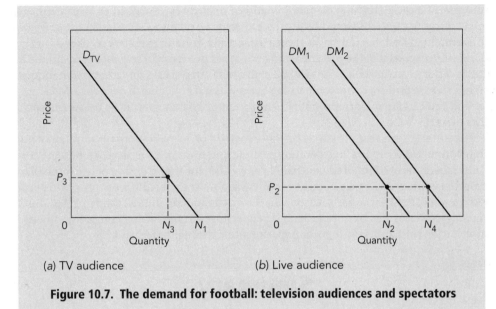

Figure 10.7. The demand for football: television audiences and spectators

Does society as a whole benefit?

Are the best interests of society as a whole being served by the ongoing relationship between football and BSkyB? As in any discussion of monopoly and competition, this question raises a host of normative issues. We know the monopoly outcome is generally undesirable because output is restricted in order to raise profits; society as a whole loses out because the product does not get made even though the willingness to pay exceeds the marginal cost of production. The television company that wins the bid becomes a monopoly supplier of live Premier League football. As a result, it will want to limit the amount of coverage to increase its profits. BSkyB realizes that it can raise the subscription fee for its package of programmes if it owns the most popular sporting events (such as live Premier League football), while ITV can charge advertisers more for slots during football matches if there are fewer of them.

The Premier League acts as the sole supplier of matches. The increase in monopoly power helps to explain the increase in the broadcasting fee paid in recent years. In 1983 the BBC and ITV jointly paid to the Football League £2.6 million per season for the coverage of live games. In 1986 the figure was increased to £3.1 million per season. ITV's exclusive contract in 1988 injected £11 million per season into the game. Since BSkyB's involvement the price paid to show live football has grown dramatically. In 1992 the Premier League secured for itself £304 million over five years (£60.8 million per season), while the 1996 contract was signed for £670 million over four years.

The large increases in the cost of showing live football would seem to reflect the monopoly power of the Premier League (Premiership). Currently, it sells a complete package of matches, in the belief that this will secure a higher total payment from television. But if it wished, it could price and sell matches individually. What would the situation be like if there were competition? Each football club would act as a separate potential supplier of matches to the television companies, and each television company would compete to screen matches. Because the bargaining power of the clubs would be greatly reduced, we ought to see a fall in the price paid. Also, we ought to find that football is shown to a greater or lesser extent on all television channels. All this suggests that the present arrangement for live football coverage is not in the best interests of society as a whole. The football clubs' best interests are served by maintaining the **cartel** so as to maximize the income to the League as a whole. But this tends to force up the price and reduce the amount of football shown on television (output is below the socially efficient level).

This example shows that the coverage of live football on television raises a number of interesting economic questions. Consideration of these questions helps us understand the enormous increase in the amount of money paid by television for the screening of live football over the past ten years. BSkyB's tactic of using football as a way of inducing more people to become BSkyB viewers provides the basic reason why it won the auction in 1992 (and in 1996). But the monopoly power of the Premier League (Premiership), in the face of competition between rival television companies, is important in explaining the high price paid.

Summary

1. This chapter has shown how we can use some basic ideas in monopoly theory to help explain the pricing of CDs, the profitability of British Telecom, and the relationship between the football industry and television.

2. A monopoly in the supply of CDs helps explain why price is well above the marginal cost of production. The problem of high prices may be compounded by retailers who exploit the fact that many people do not 'shop around' for bargains. If more people looked around for cheap CDs, competitive forces would drive down prices in the UK.

3. The high profits made by British Telecom benefit its shareholders at the expense of consumers. But the distribution of benefits between consumers and shareholders is a normative issue: you might legitimately hold the view that shareholders need high profits. To deal with this problem, we look at the efficiency of profitable firms. One indicator of efficiency is the output that maximizes the total surplus (or total economic welfare) in a market. If British Telecom maximizes its profits it will set a price that yields too little consumption relative to that which maximizes total welfare.

4. The increase in the fees paid for the broadcasting rights to live football in recent years reflect (i) BSkyB's tactic of using football as a way of inducing more people to become BSkyB viewers, and (ii) the monopoly power of the Premier League (Premiership) in the face of competition between rival television companies.

Key terms

allocative efficiency

cartel

consumer surplus

deadweight loss

distribution of welfare

economic efficiency

economic profit

expected profit

monopoly power

open-cry auction

sealed-bid auction

Review questions

1. Alan Warner (of Warner Brothers) contends that the current price of CDs in the UK is a competitive price. Figures suggest that the retail price of CDs is about twelve times the production cost. Do you agree with Mr Warner?

2. Consumer groups frequently complain that British Telecom's profits are too high and that prices could be even lower than they are whilst allowing reasonable profits to be made. What criteria would you use to assess whether British Telecom is too profitable?

3. Why is it in the interests of the Premier League to restrict the amount of football that is shown live on television? What might happen if the teams are forced to sell the television rights to their home games individually, rather than as a cartel?

Notes

1. This is adapted from Alan Ingham, 'Monopoly and the Price of Compact Discs', *Economic Review*, 11.1 (Sept. 1993), 38–40.

2. This is adapted from Martin Chalkley, 'Is British Telecom Too Profitable?', *Economic Review*, 10.3 (Feb. 1993), 13–15.

3. This is adapted from Alan Ingham, 'Football, Television and Monopoly', *Economic Review*, 10.1 (Sept. 1992), 37–9.

CHAPTER 11

The market for labour

So far our analysis of different market models has concentrated on the behaviour of firms as sellers of products. This chapter recognizes that firms are also buyers of factors of production (labour, capital, raw materials, and so on). The amount of a particular factor a firm will use and the price it will pay for the resource depends on the extent to which competitive forces operate in the market. In competitive factor markets, the forces of supply and demand determine quantities and prices; individual firms take resource prices (say, wages) as given. But where there is monopoly power, buyers of factors (firms) can affect resource prices because the individual firm faces an upward-sloping supply curve.

Factors of production are only demanded because they can produce goods and services for consumption. So, the demand for labour, for example, is derived from the demand for the goods and services workers produce. It is therefore known as a **derived demand**. Here, we examine how profit-maximizing firms choose the optimum amount of labour to hire, and how this alters according to the degree of competition in the market. We also consider the effect of a minimum wage in a labour market: is it good or bad for jobs?

The demand for labour in competitive markets

The amount of labour demanded by a competitive firm depends on the additional revenue each extra worker brings to the firm. If each additional worker adds more to revenue than to cost, the owners of firms will hire more labour.

The additional revenue a firm receives from employing an extra worker is called the **marginal revenue product of labour** (MRP_L). It depends on two things: first, on how much extra output that worker produces: this extra output is called the **marginal product of labour** (MP_L). Second, it depends on how much the firm's revenue increases when the extra output is sold: this is the firm's marginal revenue (MR). So, for all firms, the marginal revenue product of labour is equal to the marginal worker's output times marginal revenue:

$$MRP_L = MP_L \times MR.$$

The marginal revenue product of labour (MRP_L) is the maximum price the firm will pay for an extra unit of labour. Therefore, the firm's demand-for-labour schedule is simply its schedule of marginal revenue product for labour.

As we have seen, in competitive goods markets firms are price takers; hence, marginal revenue is constant and equal to (the constant) product price (P). So, the above equation becomes:

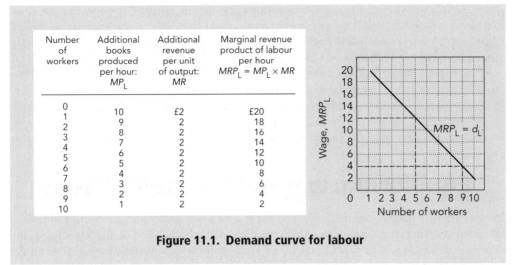

Number of workers	Additional books produced per hour: MP_L	Additional revenue per unit of output: MR	Marginal revenue product of labour per hour $MRP_L = MP_L \times MR$
0			
1	10	£2	£20
2	9	2	18
3	8	2	16
4	7	2	14
5	6	2	12
6	5	2	10
7	4	2	8
8	3	2	6
9	2	2	4
10	1	2	2

Figure 11.1. Demand curve for labour

$$MRP_L = MP_L \times P.$$

In the short run, the competitive firm's demand-for-labour schedule is downward-sloping because the marginal product of labour (MP_L) falls as more workers are hired. This is due to the law of diminishing returns, which we discussed in Chapter 7. Each additional worker adds less to total output, because additional workers (variable input) are combined with a constant amount of capital (fixed input). As a result, each extra worker is less productive than the previous one. So, if each worker's marginal output is diminishing (marginal product of labour is falling), while the price of the product is constant, the demand for labour (MRP_L) falls as more labour is hired. Therefore, the labour demand schedule for the competitive firm slopes down from left to right.

Figure 11.1 shows an example for a firm (Steely Dan & Co.) publishing books on rock music. The demand curve for labour, d_L, slopes downward to the right because of the firm's falling marginal product of labour. For example, the fifth worker hired is worth £12 per hour to the firm, whereas the ninth one adds only £4 per hour to total revenue. Steely Dan & Co. must be a competitive firm because its marginal revenue is constant (price does not fall as output is increased). Thus, its downward-sloping demand curve for labour is the result of a diminishing marginal product of labour as the firm adds more workers.

The supply of labour in competitive markets

Individuals offer themselves for work for a price: the wage rate. It is opportunity cost (the value of the worker's next best alternative use of time) that is the most important factor in determining the quantities of labour supplied at various wage rates. Your next best alternative to a particular job may be to work for a different firm, or run your own business, or watch television. You also have the option to stay in bed all day, or go down to the pub, or play tennis, and so on. Generally speaking, firms will attract more labour when they offer wages that are equal to or greater than potential workers' opportunity costs. Therefore, at the level of the market, labour supply curves are usually upward-sloping; the higher the wage rate, the greater the amount of labour offered for sale.

While market labour supply curves slope upwards, individual *firms* in competitive markets face a horizontal labour supply curve. This reflects the fact that a firm that is small relative to its labour market (it may be one firm out of a hundred) can hire all the labour it requires at the 'going' wage rate. Because the firm is small, it has no power to affect the market price (wage); hence, a single firm can take on a few extra workers without affecting the equilibrium wage.

Equilibrium wages and employment

In a competitive market, the demand and supply for labour determine the equilibrium wage and total employment. This is shown in part (*a*) of Figure 11.2. The market supply and demand curves for labour (S_L^{market} and D_L^{market}) establish the equilibrium wage rate at £8 per hour (W_e). At this wage, 40,000 workers are hired by all firms in this competitive labour market. Note that more than 40,000 people are willing to offer themselves for work, but only if the wage rate is higher than £8 per hour. On the other hand, several thousand people are willing to work for a wage below £8 per hour but they are paid £8. This is because everyone doing the same work gets paid the same amount, and £8 per hour is what firms must pay to attract the marginal (or 'last') worker. Thus, everyone receives the wage of the marginal worker.

How many workers does Steely Dan & Co. hire, and what does it pay them? Because Steely Dan & Co. is just one firm operating in a competitive market, it faces the horizontal labour supply curve, s_L^{firm}, at the going wage rate of £8 per hour (see part (*b*) of Figure 11.2). As a price (wage) taker, Steely Dan & Co. can increase the quantity of workers (employment) from one to ten without affecting the equilibrium price (wage rate) of £8.

A firm's decision as to how many workers to hire is similar to its decision regarding the amount of output to produce. In equilibrium, Steely Dan & Co. hires seven workers

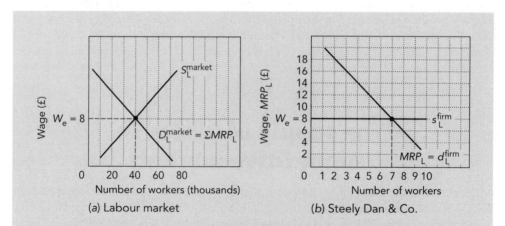

Figure 11.2. Equilibrium wage and employment: market and individual firm

at the market wage of £8. Each worker up to the seventh adds more to revenue than to cost ($MRP_L > W_e$), thus increasing profit. If the firm hired an eighth worker, profit would fall, because that worker's marginal revenue product is less than the wage rate. Note that in equilibrium, each firm in a competitive market pays a wage rate equal to each worker's marginal revenue product of labour. This means each worker receives the value of his or her contribution to the firm—no more and no less. The allocation of workers in perfect competition is efficient in the same way as the allocation of output is efficient.

The labour market and monopoly

Monopoly power can affect labour markets. We said earlier on that the demand for labour is the marginal product of labour times marginal revenue, or $MRP_L = MP_L \times MR$. In perfect competition, when product price and marginal revenue are equal, each worker hired receives exactly what he or she is worth to both society and the firm.

But the economic value of a unit of labour is not the same in monopoly. In Chapter 9, we saw that product price and marginal revenue are not the same in monopoly. Marginal revenue is below price in a monopoly, because the firm has to lower its price on all units to sell one more unit of output that an extra worker would produce. So, in monopoly the demand curve for labour is downward-sloping as a result of both a falling marginal product of labour and a declining marginal revenue. As a result, monopolists hire fewer workers and produce less output than do competitive firms.

Figure 11.3 shows this result. The demand for labour for a competitive firm and for a monopoly are shown as D_c and D_m, respectively. The demand curve for the competitive firm lies above the monopolist's demand curve, because product price is greater than marginal revenue for every level of output under monopoly. If the labour supply curve is S_L (equal to the

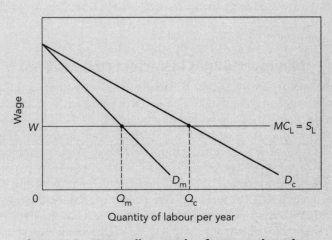

Figure 11.3. Monopolists employ fewer workers than competitive firms

constant **marginal cost of labour**), the monopolist employs Q_m units of labour. If the industry were a perfectly competitive one, the total number of people hired by the competitive firms combined would be Q_c. A competitive industry hires more workers and produces more output than a monopoly, *ceteris paribus*.

Minimum wages and employment[1]

In many countries there is a **national minimum wage** which employers are forced to pay. In the UK there has never been a national minimum wage, but the Labour government is currently committed to introducing one. At the moment, the debate concerns the appropriate rate for the minimum wage. Until now, the nearest thing to a national minimum wage in the UK has been the wages set by the Wages Councils, introduced in the early twentieth century. Wages Councils had the ability to impose minimum wage limits on employers in industries where wages were often low, such as agriculture, hairdressing, and catering. In 1992, there were 26 Wages Councils covering 2.3 million workers.

The Wages Councils were abolished by the Conservative government in 1993. The Conservatives opposed intervention in the labour market, preferring instead the virtues of a competitive market where wages are set by the forces of supply and demand. The abolition of the Wages Councils reopened the debate about minimum wage legislation. Here, we examine the traditional arguments for and against minimum wages, and consider the results of some recent research into the expected employment losses resulting from a national minimum wage.

Income from wages and salaries accounts for more than 80 per cent of all income. For this reason, the prices paid by firms for their labour inputs are among the most contentious of all prices paid. It is not surprising, therefore, to find that people are extremely concerned about the determination of wage rates. To help reduce poverty, it has frequently been proposed that some floor should be set to wage levels. But the traditional response of economists (and some politicians) to the idea of a national minimum wage is to point to undesirable consequences. Since price floors tend to reduce quantities traded (as we saw in Chapter 4), the opponents of a minimum wage argue that, while it may improve the income of a few people, it will deprive lots of others of almost all their income.

Minimum wages in perfect competition

What is the traditional argument against the imposition of a national minimum wage? The determination of wages and employment in a perfectly competitive market is shown in Figure 11.4. The intersection of the demand and supply curves for labour establish the equilibrium wage and employment in the market as W_e and Q_e, respectively. The effect of imposing a minimum wage of W_m is to cause a **disequilibrium**. At the wage W_m, the number of low-skilled workers that employers wish to employ (Q_m) is less than the number of people wishing to sell their labour (Q_s). Since the buyers of labour (firms) cannot be forced to buy what they do not want, employment falls to Q_m. The minimum wage therefore reduces employment from Q_e to Q_m. The flatter the labour demand curve, the greater the effect on employment.

Although the effect on employment tends to take centre stage in any discussion of minimum wages, there is another aspect which is equally important: this is the effect of the minimum wage on the total income of labour suppliers. In Figure 11.4, the minimum wage reduces the

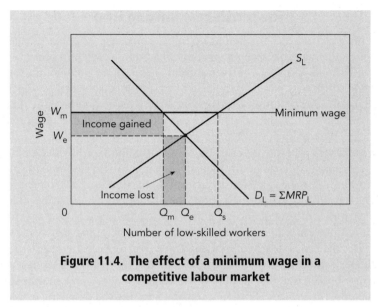

Figure 11.4. The effect of a minimum wage in a competitive labour market

quantity of labour that is bought and sold to Q_m. In the competitive equilibrium, total **labour income** is $W_e \times Q_e$. With the imposition of the minimum wage, total labour income becomes $W_m \times Q_m$. In Figure 11.4, Q_m people keep their jobs and gain income (indicated by the area of the rectangle), while others ($Q_e - Q_m$) lose their jobs at the higher wage—this represents lost income. It is the slope of the labour demand curve that determines whether total labour income after the minimum wage is greater or smaller than $W_e \times Q_e$. You should be able to confirm for yourself that the flatter (or more elastic) the demand-for-labour curve, the more likely it is that total labour income will fall with the imposition of a national minimum wage.

The model of a perfectly competitive labour market suggests that minimum wages reduce employment, and that they may reduce total labour income. The more elastic (flatter) the demand for labour, the more harmful is the effect of a minimum wage. Given this, economists have focused on measuring the elasticity of the demand for labour when assessing the likely impact of a minimum wage. From this perspective, a national minimum wage seems to be ineffective in raising the well-being of the poorest members of society. Most research indicates that the demand for low-skilled workers is relatively wage-elastic (the demand-for-labour curve is quite flat). In other words, a small increase in the wage would cause a more than proportionate fall in employment; the effects of a minimum wage on employment are said to be large.

But recently, research has begun to examine the employment effect of a minimum wage from a different perspective. If labour markets are not perfectly competitive, the predictions of the model of perfect competition may not be appropriate. The gradient of the demand curve for labour (**elasticity of labour demand**) may not give a good guide to the likely impact of a minimum wage on employment. To examine this idea we need to consider how a profit-maximizing firm chooses its wage–employment combination in circumstances other than a perfectly competitive market.

The profit-maximizing firm

To maximize profit, a firm will hire labour up to the point where the marginal cost of labour (MC_L) just equals the marginal revenue product of labour (MRP_L). In other words, the firm hires labour until the addition to costs from employing one more worker is the same as the revenue that worker is able to generate. If the firm hires labour in a perfectly competitive market, the marginal cost of labour is simply the constant wage. This means the individual firm faces a horizontal supply curve of labour ($s_L^{firm} = MC_L$ in Figure 11.2). If the wage offered by the firm falls slightly below the equilibrium wage, no-one will offer themselves for work with that firm.

But this is not a very accurate description of the situation faced by the employers of low-skilled labour, because people do not immediately change jobs in response to small variations in the wage. Finding a new job can be costly in terms of the time and effort spent searching, and individuals can never be fully informed about the likelihood of alternative offers of employment. A straightforward consequence of a firm being able to vary the wage it pays without losing all of its employees is that the *firm* faces an upward-sloping supply curve for labour. Because this gives the firm a degree of market power (it can affect the wage), the labour market cannot be perfectly competitive. In this situation, the firm has a degree of *monopsony* power. (As a monopolist is a sole supplier of goods and services, so a **monopsonist** is a sole purchaser of goods and services.) So, a monopsony firm, instead of having to take the wage as given, can affect the wage through its own actions. How does a monopsonist determine the equilibrium quantity of labour to employ?

When a firm with monopsony power decides to hire more workers, it must anticipate paying higher wages. These higher wages are paid not only to the last person hired but to all the other workers that are currently employed. This means that the marginal cost of labour (MC_L) differs from the labour supply curve facing the firm. To maximize profit, the monopsonist employs workers up to the point where $MC_L = MRP_L$.

In Figure 11.5, the equilibrium occurs where the MC_L curve intersects the MRP_L curve; the monopsonist hires Q_1 workers and pays a wage of W_1. The crucial point is that the monopsonist pays a wage below the marginal revenue product of labour (compare W_1 with W_e). The larger the gap between the marginal cost of labour (W_1) and the marginal revenue product of labour (W_e), the more profit the firm will make on the marginal employee. If a minimum wage is now imposed on the firm, it is forced to pay higher wages but, because of the gap between W_1 and W_e, this higher wage does not necessarily make the employment of workers unprofitable. In Figure 11.5, if the minimum wage is set at W_m, no-one will supply their labour below this level, so the firm will employ workers at the point where the new labour supply curve ($W_m X$) cuts the MRP_L curve. There is an increase in employment (from Q_1 to Q_2) as well as wages. Consequently, total labour income will definitely increase.

This observation is very important. If firms have monopsony power, economic theory suggests that the imposition of a minimum wage might lead to an increase in employment, and not a reduction. The problem for economists has been to determine just how much monopsony power actually exists in low-wage labour markets. Recently, research has begun to try to measure the extent of the gap between the marginal cost of labour and the marginal revenue product.

Measuring monopsony power

Economists in both the UK and the US are now actively investigating the extent to which the wages of low-skilled workers fall below their marginal revenue product. The research is often

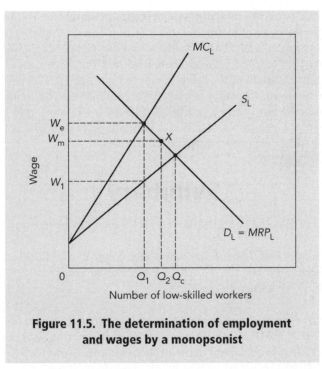

Figure 11.5. The determination of employment and wages by a monopsonist

based upon surveys specifically designed to extract the appropriate data. A recent study in the US claims that employment increased following an 18 per cent increase in the minimum wage in New Jersey in 1992. Critics of the study question this, although they can find no evidence that the increase in the minimum wage had a negative effect on employment. Most studies in the UK do not find any noticeable increase in employment following the abolition of the Wages Councils. One report into the effect of minimum wages in the agriculture sector (prior to their abolition in 1993) found that minimum wages raised the wages of low-paid workers without adversely affecting their employment prospects.

Another UK study looked at residential care homes, a traditionally low-paying sector. Ninety per cent of employees received less than £3.50 per hour, with the most common rate being £3 per hour. To put this in perspective, the Labour government is now considering a national minimum wage of between £3 and £4 per hour. The study estimated that the wages paid in the residential care sector are, on average, 15 per cent below marginal revenue product. Because this is an average figure, it does not mean that if the minimum wage was set at £3.20 there would be no unemployment effects. Where firms are paying close to marginal revenue product there would be some adverse effect on employment, but for the majority of firms there would not. Nevertheless, the study estimated that nearly 70 per cent of workers would not have their employment prospects damaged by the imposition of a national minimum wage of £3.40 per hour. If these findings are typical of low-paid labour markets, they suggest that the fears expressed about minimum wage legislation may be unfounded.

The debate about a national minimum wage is often ill-informed because it tends to take for granted the economic analysis found in most textbooks. In this approach, the imposition of a minimum wage in a perfectly competitive market creates a disequilibrium; the minimum wage acts as a **price floor**, so reducing the quantity of the good traded. The result is unemployment or a reduction in total labour income. From this perspective, a minimum wage will do most harm when the demand for labour is highly elastic. But, in the case of low-wage labour markets, the perfectly competitive model might not be appropriate. If firms have monopsony power, a national minimum wage may actually raise employment and so increase the income of low-paid workers. Recent research in the UK and elsewhere has found some evidence of monopsony power; the results suggest that a minimum wage might actually succeed in improving the welfare of the poorest workers in the economy.

Summary

1. Individuals receive income by selling the services of their labour to firms.

2. The forces of supply and demand in competitive factor markets determine the prices of factors and the quantities used. The demand for a factor (such as labour) is derived from the demand for the firm's (or industry's) product.

3. The demand curve for labour reflects the value to the firm of the extra output produced by a unit of labour: $MRP_L = MP_L \times MR$. In competitive markets, marginal revenue is equal to (constant) product price, so the labour demand curve slopes downwards because the marginal product of labour declines as extra workers are hired in the short run.

4. Where there is imperfect competition, too little labour will be hired compared with a competitive industry.

5. To maximize profit, a firm will hire labour up to the point where the marginal cost of labour (MC_L) just equals the marginal revenue product of labour (MRP_L). In perfectly competitive markets, the marginal cost of labour is simply the constant wage: the individual firm therefore faces a horizontal supply curve of labour ($s_L = MC_L$). The market wage is taken by the firm.

6. Where firms have some market power, the labour supply curve facing the firm is upward-sloping. In this situation, the firm is called a monopsony. A monopsonist can affect the wage through its own actions. When a monopsonist pays higher wages, these are paid not only to the last person hired but to all the other workers that are currently employed. This means that the marginal cost of labour (MC_L) lies above the labour supply curve facing the firm. To maximize profit, the monopsonist employs workers up to the point where $MC_L = MRP_L$.

7. The model of a perfectly competitive labour market suggests that a national minimum wage will reduce employment, and may reduce total labour income. The more elastic (flatter) the demand for labour, the more harmful is the effect of a minimum wage. But, some low-skilled labour markets may be better described by the monopsony model; here, economic theory suggests a national minimum wage may increase employment and the income of low-paid workers. Recent research has found some evidence of monopsony power, suggesting that a minimum wage might improve the welfare of the poorest workers in the economy.

Key terms

derived demand

disequilibrium

elasticity of labour demand

labour income

marginal cost of labour

marginal product of labour

marginal revenue product of labour

monopsonist

national minimum wage

price floor

Review questions

1. From what is the demand for university lecturers derived? What do you think would happen to lecturers' salaries if the number of students entering universities declined?

2. According to economic theory, in competitive labour markets workers are paid precisely what they are worth to a firm. Explain the assumptions underlying this statement. What are the two principal determinants of wage rates?

3. Steely Dan & Co. publishes books in a competitive product market. It sells its output for £2. The firm pays its workers a wage of £10 per hour. Given the following information, complete the table and calculate the number of workers hired by the firm.

Number of workers	MP_L per hour	Extra revenue per book	MRP_L
0			
	6		
1			
	5		
2			
	4		
3			
	3		
4			
	2		
5			

4. How does a monopolist decide how much labour to hire? Why is that amount normally less than the amount of labour hired by a corresponding firm in a competitive market?

5. In what sense does a monopsony firm exploit its workforce?

6. The Conservatives abolished the Wages Councils in 1993 on the grounds that their ability to set minimum wages had adverse consequences for employment. The present Labour

government is committed to introducing a national minimum wage. What is the traditional argument against a minimum wage? In what circumstances might a minimum wage improve the welfare of the poorest members of society?

Note

1. This is adapted from Martin Chalkley, 'How Much do Minimum Wages Reduce Employment?', *Economic Review*, 12.1 (Sept. 1994), 15–17.

Further reading

- Mabry and Ulbrich, chapters 7 and 8

- Lipsey and Chrystal, chapters 15 and 17
- Sloman, chapter 9

CHAPTER 12
Market failure

In the chapters on imperfect competition, we saw that monopoly power results in an output level that is inefficient from the point of view of society as a whole; in other words, the market fails to work efficiently. Market failure of this nature leads to government action to try to make markets more efficient (for example, laws prohibiting cartels and regulating monopolies). We also saw that competitive markets produce goods and services in the correct quantities and at the lowest possible cost. That is, competitive markets produce an efficient outcome.

However, in reality, markets do not always work in the way predicted by economic theory. Under certain conditions, competitive markets 'fail' to produce an efficient result. In this chapter, we look at another set of market problems that may call for corrective government action. In doing so, we return to a topic from earlier on—health care. Why might a market in health care fail?

Market failure in health care

Because an ideal market can transmit all the information about benefits and costs between producers and consumers, it is able to provide the right goods at the lowest possible cost. In essence, a market is an information system. If this information is less than perfect, **market failure** will result. Imagine you are about to buy a CD. You know what a CD is and you are also well informed as to the kind of music on the disc. This means you can relate your benefit to the price of the CD. In an ideal market, CDs are bought until the extra satisfaction from the last CD bought is exactly the same as the price of the CD. In other words, the 'correct' quantity of CDs is being consumed since we gain the maximum satisfaction given the price.

But buying health care is a lot different from buying CDs. There are acute information problems that render rational buying decisions almost impossible. For instance, because most people do not know the best way to treat a stomach ulcer, they find it difficult to buy such treatment. Also, we assume that it is only the person buying the CD that receives any benefit from it. The possibility of **externalities** is ignored. For example, if someone else enjoys hearing your CD they gain satisfaction from the disc. But, the market cannot provide any information about their benefits because they have not contributed to the cost of buying the CD. In this case, there is a **positive externality** in consumption: the other person benefits but he/she does not contribute towards the cost of creating the benefit received. (Equally, your purchase of a CD may impose a cost on another person if that person does not like the music. As an undergraduate student, one of the authors was responsible for imposing an external cost, or **negative externality**, on his room-mate; the other person had to listen to Steely Dan albums almost all the time without receiving any compensation for having to listen to the 'unpleasant' noise!)

Where externalities are present, the market fails to work efficiently (resources are misallocated). We look in more detail at the role of externalities later. For the moment, we consider the problems that risk and uncertainty pose for consumers in a health care market.

Risk and uncertainty

If we wish to buy health care in a free market, then we need enough money to pay for it. But health care is expensive, and we do not know for certain when we are going to be ill. What makes matters worse is that postponing the purchase of health care is often risky. So, as consumers we face the twin problems of **uncertainty** and **risk**. The market's response to this situation is to develop an **insurance market**. An efficient insurance market removes the uncertainty and risk from health care spending. By purchasing health insurance, we know that it is the insurer who will pay the bill when we need treatment. So, an effective health care insurance market is needed if there is a free market in health care. Unfortunately, the market for health care insurance often fails to work efficiently, primarily because of the problems of moral hazard and adverse selection.

Moral hazard

The way we behave may alter once we have bought insurance. Imagine you are in a cinema and the film is about to start. You then remember that your car is unlocked. If you are insured against all losses you are much more likely to carry on watching the film. Your attitude has been altered by the fact that you have bought insurance—this is an example of what economists call **moral hazard**, where people act less carefully because they themselves do not have to bear the cost of their carelessness. Moral hazard is a particularly serious problem for health care insurance.

Where consumers have purchased insurance they have an incentive to over-consume health care—they want operations and other treatment which they would not choose if they had to pay for them. It is also possible that they may not follow a healthy lifestyle. As a result, when people become ill, the cost of treatment is higher than it would otherwise have been. But moral hazard not only affects consumers; doctors are also affected. Doctors know that the cost of any treatment will be covered by the insurance company, so there is a temptation to over-treat and over-prescribe. Thus, moral hazard leads to an inefficient allocation of resources in the market for health care.

Adverse selection

When companies sell health care insurance, they need to estimate the level of risk accurately. But this is not easy, because the companies have incomplete information on the risk status of the person being insured. One way around this problem is to set the insurance premium at a risk level for the 'average' person. Doing this, however, makes the policy expensive for low-risk people, who may choose not to buy any insurance. This process whereby low-risk people select themselves out of the insured group is called **adverse selection**. Essentially, it means that only sick people buy insurance. Because insurance companies know that this may happen, they offer different insurance premiums according to the level of risk and the person's history of poor health. So, low premiums are offered to low-risk groups, and high premiums are offered to high-risk groups, such as the elderly or chronically sick. Therefore, in a free market, health care insurance is likely to be too expensive for many people.

A free market in health care insurance is likely to be inefficient because of the problems of moral hazard and adverse selection. However, health care markets face even more fundamental information problems. We now examine the problems caused by unequal information, and the role played by doctors as agents.

Unequal information

When you go into a shop to buy a CD you have enough information to make a rational choice: you do not need the shop assistant to tell you what to buy. But, a market in health care is clearly very different. Imagine that you need to see your doctor. You know you are feeling unwell and that you have certain symptoms, but (like most people) you cannot diagnose your complaint—you want your doctor to do that. Furthermore, if you are told by your doctor that you need an expensive operation, then, in all probability, you will buy it.

Information between buyers and sellers is not equally shared in the health care market. The seller of health care (doctor) has much more information than the buyer (patient). The market is characterized by **asymmetric information**, and this undermines the separation of buyers and sellers. A number of factors make this asymmetry especially acute. (i) Most medical information is technical and not easily understood by the layperson. (ii) Because many illnesses do not repeat themselves the problem is made worse: the cost of acquiring the information is high. Becoming a doctor is the only way to become fully informed. (iii) The cost of a making a wrong choice is much greater and less reversible than in other cases. If you do not like the CD you have bought you can buy another one next week. In health care, making a wrong decision can prove fatal.

Doctors as agents

The fact that the doctor knows more than the patient (information is asymmetric) means the relationship between patient and doctor is different from that between buyers and sellers in most markets. We rely upon doctors to act in our best interests; that is, to act as our agent. This creates divided loyalties for doctors—on the one hand, they are required to act in the best interests of the buyers of health care, but, on the other hand, they have to act in their own interests as the sellers of health care. In a free market, doctors are primarily motivated by profit. So, it is possible that doctors may exploit patients by advising them to buy more treatment than they need. This is known as **supplier-induced demand**. So, without any ethical code of practice, we would expect supplier-induced demand to be a major problem. For this reason, the behaviour of doctors has traditionally been controlled by a professional code and a system of licensing. This means a licence is needed to work as a doctor, and the provision of the licence depends on acceptance of a code which makes explicit the obligations of being an agent.

Imperfect competition

In the competitive market model, buyers and sellers have no power to influence the market price. However, a large amount of health care is delivered by hospitals. These hospitals are often able to exercise monopoly power within the health care market. The reason hospitals can act like monopolies is that they have an incentive to grow in size. Eventually, this will lead to there being one large hospital in an area rather than many small hospitals. The incentive for hospitals to grow is because of falling average costs—what economists call **economies of scale** (see Chapter 7). There are two main reasons why the average cost of providing some treatments may fall as a hospital becomes larger.

(i) A large hospital has more opportunity to specialize; the hospital can employ highly skilled surgeons within its specialist medical units, and make use of the talents of specialized managers and ancillary staff. It may also have access to the latest equipment. All this allows the hospital to function more efficiently.

(ii) A large hospital prevents wasteful duplication of facilities. Within any town or city, there will only be a limited number of people with a particular medical condition needing particular specialist skills and equipment. Concentrating the treatment in one place allows resources to be used efficiently.

Once a hospital becomes relatively large it has considerable bargaining power over the price at which it sells its health care services. The hospital is a price maker rather than a price taker. Furthermore, if the hospital is a profit maximizer it will set price above marginal cost: the outcome will, therefore, be allocatively inefficient (a result we saw in Chapter 9). Also, in the absence of any competition, it is likely that the hospital will be productively inefficient because it lacks the incentive to reduce costs.

Externalities

We mentioned earlier in the chapter that externalities provide a source of market failure. Again, the problem is related to information. When externalities are present the market price does not fully reflect all the information about the costs and benefits of the market transaction. Earlier, we illustrated how this might occur when you buy a CD. Now we are interested in how this might operate in a health care market.

Suppose the buying and selling of vaccinations takes place in a free market. You are thinking of the benefits to yourself of not catching measles. The price you are willing to pay for a vaccination will depend on your personal, private valuation of the expected benefits. If we extend the idea from a single consumer to the level of the market as a whole, we can illustrate the market situation with a supply and demand diagram. In Figure 12.1, the line labelled D represents the market demand curve for vaccinations. The number of vaccinations that private individuals are willing to buy at each price depends on the expected benefits from not catching measles. Formally, this means that the demand curve represents the **marginal private benefit** (MPB) that consumers receive. The line S represents the market supply curve for vaccinations. The free market equilibrium occurs at point E, giving Q_e vaccinations.

But, you are not the only person to benefit when you are vaccinated against measles. Other people benefit as well because they no longer risk catching measles from you. This positive externality goes unnoticed by the free market. This effect is shown in Figure 12.1. The MSB curve represents the **marginal social benefit** from vaccination; that is, all the benefits received by society. The MSB curve thus comprises the private benefits to consumers (along the demand curve) plus the **marginal external benefit** (MEB). We can therefore write the marginal social benefit as $MSB = MPB + MEB$. The efficient equilibrium is at E', corresponding to Q_s vaccinations. So, a free market will not provide enough vaccinations from society's point of view ($Q_e < Q_s$). This underprovision imposes a cost on society, shown by the shaded area EFE'.

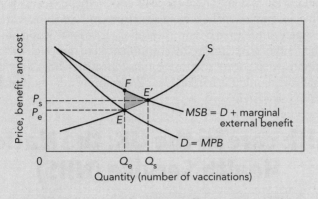

Figure 12.1. A positive externality in consumption

Uncertainty, risk, unequal information, **imperfect competition** (monopoly power), and externalities all help to explain why a free market in health care will lead to serious problems. But, these are not the only reasons why many people are unhappy about the idea of a market in health care.

Equity and health care

Although efficiency is important it is not everything. We also need to concern ourselves with what is fair. If health care is provided via a market, then only those with enough money can buy it. For many people, this situation is regarded as unacceptable. This is one of the main reasons why health care is treated differently from other commodities in most societies. In most countries, there is a concern that the distribution of health care resources and benefits should be fair.

A concern about equity was one of the main motivating forces behind the creation of the National Health Service (NHS) in the UK. The architect of the welfare state, William Beveridge, argued that the health service should provide treatment to everyone 'without remuneration limit and without an economic barrier at any point to delay recourse to it'. Equity remains a goal within the UK system. Both Conservative and Labour governments have stated that they are committed to providing a health service for all, irrespective of the ability to pay. In other countries too a concern about equity has influenced the development of the health care system. In the 1980s the Australian government introduced Medicare to ensure that everyone has access to medical treatment on the basis of need. In the 1960s, the US government introduced the Medicare scheme to help the elderly afford health care, and, in the 1980s, Medicaid for the poor under retirement age.

Market versus state?

In practice, the choice between a free market in health care and a government-controlled system is not that simple. It is agreed that to some extent health care markets fail and that there are equity considerations. But this does not necessarily mean that society is better off with a state-controlled allocation system. There are costs and inefficiencies associated with government intervention. For instance, management structures are often bureaucratic and inflexible. This can mean resources are wasted because health service outcomes do not reflect consumer demand. So, the benefits of government intervention need to outweigh the costs.

The real question is what sort of mixture is most effective—how should the government intervene and what role should the market play? We examine this question below in the context of the UK health care system.

Health care in the UK: the National Health Service (NHS)

How does the health care system in the UK relate to the economics you have learned so far? Most health care in the UK is provided by the NHS. It was set up by the Labour government in 1948. Essentially, the NHS represents an interventionist solution to the problem of allocating health care. The government decides how much health care is to be produced and who is to receive it. The state also gets involved with the production of health care, in the sense that most of the medical facilities (such as hospitals) are owned by the state. Also, those working in the NHS are employed by the state, either directly or as independent contractors.

Almost all health care spending is financed out of general taxation. This means that people have no direct say in whether they pay for health care or how much they pay. But, on the other hand, apart from prescription charges (which account for about 5 per cent of NHS income), health care in the UK is free and is available to everyone who needs it. In 1990 the Conservative government introduced a number of key reforms which altered the organization and structure of the NHS. Before examining these reforms, we consider how the system worked prior to 1990.

Prior to the reforms, your doctor would diagnose your illness and either give you a prescription or arrange for an appointment to be made for you to see a hospital specialist. You might then require treatment in hospital either as a day patient or as an in-patient. Throughout this sequence, the health care professionals gave you the medical care which they thought you needed. In other words, these professionals acted as your agent to overcome the information problems we mentioned earlier. But, in this system, the quantity and type of medical care produced is independent of your preferences. There is no market mechanism whereby you can express your consumer demand.

In debates about the NHS feelings often run high. Many people argue that it is the NHS that makes the UK a civilized society. But, for others, the NHS means slum hospitals run by unaccountable bureaucrats, and staffed by surly trade unionists. So, what are the facts? The positive achievements of the NHS include the following:

(i) The NHS is cheap by international standards. For example, in 1990 the UK spent 6.1 per cent of its gross domestic product (GDP) on health care; the average for developed nations was 9 per cent.

(ii) The NHS avoids many of the problems of insurance-based systems. Because doctors are either salaried or under contract (that is, not paid a fee for services), the incentive to oversupply is reduced. This makes producer moral hazard much less likely.

(iii) Doctors decide who needs treatment. In particular, because doctors act both as a guide to the appropriate specialist and as a filter, the problems of consumer ignorance are overcome, and the level of demand can be controlled. Furthermore, since health care is funded out of taxation and is free at the point of use, there is no stigma attached to receiving care.

What about the criticisms? Some people argue that the system has been plagued by a number of serious problems, including these:

(i) Not enough resources have been devoted to health care; in other words, consumers would like more care than is actually provided. This is a consequence of funding the service out of taxation. In the NHS, there is no mechanism whereby consumers can signal that they are prepared to pay more. This also explains the apparent continual financial crisis in the NHS— long waiting lists, ward closures, and an inability to treat particular patients all reflect the fact that insufficient resources have been devoted to health care.

(ii) The system is insensitive to consumer preferences. Doctors have considerable clinical autonomy. They make decisions about the treatment of patients with little reference to either the patients or the managerial structure of the NHS. The consequence of this is a system which is unwieldy and difficult to control.

Reforming the NHS

The weaknesses in the NHS help to explain why the Thatcher government embarked upon a major series of reforms at the end of the 1980s. The principal aims of the reforms were twofold:

(i) To improve the government's ability to control the finances of the NHS. In practice, this meant doctors had to be made more accountable to government. The clinical autonomy of doctors meant that only their professional peers were allowed to question their judgement. This made it difficult to restrict excessive prescribing or set performance targets for doctors.

(ii) To improve the efficiency of the NHS. To achieve **productive efficiency** the NHS needs to produce the maximum possible health care from the resources allocated to it. Achieving **allocative efficiency** requires that the NHS produce the type of health care that consumers want and in the correct quantities.

To achieve these objectives the Conservative government introduced elements of a market system into the NHS. This internal market split the health service into providers and purchasers. The providers are the hospitals, NHS trusts, general practitioners (GPs), pharmacists, dentists, and opticians. Initially, the purchasers included GP fundholders, District Health Authorities (DHAs), and Family Health Service Authorities (FHSAs), but in April 1996 the number of buyers was reduced with the merging of DHAs and FHSAs. These purchasers 'buy' health care services for their patients from the providers.

GPs appear as both purchasers and providers. Those GPs that have been given a budget for the purchase of secondary health care for their patients are called GP fundholders. At the time of writing, this grouping of GPs has become quite common in both large and smaller practices. The main providers of secondary health care are the NHS trusts. These are self-governing, public corporations operating within the NHS. At the moment, about 96 per cent of all secondary health care services are provided by NHS trusts.

Market discipline and the NHS

What did the Conservative government expect from these reforms? Its hope was that by introducing market discipline and a more streamlined control structure, the medical profession would be brought under control and efficiency would improve. The objective of reducing the clinical autonomy of doctors was assisted by the new contract for GPs, which made family doctors far more accountable to government; the system of targeted incentive payments, designed to promote activities such as increased childhood immunization, seriously limited the autonomy of GPs.

In theory, competitive markets are efficient. It was hoped that the internal market would improve efficiency. Specifically, the government of the day hoped that if it could separate the providers from the purchasers, then a mechanism would exist whereby inefficient providers would lose customers (patients). These inefficient providers would either disappear or change their behaviour in order to become more efficient and, hence, more competitive. Because money would follow patients, the efficient producers would be rewarded. This ought to have encouraged the NHS trusts to minimize costs and switch to new (more efficient) treatment methods as they became available.

As for allocative efficiency, the tradition in the NHS has been not to respond to consumer demand. It was hoped that this would change after the reforms, because with the introduction of GP fundholders, consumers would be able to express their preferences for a range of hospital and community health services. If you are unhappy about the range of health care offered by your GP, then you can transfer your registration to another GP. Since the payment of GPs depends on the number of patients on their list, they will respond to the disciplines of the market by providing the care consumers want.

The 1990 reform of the NHS remains controversial. Some studies into the performance of the NHS since the reforms have been favourable, while others have not. Although opinion is divided on the merit of the changes, the main findings in the reports have been:

(i) There has been no increase in patient choice or any improvement in the availability of services.

(ii) Administrative costs have increased.

(iii) GP fundholding has generated benefits. Patients in fundholding practices have shorter waiting times and can get X-rays and blood tests more quickly. However, the Labour government has said there must be common waiting times for all patients. In other words, NHS trusts must not (from April 1998) show preferential treatment to patients of GP fundholders.

(iv) There is competition between NHS trusts but so far patients have seen few benefits.

(v) Patients' choice of hospital or consultant has not improved.

Whatever the merits of the reforms the present Labour government is committed to dismantling the internal market. For Labour internal competition (and GP fundholding) is not the route to a more efficient service. But, whatever structure is put in place how do we tell whether efficiency has improved or not? We need information about health care outcomes if we are to measure efficiency. But, as yet, there is little information about the effectiveness or otherwise of different treatments.

Summary

1. In health care markets consumers face the twin problems of uncertainty and risk. We do not know for certain when we are going to be ill, and postponing the purchase of health care is

often risky. Insurance markets are designed to remove the risk and uncertainty from health care spending. But, the market for health care insurance is unlikely to be efficient, because of the problems of moral hazard and adverse selection.

2. Moral hazard occurs when individuals adopt riskier behaviour once they have bought insurance. A market for health care insurance creates an incentive for individuals to over-consume health care. Doctors may over-prescribe because they know that the cost of any treatment will be covered by the insurance company. Adverse selection is the process whereby low-risk people select themselves out of the insured group. This leads to low premiums being offered to low-risk groups, and high premiums being offered to high-risk groups, such as the elderly or chronically sick.

3. Information between buyers and sellers is not equally shared in the health care market— there is asymmetric information. The sellers of treatment (doctors) know more than the buyers (patients).

4. In a market for health care, doctors face divided loyalties; they have to act in the best interests of the buyers of health care, as well as acting in their own best interests as the sellers of health care. If they are primarily motivated by profit they may exploit patients by advising them to buy more treatment than they need. This is known as supplier-induced demand.

5. Hospitals have an incentive to grow in size. Once a profit-maximizing hospital becomes relatively large it has the power to set its price above marginal cost. This is another source of market failure.

6. The activities of consumers (and producers) can impose external costs and benefits, called externalities, on other people. Where externalities are present, the market fails to work efficiently (resources are misallocated). Many economists argue that there are strong externality effects related to health care. If you are vaccinated against a particular illness, you are not the only person to benefit. Other people also benefit because they no longer risk catching the illness from you. This externality, or extra benefit, goes unnoticed by the free market. The free market outcome is one where there are not enough vaccinations from society's point of view.

7. The 1990 reforms to the NHS were chiefly designed to give more financial control to government and to improve the efficiency of the service. To achieve these objectives, the Conservative government introduced an internal market into the NHS, so splitting the health service into providers and purchasers. A mechanism would exist to identify inefficient providers, who would lose customers (patients). These providers would either disappear or change their behaviour in order to become more efficient. If consumers were not happy with the service being provided they could switch from one GP to another.

8. Patient choice has not improved since 1990 but GP fundholding has generated benefits for some patients. The labour government proposes to reduce competition between NHS trusts. Without much better information on health care outcomes it is difficult to make judgements about the efficiency of the system which provides health care.

Key terms

adverse selection

allocative efficiency

asymmetric information

economies of scale

externalities

imperfect competition

insurance market

marginal external benefit

marginal private benefit

marginal social benefit

market failure

moral hazard

negative externality

positive externality

productive efficiency

risk

supplier-induced demand

uncertainty

Review questions

1. Why is there moral hazard and adverse selection in the market for health care insurance?

2. How are resources misallocated when externalities are associated with some goods? Does it matter whether the externalities are positive or negative?

3. What might be the externality effects of smoking?

4. Why is a positive externality likely to be associated with the purchase of household smoke alarms? Draw a diagram to illustrate this effect. How might the government deal with this externality?

5. How were the reforms to the NHS expected to improve efficiency?

Further reading

- Mabry and Ulbrich, chapter 9
- Lipsey and Chrystal, chapter 18
- Sloman, chapters 11 and 12

PART II
macroeconomics

CHAPTER 13

The focus of macroeconomics

What is macroeconomics?

Macroeconomics is the study of the economy as a whole. We look at the big issues such as economic growth, unemployment, and inflation. Each of these affect the life of an individual, or the decisions made by an individual firm, but in the study of macroeconomics we focus on the aggregate. In other words, we look at the total picture: total spending in the economy, the total output of the economy, the country's average rate of price increases in a year, and so on. The fate of the individual is caught up in the overall picture, but the action of any one individual cannot affect the overall picture.

Although macroeconomic issues have been studied for over two centuries, modern macroeconomics is in many ways the result of the Great Depression of the 1930s. The economic orthodoxy of the day seemed to have nothing useful to say about prolonged unemployment and poverty on such a vast scale and the only alternative to the market, or capitalist, economy seemed to be the central planning of communism. Against this background of uncertainty and anxiety the publication of John Maynard Keynes's *The General Theory of Employment, Interest and Money* in 1936 changed the way people thought about the economy and the role of government.

Economics has become more sophisticated since then and its tools of analysis more diverse; much more data, and more reliable data, are now available. Controversies continue, but the essential problems on which macroeconomics focuses remain the same. Economists are concerned with the short-term fluctuations in economic growth, in employment, and in price levels, but also with the conditions which foster long-term economic growth, so that living standards generally may rise. Trade between countries can play an important role and a country's balance of payments may act as a constraint on the performance of the domestic economy. All this, and more, is the province of macroeconomics. Finally, economists consider how the policies of governments, central banks, and bodies such as the World Bank and the International Monetary Fund may best be devised and implemented for the greater good.

In Part II of this text we have chosen to examine three models of the economy as a whole, each one of increasing complexity, and then to examine the role of money in the economy. This leads us to consider the nature and scope of fiscal policy and monetary policy. A discussion of the impact of the global economy on a country's internal economy may be found at the end of the book. Throughout we pay attention to the relevance of the macroeconomic models described to the key concerns of growth, employment, and stable prices.

Using macroeconomic models

A macroeconomic model is a deliberate simplification of the real world. We could try to study a country's economy in elaborate detail, looking, for example, at the spending patterns over ten years of every household and trying to draw conclusions from masses of detail. The result would be a nightmare, time-wasting and ineffective, because we do not have the computer power or the money for such a study to work; it would be a case of not seeing the wood for the trees.

Instead a macroeconomic model focuses on key elements relevant to the question under investigation. In one model the use of total spending in the economy may be appropriate; in another, total spending may split into three parts—households' spending, government spending, and firms' spending. In both cases the level of detail would be just enough to make the analysis useful, without unnecessary detail getting in the way.

Some aspects of the diagrams, in particular, will remind you of the diagrams used in the microeconomics section of the book. We look, for example, at a demand and supply diagram and find an equilibrium price and quantity. But, since this is macroeconomics, the demand line is **aggregate demand** (total demand in the economy), the supply line is **aggregate supply** (total supply in the economy), the equilibrium price is the average level of prices in the economy, and the equilibrium quantity is the total output of the economy.

The circular-flow model

The simplest macroeconomic model you will come across is known as the **circular-flow model**. At its most basic the model is of an isolated economy with only two groups of economic agents: firms and households. Households own the factors of production—land, labour, and capital—while firms employ the factors of production and organize them to produce the economy's output, which is bought by households. The circular flow is best thought of as two flows, one of **goods and services** and the other of money in payment for these goods and services. Figure 13.1 shows how this works.

The outer circle shows the **real economy**, round which circulate the factors of production and the goods and services produced. The inner circle shows the **money economy**, illustrating the flows of payments for the goods and services and factors of production. Notice the flows go in opposite directions; this makes sense, as money goes from the buyer to the seller as the goods bought go from the seller to the buyer.

In this simple economy you can see at a glance that the incomes received by households for the use of the factors of production are equal to the amount of money spent on goods and services by households; in other words, total income equals total expenditure. The value of the output of goods and services is equal to the amount spent on those goods and services; so total output equals total expenditure, which equals total income. This is a key idea to which we return later.

The other important idea, which follows from that above, is that we have three ways of measuring the level of economic activity in this economy: either we add up the value of output, or we use total spending, or we use the total of all incomes.

Figure 13.1 shows the circular-flow model at its simplest. We will return to this model later in the book and will gradually build in greater complexity as we make it a little more like economies in the real world.

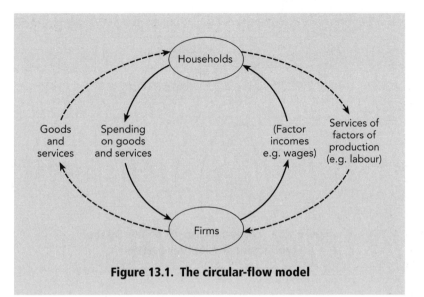

Figure 13.1. The circular-flow model

Macroeconomic goals

One reason why people study and use macroeconomics is that they wish to make the world a better place; they have ambitions and goals. Policies designed to achieve these goals may come from an understanding of macroeconomics. The main goals of macroeconomic policy are, in essence, the long-term growth of the economy, stable prices, low levels of unemployment, and the avoidance of large deficits on international payments for foreign trade. Sometimes progress towards one goal involves a retreat from the achievement of another: low inflation, for example, is often associated with high unemployment. Balance of payments crises in the 1960s acted as a major constraint on British economic policy at the time but have not occurred in the same way in more recent years. In this book we focus on the first three goals—growth, stable prices, and low unemployment—and deal with international payments briefly at the end of the book.

Economic growth

Economic growth increases the size of the economic cake, but the larger cake does not necessarily mean that all have more to eat. More formally, growth can be shown as an outward shift of the **production possibilities frontier**, as in the two-good economy producing guns and butter in Figure 13.2. (The production possibilities frontier was introduced in Chapter 2.)

This outward shift of the production possibilities frontier indicates that more goods are being produced: it is particularly important, in periods of a general upward or downward movement of prices in an economy, that we consider **real output**, rather than the money value of output, as our indicator of growth. Figure 13.3 shows how misleading it can be to look at the money value of output in a period of a sustained rise in prices. The money value of UK output rose 93 per cent between 1986 and 1996 while the real value of UK output rose by a less

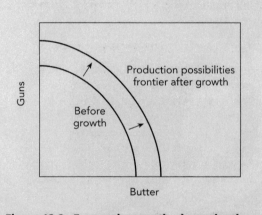

Figure 13.2. Economic growth, shown by the production possibilities frontier

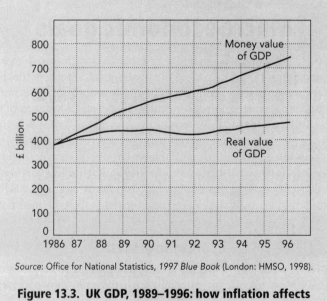

Source: Office for National Statistics, *1997 Blue Book* (London: HMSO, 1998).

Figure 13.3. UK GDP, 1989–1996: how inflation affects the figures

spectacular 23 per cent over the same period, in which the inflation rate was lower than the UK post-war average inflation rate.

Is economic growth a 'good thing'?

Many obvious benefits result from economic growth over a long period: a country will be able to spend more on education and health care, on overseas aid, on bridges, on monuments, on theatres, and so on, but there are also costs associated with growth.

Growth implies change and when change occurs there are always some who benefit more than others, and there may also be some who become worse off. For example, the industrial revolution in Britain during the eighteenth and nineteenth centuries saw a rapid rise in real output, but for some people it involved enormous changes in their way of life. Handloom weavers were highly skilled artisans who worked at home and had a certain status and independence. As weaving became more mechanized and increasingly took place in larger and larger factories, the handloom weavers were outpriced—relatively unskilled factory workers could produce cloth much more cheaply. The handloom weavers and their families starved. The population as a whole, however, enjoyed the opportunity to buy much cheaper cloth and could therefore afford to live a more comfortable life.

A second cost of growth involves the depletion of resources. Some resources are renewable and, if used at an appropriate rate, will regenerate themselves—fish are an example—but if over-exploited their capacity for regeneration is damaged. Other resources, such as coal, are non-renewable.

A third cost of growth may be increased pollution—noise, dirt, smog, and the poisoning of rivers. This is not inevitable and as countries get richer they sometimes feel able to tackle such problems.

In spite of these well-recognized costs of growth, in general the benefits seem to outweigh the costs. Not least among the benefits is the possibility of improving the living standards of the poor without drastically reducing the living standards of the rich, which makes improvements for the poor much more likely to happen.

Stable prices

Inflation is a sustained upward movement in the average level of prices: it is a decrease in the **purchasing power** of money. The opposite is called **deflation**, when the average level of prices falls and the purchasing power of money increases. Inflation has been a much more frequent experience in many parts of the world in recent decades, but deflation has occurred recently in Japan and was widespread during the Great Depression of the 1930s. Both inflation and deflation can cause problems; the main cause of these problems is uncertainty over the future value of money. Our examples illustrate problems arising from inflation.

First, inflation leads to arbitrary redistributions of wealth. Such redistributions can be significant over several years, but have never been in a political party's manifesto or been voted upon by an electorate, and if they were proposed by a politician would cause an outcry. Inflation favours those with debts at the expense of those with savings, and it favours the financially aware at the expense of the unaware. Younger people tend to have greater debts than older people because over a working lifetime they expect to be able to pay off their debts and then to save for their old age. With inflation the real value of a debt is reduced, so that paying off the debt becomes less of a burden the more that money loses its value. Similarly, savings lose their value in real terms. These changes may be partly compensated by adjustments in interest rates, but this is by no means certain. Inflation therefore tends to penalize the old and reward the young, by redistributing wealth from the old to the young.

A second undesirable feature of inflation is the efforts and resources that people devote to beating the expected effects of inflation. Many of those flexible and inventive minds employed in the financial sector might otherwise be more productively employed elsewhere.

Inflation is at its most alarming and destructive during **hyperinflation**. On 1 February 1997 the *Independent* newspaper carried a report of the hyperinflation in Bulgaria. It was accompanied by a picture of miners at a rally demanding a pay increase of 800 per cent, against a reputed rise in prices of 50 per cent in January alone and a predicted inflation rate in 1997 of 3,600 per cent. In such circumstances salaries become worthless, the able-bodied devote much of their effort to finding enough to eat, and people with any savings are ruined.

The costs to society of uncertainty about future prices are serious, and can sometimes be extremely serious, which is why price stability is one of the goals of macroeconomics.

Full employment

For most people employment means having paid work and unemployment means that there are not enough jobs for all those who wish to work. However, labour is only one of the factors of production and, strictly speaking, full employment involves all the factors of production available being in use. In this sense full employment can be illustrated by the production possibilities frontier, as in Figure 13.4. At point A resources are being wasted, while any point on the production possibilities frontier, such as B, represents full employment, with all the factors of production being used efficiently to produce maximum output.

Nevertheless, the macroeconomic goal of **full employment** is always understood to mean the full employment of labour, rather than of all the factors of production. What full employment actually means in terms of unemployment rates, or other available measures, can be difficult to pin down. Chapter 15 goes into this in more detail.

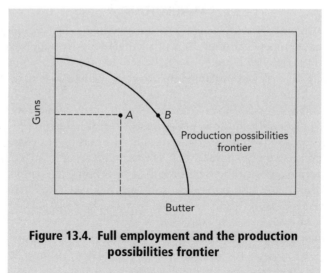

Figure 13.4. Full employment and the production possibilities frontier

We can identify three kinds of unemployment: frictional, structural, and cyclical unemployment. **Frictional unemployment** occurs when people are between jobs; they leave one job to look for another and feel confident of finding one. **Structural unemployment** is caused by long-term changes in the economy, such as the decline of coal mining in Britain as oil and North Sea gas take an increasing share of the energy market. Frictional unemployment is a necessary part of a free labour market and some structural unemployment is inevitable if the economy is to change and grow—we would not all care to be stuck with the same jobs as were available in 1910. What is less inevitable is the length of time that some structural unemployment persists.

It is the third kind of unemployment, **cyclical unemployment**, which is the main focus of macroeconomic policies to achieve full employment. Cyclical unemployment grows when there is a periodic downturn in economic activity, during a recession or a slump, and is reduced when the economy picks up again. Full employment occurs at the peak of economic activity, during the boom period of the business cycle.

Even at full employment a percentage of the labour force will be unemployed and the causes will be frictional and structural unemployment. In 1944, when the US economy was mobilized for war, there was an unemployment rate of 1.2 per cent. A sixth of the labour force was in the services, teenagers were asked to leave school early, older people came out of retirement, those in work did a six- or seven-day week, and still there was unemployment. In Chapter 15 we look further at the unemployment which exists when there is 'full employment'.

Because cyclical unemployment has such an effect on the level of unemployment most attempts to achieve full employment have tried to smooth out the peaks and troughs of the business cycle. We look in greater detail at the business cycle in Chapter 16 but before we can study the causes and effects of fluctuations in economic activity we need to consider how the economy can be measured so that we can make comparisons, discern trends, and gain an idea of the relative importance of any changes.

Summary

1. Modern macroeconomics dates from the 1930s. Economic data have improved since then so that macroeconomics now employs a wider range of analytical techniques.

2. Macroeconomic models are tools used to analyse the economy. They may be very simple or more complex.

3. The circular-flow model shows the flows of money and of goods and services around the economy. It distinguishes between the money economy and the real economy.

4. Macroeconomic goals are growth, stable prices, and full employment.

Key terms

aggregate demand	hyperinflation
aggregate supply	inflation
circular-flow model	money economy
cyclical unemployment	production possibilities frontier
deflation	purchasing power
frictional unemployment	real economy
full employment	real output
goods and services	structural unemployment

Review questions

1. Consider three generations of your family. Can you identify any members of your family who have benefited from inflation or any who have suffered because of inflation? Is there any pattern to your answer?

2. 'Unemployment is always a bad thing.' Is this so?

3. What do we mean by the 'real economy'?

4. What do you understand 'full employment' to mean?

5. Why are some people uncertain about the benefits of economic growth?

Further reading

- Mabry and Ulbrich, chapter 11
- Lipsey and Chrystal, chapter 20
- Sloman, chapter 13

CHAPTER 14

Measuring the economy: output and living standards

Economic statistics measure the performance of an economy and whether or not it achieves the macroeconomic goals discussed in Chapter 13. Economic statistics may also be used to develop and test economic theories in a way which was impossible when Keynes was writing in the 1930s. This chapter focuses on GDP, or **gross domestic product**, the first of the three statistics most frequently used by economists, commentators, and policy makers. Gross domestic product gives us the output of goods and services produced by the economy. In Chapter 15 we look at the Retail Prices Index, or RPI, which measures the cost of living, and at the unemployment rate.

Measuring output

The statistics as we know them now only began to be collected in a systematic way in Britain during the Second World War, when the government realized how important it had become to have a reliable indication of the output both of the economy as a whole and of the different sectors of the economy. The Central Statistical Office was set up early in 1941 and in the next few years the framework of the **National Income Accounts** was established. Although the range of statistics collected has grown, and the Central Statistical Office has recently become the Office for National Statistics, the ideas behind the National Income Accounts are unchanged.

Unfortunately there are differences of method in the way that some countries collect their statistics—the most striking being between the output statistics of the old Soviet bloc and those of other industrialized countries. Another difference lies in the accuracy of statistics, which can be a problem in the best-run countries but a much greater problem in the more dishonest or ill-organized. There can also be differences of emphasis, such as the focus until recently of the US figures on **gross national product** (GNP), while many countries pay more attention to gross domestic product (GDP). In spite of all these difficulties, comparisons using national economic statistics are made both between countries and over time.

GNP or GDP?

GNP is the output produced by factors of production owned by the residents of a country. GDP is the output produced by the factors of production within a country's boundaries, whoever owns them. Most countries have enterprises owned by foreign individuals or companies: think for example of the Japanese-owned car plants in Britain or the Marks and Spencer shops in Hong Kong and Paris. The profits made by Nissan in Britain are included in the British GDP figures but that part of those profits which is sent back to Japan will appear as part of the Japanese GNP.

For many countries the difference between GNP and GDP is negligible, but for others it is very significant. A country which owns a number of large multinational companies, for example, or which has many citizens who have migrated abroad to find work and send money home to support their families, may have a higher GNP than GDP. Conversely, a country such as Mauritania has a much greater GDP than GNP because its most productive resource is the waters of the Atlantic Ocean, up to 200 miles offshore, whose fish are caught partly by foreign-owned vessels and sold to foreign buyers. Fish caught by foreign-owned vessels contribute to Mauritania's GDP and to other countries' GNP.

At the level of the economy of the whole world, total GNP is the same as total GDP. At the level of an individual country GNP is a better indicator of living standards and GDP is a better indicator of productive activity.

Three ways of finding GDP

You may have thought it odd that while we talk of measuring the value of *output*, the system used in the UK is called National *Income* Accounting. It is not so odd when you are familiar with the routes statisticians use to arrive at the output figures. GDP figures are used not only as a measure of an economy's total output, but also as a measure of total incomes in that economy, and as a measure of the country's total spending on the goods and services produced. There are three ways of calculating GDP—the output method, the income method, and the expenditure method. How can this be so?

The circular-flow model can be used to explain these relationships. Figure 13.1 (in Chapter 13) was of the simplest form of the circular flow. From that diagram it is easy to see why income equals expenditure, and why expenditure equals the value of output. Does this work with a more realistic, and therefore more complicated, version? Figure 14.1 shows an economy, again with households and firms, in which the households do not spend all their income but

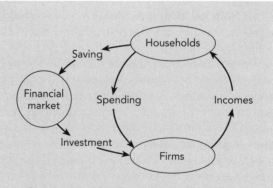

Figure 14.1. The financial sector and the circular flow of income

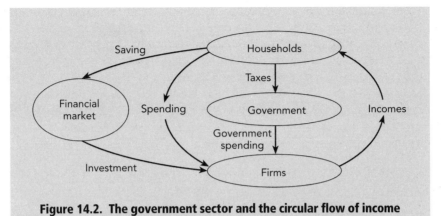

Figure 14.2. The government sector and the circular flow of income

save a proportion, and in which the firms spend money on new equipment. The firms' source of money for this investment is the financial market, which looks after the households' saving. In Figure 14.1 we show only the money circular flow, known as the circular flow of income, because at this stage we are not interested in the flow of goods and services. The money which goes into the financial market as saving does not circulate around the circular flow of income and is often described as a **leakage** from the circular flow, while the money invested by firms is in addition to the spending by households and is often described as an **injection** into the circular flow. If there were no investment by firms, but households continued to save, the circular flow would shrink and the size of the economy as indicated by total spending would become smaller.

The government takes part of people's income as taxes and indulges in some spending of its own; taxes reduce the spending power of households and so are another leakage from the circular flow. Government spending on goods and services becomes another injection into the circular flow. Figure 14.2 shows our economy with a financial sector and a government but no foreign trade. Again, if the leakages of saving and taxes were larger than the injections of investment and government spending, the circular flow would shrink.

Finally, the all-singing, all-dancing version extends the model so that the economy is open to foreign trade. Exports are goods and services produced by the domestic economy but bought and paid for by foreign buyers. The flow of goods and services is out of the domestic economy but the payment flows in, therefore exports are another injection to the circular flow of income. Imports, on the other hand, involve a payment leaving the domestic economy, while the goods and services come in. Imports, therefore, are a leakage from the circular flow of income. Figure 14.3 portrays this more complicated version. There is no reason why exports and imports should be equal. As with the previous versions of the model, the circular flow of income only stays the same size if the total flows in (injections) are equal to the total flows out (leakages). The injections and leakages are summarized in Table 14.1. (Another term in common use for leakages is **withdrawals**.)

In any time period, such as a year, the spending side of the circular flow of income, after its leakages and injections, equals the income side. The GDP figures measure both total spending and total income, but they also measure total output. The total spending on the goods and

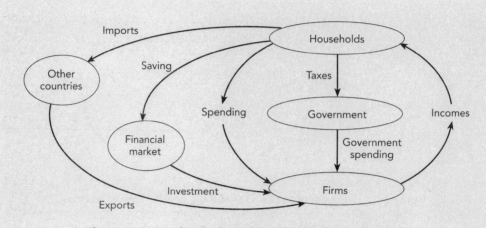

Figure 14.3. Foreign trade and the circular flow of income

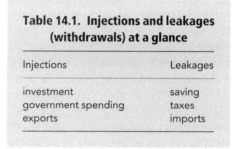

Table 14.1. Injections and leakages (withdrawals) at a glance

Injections	Leakages
investment	saving
government spending	taxes
exports	imports

services produced in any time period in an economy will give the value of the output of the goods and services purchased, and the total incomes of the factors of production used in the production of that output will be another measure of the value of that output. So any of the three methods of measuring GDP should give the same answer. Unfortunately, in the real world rather than the world of theory, the sums never quite add up because it is too difficult to collect such a vast array of statistics with complete accuracy. The necessary adjustment between the three totals is made by using what is quaintly known as the 'statistical discrepancy'. Next we look in a little more detail at each of the three methods of computing GDP.

The output method

The **output method** adds together the value of the output of goods and services produced in the economy, during the appropriate time period. The great difficulty faced by this method of arriving at GDP is that many firms' output forms the input of another firm, so that the method of calculating the value of output must avoid **double-counting** if it is to give a meaningful figure for GDP. This is achieved by counting only the **value added** at each stage of the production process, where value added is the difference between the value of the goods and services

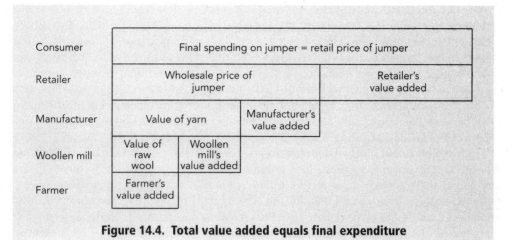

Figure 14.4. Total value added equals final expenditure

sold by a firm and the cost of raw materials and intermediate goods used in the production process. Value added is, in fact, the value of the work done by the factors of production and is equal to the sum of wages, rent, profits, and interest.

Figure 14.4 shows how value is added at each stage of the production of woollen knitwear. The wool is produced by sheep owned by a hill farmer who employs a shepherd. The farmer pays wages, rent for the land, and interest payments on a loan for the purchase of his Land Rover, and makes a profit. When the sheep are sheared and the wool sold the value of this sale is the farmer's value added. The wool is sold to a woollen mill, which washes, combs, dyes, and spins the yarn. Value is added during these processes and is reflected in the higher price received for the yarn than was paid for the raw wool. The cones of yarn are then sold to the knitwear manufacturer, who transforms the yarn into knitted garments, which are sold to the retailer at a much higher price than the cost of the yarn. Finally, the retailer provides the service of making the knitted clothes conveniently available in a range of sizes and colours on the high street. The retailer's mark-up on the wholesale price paid gives the value added at the retail stage. Only the sale of the finished garment counts as the sale of a final good; at all the other stages of the productive process the sales are of intermediate goods. When you buy yourself a jumper, the price you pay is the sum of all the value added at each stage of its production.

The income method

The **income method** aggregates all the incomes earned by the factors of production: labour earns wages, land earns rent, capital earns interest, and entrepreneurship earns profit. These standard categories used in economic theory correspond reasonably closely with those used in the National Income Accounts, which have four categories measuring income from employment, rent, gross trading profits and surplus, and income from self-employment. The first two are self-explanatory but the last two are less obvious.

The profits made by companies are either paid as dividends to shareholders or retained by the company. The word 'surplus' here refers to any excess of income over expenditure of publicly owned enterprises, which are now far fewer than they used to be. Municipally owned airports are an example, as is the city of Hull's telephone system. Income from self-employment may include elements of wages, rent, and profit, and it would be too difficult to distinguish between these elements in many cases. The self-employed include partners in professional firms such as lawyers and accountants, as well as farmers, small shopkeepers, and mobile hairdressers.

The incomes above, when added together, give us the value of **national income**, a commonly used term which does not equal GDP or GNP, though it is closer to GNP. Two adjustments need to be made to get from GNP to national income. One adjustment lies in the distinction made between the terms 'gross' and 'net', and the other in the distinction made between market prices and factor cost.

The first adjustment involves **depreciation**: as new capital—plant and machinery—is used it begins to wear out and continues to wear out over its useful lifetime. Replacement of worn-out equipment is not new investment at all, except that in many cases the new equipment is more technologically advanced than the old. The figures in the national accounts for investment are in one sense misleadingly high because most investment includes an element of replacement of older capital goods. **Gross investment** less depreciation gives us **net investment**, just as gross national product (GNP) less depreciation gives us net national product (NNP). So,

$$\text{GNP} - \text{depreciation} = \text{NNP}.$$

NNP is at **market prices**. The prices of goods at final sale do not always accurately reflect the costs of the factors of production because many carry some form of tax such as Value Added Tax (VAT) or an excise duty, for example the tax levied on cigarettes in Britain. In some countries goods are subsidized by the state so that their prices are artificially low. The difference between the figure for NNP and that for national income lies in the net value of these indirect taxes and subsidies. While NNP is at market prices, national income is at **factor cost**, and gives a clearer picture of the value of the work done by the factors of production:

$$\text{NNP} - \text{indirect taxes} + \text{subsidies} = \text{national income}.$$

The expenditure method

The **expenditure method** gathers data on all the spending in the economy to arrive at **aggregate expenditure**. This is made up of spending by households on goods and services, or consumption (C), plus investment spending (I) by firms, plus government spending on goods and services (G), and the net result of exports (X) less imports (M); in symbols,

$$\text{GDP} = \text{aggregate expenditure} = C + I + G + (X - M).$$

Consumption forms by far the largest proportion of aggregate expenditure in the UK, at about two-thirds of GDP. Consumption includes household spending on durables such as cars and washing machines, which should last for several years; spending on goods that are used up more or less quickly, such as food, newspapers, and clothes; and spending on services such as hairdressing, dentistry, opera, and football games.

Investment was about 15 per cent of UK GDP in 1996 and is made up of spending by firms on additions to the capital stock of the country. It includes plant and machinery, office buildings, warehouses, and additions to firms' stocks of unsold goods or unused inputs.

Government spending includes all the spending on goods and services by both central and local government and forms about one-quarter of UK GDP. It includes defence, education, and health. It does *not* include government spending on **transfer payments**, such as pensions and other social security benefits, or subsidies to industry. These forms of spending are merely a transfer of purchasing power.

Net exports, or exports minus imports, are a tiny proportion of UK GDP because although about 30 per cent of GDP is exported, the size of imports is roughly similar. Net exports are frequently negative; that is, imports are greater than exports.

Some forms of spending are not included in aggregate expenditure because they are not spending on **final goods**. Spending on **intermediate goods** which go to make the final product would artificially inflate the size of aggregate expenditure if included, as would spending on second-hand goods.

Some limitations of official output figures

Economists and statisticians complain increasingly that the traditional methods of calculating GDP are becoming less reliable. There are plenty of data on the production of coal, grain, and clothing, but useful date about today's fastest-growing industries—computing, telecommunications, business services, and finance—are much harder to find. Called by some the 'weightless economy', these activities cannot be seen and are not easily numbered.

Another deficiency is the exclusion of unpaid services from the figures. These 'non-market' activities include do-it-yourself work; most housework, cooking, gardening, dress-making, and knitting; and all voluntary work. All of these produce outputs which would otherwise have to be paid for and, if bought, would increase the size of GDP. Estimates of the value of unpaid housework in industrial economies are that it is about a fifth of GDP. In less developed economies, particularly those with large subsistence economies, these unpaid activities are even larger in proportion to the official output figures.

Illicit activities are a further exclusion from the official statistics. These range from the highly profitable production and distribution of illegal drugs to the plumber who prefers to be paid in cash, so as to avoid paying tax.

Another difficulty with the official figures for GDP is that they add the costs of coping with pollution to the value of output. For example, when a tanker runs aground and spills its cargo of crude oil, the costs of salvage of the vessel and of cleaning up the effects of the spillage are counted as an addition to GDP. As economies grow the costs of pollution tend to become larger, but they are not in any sense adding to the well-being of the country. This brings us to consider what is meant by 'the standard of living' and how it may be measured or assessed.

Living standards

The **standard of living** is not a well-defined concept and it may mean different things to different people. Do the social science researcher, the district nurse, the archbishop, and the politician all mean the same when they use the term? The economist takes the national income figures as a starting point, but needs to be aware of their deficiencies. GDP is the figure most commonly used to measure a country's output and growth but national income, which is more closely linked to GNP than to GDP, is more useful when considering a country's standard of living. In practice, any of the three will be used.

There are two main kinds of difficulty with using output or income statistics as an indicator of living standards: these difficulties lie in omissions and in comparisons. We consider the problems of omissions from the official statistics first. The preceding section on the limitations of output figures listed the 'weightless economy', the 'underground economy', and non-market activities as contributions to output which are poorly recorded by the official statistics, or not recorded at all. Economic 'bads' such as pollution should be deductions from figures used to indicate living standards; instead they often lead to an increase in recorded output and income, as officially measured.

Output figures are unable to show how improvements in the quality of goods and services contribute to improvements in living standards: an automatic washing machine of the 1990s is far less time-consuming than an electric washing machine of the 1950s, with its small tub and mangle for squeezing water from the washing. The hours we spend in paid employment contribute to output figures, but we value our leisure time equally; no measure of the improvements in living standards associated with the gradual shortening of the working week is possible within the existing framework of output and income statistics.

The second area of difficulty lies in making comparisons, both over time and between countries, using output and income statistics. These figures express the value of output or income in terms of the current value of money, but the value of that money may change quite rapidly, sometimes even making comparisons between one year and the next meaningless. Comparisons over several decades in terms of current money are usually pointless. Such comparisons need to be made in **real terms** rather than using **nominal figures**, that is, after adjusting for any changes in the average level of prices over the time period of the comparison. This idea is explored more fully in Chapter 15.

Figures of output per head, or **per capita GDP**, tell us rather more about the relative living standards of two countries than the total figures for GDP, but they do not tell us how income is distributed within a country, and so still cannot give us the full picture. Also, ways of life vary around the world—on a small tropical island there is no need for layers of warm clothing and expensive heating. Output-per-head figures may give a quite misleading impression of the comfort and pleasure of life on a tropical island, when compared to life in a northern industrial country.

Finally, national statistics are presented in terms of national currencies but the purchasing power of different currencies may not be reflected by the official exchange rates. So even if all per capita GDP figures were expressed in US dollars the results could still be misleading. In an attempt to overcome this kind of problem *The Economist* has produced its own 'Big Mac index' for several years; this index gives a guide to the purchasing power of different currencies buying a standardized product available from McDonald's around the world.

Summary

1. GDP is the most commonly used measure of output.

2. GNP is a better indicator of living standards and GDP is a better indicator of economic activity in a country.

3. There are three methods of calculating GDP: the expenditure method, the income method, and the output method.

4. Official figures exclude the value of both non-market goods and services and the underground economy.

5. Omissions from official statistics can make international comparisons of living standards less meaningful, as can differences between a country's exchange rate and its currency's internal purchasing power.

6. Rising prices (or falling prices) make comparisons over time misleading. Such comparisons must be made using figures in real terms.

Key terms

aggregate expenditure

consumption

depreciation

double-counting

expenditure method

factor cost

final goods

government spending

gross domestic product (GDP)

gross investment

gross national product (GNP)

income method

injection

intermediate goods

investment

leakage, or withdrawal

market prices

national income

National Income Accounts

net exports

net investment

nominal figures

output method

per capita GDP

real terms

standard of living

transfer payments

value added

withdrawal, or leakage

Review questions

1. Why are there three possible methods of calculating GDP?

2. What is the difference between (i) a statistic at market prices and at factor cost; (ii) GNP and NNP; (iii) intermediate goods and final goods? In each case, explain why the distinction matters.

3. What difficulties might you expect to meet when comparing living standards in China, Brazil, Sweden, and Angola?

4. 'Never make the mistake of confusing GNP with gross national well-being.' Why not?

Further reading

- Mabry and Ulbrich, chapter 11
- Lipsey and Chrystal, chapter 20
- Sloman, chapter 14

CHAPTER 15

Measuring the economy: inflation and unemployment

In this chapter we look at two of the most familiar **economic indicators**, the inflation rate and the unemployment rate. A rise in either is bad news on the front pages of the newspapers, and a fall in either is often a cause for self-congratulation by government politicians. We also consider a less familiar economic concept, the natural rate of unemployment.

The Retail Prices Index

The most commonly used measure of inflation in Britain is the **Retail Prices Index**, or RPI, which measures the cost of living. This is sometimes called **headline inflation** because it is the measure of inflation which hits the newspaper headlines most frequently. There are other measures of inflation in use and we will discuss some of these later in this chapter.

The RPI measures changes in the prices of goods in the shops, or retail prices, and changes in the prices of services bought by households; new figures are published every month. You may wonder how this mammoth task is performed—it would seem impossible to go into every shop, every month, and record the price of everything for sale. A carefully considered sample of goods and services is taken and this sample is intended to reflect the spending pattern of a typical household. The sample is cosily referred to as a 'basket' of goods (and services), though not very many people now go shopping with a basket.

Every month price collectors note prices of the goods and services in the 'basket'. The countrywide results are put together and an index calculated by the Office of National Statistics (ONS) to show the overall effect of changes in those prices. Obviously, a 10 per cent rise in the price of tinned anchovies is going to have less of an impact on households than a 10 per cent rise in the cost of petrol. To reflect the relative importance of different goods each item is weighted according to its significance in the scale of household spending.

How to calculate a simple price index

Table 15.1 shows how a **price index** may be calculated. Goldilocks leads an uncomplicated life, spending her money only on porridge and hair dye; the price index shows how her cost of living in 1998 compares with her cost of living in January 1990, the **base period**. To calculate this

Table 15.1. How to calculate a simple price index

Goods in the basket	Base period 1990 Quantity (= weight)	Price (£)	Total spending (£)	1998 Price (£)	Total spending (£)
Porridge	4	2	8	2.50	10
Hair dye	2	5	10	7	14
			18		24

Price index for base period (i.e. 1990) = 100
Price index for 1998 = price index for 1990 × (spending in 1998 ÷ spending in 1990)
$$= 100 \times (24 \div 18)$$
$$= 100 \times 1.33$$
$$= 133$$

we first take Goldilocks' expenditure in January 1990. In that month she bought four packets of porridge at £2 each and two packets of hair dye at £5 each, making her total expenditure £18. In 1998 she faces prices of £2.50 for a packet of porridge and £7 for each packet of hair dye. A feature of this index is that the weights attached to spending in later time periods are those of the base period, so Goldilocks' expenditure for a month in 1998 is calculated using the quantities she bought in the base period, but at the new prices, and is thus £24. The index for expenditure in the base period is 100 and the index for the month in 1998 is expressed as a percentage of the base period expenditure, that is, (24/18) × 100 = 133. So Goldilocks faced an increase in her cost of living of 33 per cent over the time elapsed since the base period of January 1990.

A price index needs to give a realistic picture of the average level of prices and it needs to be not impossibly difficult to calculate. Different countries use subtly different methods of calculating such an index. You can see from the example above that by 1998 the quantities used in 1990 might not be all that relevant. Currently, in the UK the contents of the RPI basket and the weights attached to them are altered every year in line with a survey of family spending patterns, while the base period in which RPI equals 100 remains January 1987. In the USA, the Consumer Prices Index (CPI) is calculated on a basket of goods and weights updated every decade. In recent years this has led to suggestions that the CPI has overestimated US inflation.

Some problems of the RPI

Price indices are particularly useful when making comparisons between countries, or over time, or between the cost of living of different kinds of consumer. But in any of these comparisons the use of an index immediately throws up some problems.

Goods and services included in one country's basket will not be the same as those in another country's basket. This may not always be particularly significant, but in the case of the RPI there is one major difference which makes comparisons with similar indices of other countries sometimes quite misleading. The RPI includes two kinds of housing costs—rents and mortgage payments—since housing is an important part of household expenditure and a relatively large proportion of UK households own or are buying their own home. Other countries' consumer price indices tend not to include mortgage payments. Houses are not a retail purchase but a form of investment, and mortgage payments are affected by the current interest rate, which can be very volatile.

In recent years one anti-inflationary tool used by the government and the Bank of England has been to raise the rate of interest. This puts up the cost of mortgages and causes an increase in the RPI, apparently raising inflation while trying to lower it. Should the rate of interest fall, the RPI may understate inflation, since the weight attached to housing costs is relatively large. The RPI is, politically, a particularly sensitive indicator and British governments in recent years have tended to try to emphasize **underlying inflation**, that is, the RPI without the mortgage interest payment element—this form is sometimes called the RPIX.

Another influence on retail prices is the rate of indirect tax, principally Value Added Tax (VAT) but also some excise duties such as the tax on beer or cigarettes. When these sorts of taxes go up, so does the RPI. A measure of inflation which excludes the influence of changes in indirect tax (and the influence of mortgage interest payments) is known as the RPIY, but it is not as frequently quoted as the underlying rate of inflation, or RPIX.

A further difficulty of price indices is that they are not as clever as consumers. When relative prices change, consumers tend to buy more of the cheaper good and less of the relatively more expensive good, especially when a price rises quickly; even a price index whose weights are revised annually cannot deal well with this. Also, consumers often take advantage of sales, special offers, and discounts, none of which influence the RPI or similar price indices. Neither can a price index deal adequately with changes in the quality of goods and services. A domestic refrigerator bought in 1995 may well be larger than one bought in 1955, and may have more 'features' such as an automatic defrost, but it is unlikely to be as sturdily built and may not last as long as a 1955 model. So for a variety of reasons commentators suggest that consumer price indices tend to overstate the rate of inflation a little—the US measure, the Consumer Price Index (CPI), is thought by some to have been one percentage point too high in 1996.

The GDP deflator

The RPI and other consumer price indices are just that—they measure changes in the prices paid by consumers but ignore prices of goods and services never bought by consumers. Some of these omissions are of goods and services of some importance to the economy but which do not directly affect the cost of living. A Tornado aircraft, for example, or a Chieftain tank, are not part of the contents of the average household's shopping basket. When looking at changing prices in the economy as a whole the **GDP deflator** is a more appropriate index than the RPI because it measures the average level of prices of all the goods and services included in gross domestic product.

The GDP deflator is calculated by dividing nominal GDP by real GDP and expressing the result as a percentage:

$$\text{GDP deflator} = (\text{nominal GDP/real GDP}) \times 100.$$

Nominal GDP is the value of GDP at the prices current at the time of measurement and is a relatively easy figure to get hold of, but how do we discover what real GDP is? **Real GDP** measures the physical quantity of output of goods and services and is calculated by valuing the current quantity of output at the prices of the output of the base period. The base period is currently 1990 so the quantity of mountain bikes produced in 1998 would be valued at the price of mountain bikes in 1990 to get their 'real value' in terms of 1990 prices. This is repeated for the output of goods and services of all sectors of the economy to arrive at real GDP. If the prices of goods and services are generally rising then the GDP deflator gets larger—in Britain it rose from 100 in the base period (1990) to 123.4 in 1996.

The GDP deflator is a wider measure of price changes than the RPI, but it is of less immediate interest to the man or woman in the street. Both the RPI and the GDP deflator tend to show a similar pattern of price changes over several years, and tend to move in the same direction, but they do not always agree. The RPI is prone to greater fluctuations than the GDP deflator and both have a tendency to overstate inflation, for the reasons outlined above.

Finally, you may wonder why statisticians bother with the complicated and frequent calculations needed to construct these price indices. The great advantage of using index numbers rather than the raw figures is that they make two kinds of comparisons much easier. Comparisons over time are more obvious at a glance, as are comparisons of different series of figures, such as the cost of living for pensioner households and the cost of living for students.

Measuring unemployment

Achievement of the third macroeconomic goal of full employment is measured by the **unemployment rate**, which, with the RPI, is one of the most politically sensitive economic indicators. Internationally, the unemployment rate is understood to show the number of people without a job and looking for work as a percentage of the **labour force**.

In practice this is not easy to measure and depends very much on definitions of what is meant by 'without work', 'looking for work', and 'the labour force'. You might think these definitions are obvious but, partly because of the politically sensitive nature of the resulting figures, definitions have been changed several times in the UK in the last twenty years. This makes comparisons over any period of time difficult and has led to a widespread and unfortunate cynicism about the validity of government statistics in general. Until April 1998, the UK unemployment figures were based on a **claimant count**: they showed the numbers of adult workers not employed and claiming the Job Seeker's Allowance. Therefore the unemployment figures excluded those under 18 and those over 60 years of age, even though the retirement age for men is 65, while the UK employment figures showed the number of workers over 16 with a job and those on government work-related schemes—an obvious inconsistency.

Changes in the bases on which the unemployment data were collected in recent years have generally had the effect of reducing the quoted unemployment rate. In particular, the unemployed have been shown as a percentage of the working population rather than of the labour force. The working population is larger than the labour force because it includes the armed forces and the self-employed; therefore the unemployment rate looks lower than it might, had the previous definition been still in use.

There are several other ways in which the published unemployment statistics underestimate unemployment as the term is understood by most people. Women who stop working to raise a family and then wish to return to work may not claim unemployment benefits and so are excluded from the recorded unemployment figures, as are school leavers and men between the ages of 60 and 65. People who are unemployed for only a brief period are also excluded. There is no way of indicating the extent of underemployment either, whether of the part-time

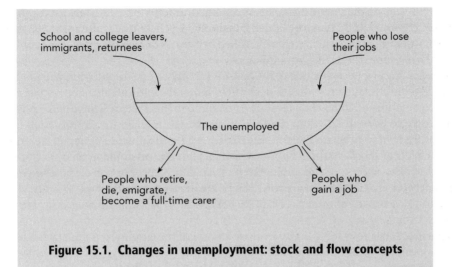

Figure 15.1. Changes in unemployment: stock and flow concepts

employee who would prefer full-time work, or of the over-qualified employee such as a bio-logist with a Ph.D. who works in McDonald's serving hamburgers.

However, from April 1998, the published UK unemployment rate has conformed to inter-national standards of computation and has been based on a monthly estimate of the number of people seeking jobs and available to work, derived from the quarterly Labour Force Survey. This change added about half a million people to the jobless total, overnight.

On the other hand government figures may also overestimate unemployment. Some claims for unemployment benefits are fraudulent because those claiming have an undeclared income from employment in the underground economy; similarly some people with seasonal work may prefer not to work all year round but may sign on the unemployment register when not employed.

Stocks and flows

Unemployment is a **stock**, measured at one point in time, while people becoming unemployed or finding a job are a **flow**, measured over a period of time. Stock and flow concepts are cent-ral to macroeconomics—they are, for example, relevant to the first model in this book, the circular-flow model. Figure 15.1 shows how the pool of unemployed people is added to by those who lose their jobs or who return to or join the labour force; it is reduced by those who leave the labour force by retiring, emigrating, dying, caring for children or relatives, or giving up the search, and by those who get a job. If the flows into the pool are greater than the flows out then the level of the pool will rise, that is, the stock or the number unemployed becomes larger and the unemployment rate rises. In any one year the flows in and out of the pool are significantly greater than the number unemployed at any one moment.

The natural rate of unemployment

The **natural rate of unemployment**, or *NRU*, is the unemployment rate at **full employ-ment**, or when the labour market is in equilibrium. For the reasons described at the end of

Chapter 13, full employment does not mean a zero unemployment rate: there will always be some **frictional** and **structural unemployment**. **Cyclical unemployment**, or **demand-deficient unemployment** such as that identified by Keynes during the inter-war depression, is not part of the natural rate of unemployment.

There is some evidence that one of the reasons for higher rates of unemployment in Britain in the 1980s and 1990s than in the 1950s or 1960s is that the natural rate of unemployment has risen. Explanations include changes in the tax and benefits system which make it easier for some people to be without work; rigidities in the labour market due to legislation or to the power of trade unions which make it difficult for wages to adjust to a market clearing level; and the effects of shocks to the economy which increase the unemployment rate. Some argue that such shocks increase the unemployment rate and that a proportion of those unemployed, particularly if they are out of work for a long time, never return to work. It is not clear why shocks to the economy should have had this effect in the last two decades only, rather than over the past fifty years.

The size of the labour force is greater than the size of the employed population but smaller than the population of official working age. Over the years changes in society have meant that the composition of the labour force has altered and changes in the economy have meant that the sort of work offered by employers has also altered. In the last fifty years an increasing proportion of women has entered the labour force; the school-leaving age has risen and a higher proportion of school leavers go on into further or higher education, thus entering the labour force several years later; and the average retirement age has fallen but average life expectancy has risen. During the same period there has been a decline in employment in heavy industry and a rise in employment in the service sector; there has been a decline in employment in manual labour and a rise in employment in high-technology industries; and there has been a significant growth in the numbers of those in part-time employment. All these factors may combine to affect the natural rate of unemployment, since much of the labour force is relatively immobile geographically and retraining is not universally available or acceptable.

Summary

1. The Retail Prices Index (RPI) is a cost of living index based on the spending pattern of the average household.

2. The RPI includes housing costs but because the mortgage interest payment element changes as the interest rate changes, the RPI can sometimes give a misleading impression of the behaviour of retail prices. The RPIX is designed to avoid this.

3. Consumer price indices in general have a tendency to overstate the rate of inflation, particularly if the weights used in their calculation are infrequently revised.

4. The GDP deflator is a price index which measures the average level of prices of all the goods and services produced in the economy.

5. Price indices make comparisons over time and comparisons between different series of figures much easier.

6. The unemployment rate is the number of people without a job and looking for work as a percentage of the labour force. This is the international definition and needs to be distinguished from the claimant-count measure in use in Britain in recent years.

7. Ways of measuring the unemployment rate in Britain have changed several times in the last twenty years. This makes comparisons over time and comparisons between countries more difficult.

8. The natural rate of unemployment (NRU) is the unemployment rate at full employment. It includes frictional and structural unemployment.

Key terms

base period

claimant count

cyclical unemployment

demand-deficient unemployment

economic indicator

flow

full employment

frictional unemployment

GDP deflator

headline inflation

labour force

natural rate of unemployment (NRU)

nominal GDP

price index

real GDP

Retail Prices Index (RPI)

stock

underlying inflation

unemployment rate

Review questions

1. When would you find each of the following the most useful measure of inflation?

    (i) the RPI
    (ii) the GDP deflator
    (iii) the RPIX
    (iv) the RPIY

2. Why do statisticians use weights when calculating a price index?

3. What is the generally understood definition of an unemployment rate?

4. How might a figure for an unemployment rate based on a claimant count be misleading?

5. What sort of factors might influence the natural rate of unemployment?

Further reading

- Mabry and Ulbrich, chapter 11
- Lipsey and Chrystal, chapters 20, 30 and 31
- Sloman, chapter 13

CHAPTER 16

Macroeconomics and history

Well before the advent of economic statistics people were aware of widespread changes in their local and national economy. Sometimes they found a pattern to these changes; during the twentieth century improved statistics have given greater precision to analysis of the economy. In this chapter we consider, first, the pattern of changes in the economy over the business cycle and second, the way macroeconomic ideas have developed over the past two and a half centuries.

The business cycle

There can be marked swings up and down in the rates of unemployment and inflation. We now consider the patterns made by these fluctuations, as well as the accompanying changes in the rate of growth of real output, and bring all three together in this section on the **business cycle**.

Business cycles are the periodic up-and-down movements in economic activity, measured by fluctuations in real output, but reflected too by other macroeconomic variables. The business cycle is also known as the **trade cycle**.

The business cycle and real output

During the business cycle the growth of real output fluctuates around the long-term *trend* growth rate of real output; we look first at what this trend means. Over the past 160 years the average rate of growth of real GDP in Britain has been 2 per cent a year, which means that real GDP has doubled every 35 years. The average growth rate is the **trend** in real GDP. Should this trend continue, by the time each of us reaches the biblical span of threescore years and ten, the real GDP of the British economy should be four times as great as it was when each of us was born and, since the growth rate of the population is much lower, we should notice significant improvements in living standards over a lifetime.

Figure 16.1 illustrates fluctuations in the growth of real output around the trend over the course of two business cycles. There are four distinct phases to a business cycle: peak, contraction, trough, and expansion. Other frequently used terms are: **boom, recession, slump**, and **recovery**. To be precise, if real GDP falls (that is, the growth rate is negative) for two successive quarters economists call it a recession, and a very deep trough is known as a **depression**, though often the terms 'slump' and 'depression' are used interchangeably.

Although Figure 16.1 makes the business cycle look fairly regular, and somewhat predictable, in practice business cycles are irregular both in the size of the changes in the growth rate of real output, and in the length of the four phases.

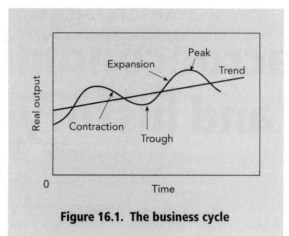

Figure 16.1. The business cycle

Unemployment over the business cycle

Changes in the unemployment rate are closely linked to changes in the rate of growth of real output, but they move in opposite directions and there is a time-lag—changes in real output precede changes in unemployment. The unemployment statistics are therefore a **lagging indicator**, of great interest and importance, but not as a pointer to what is likely to happen next to output. Norman Lamont, when Chancellor of the Exchequer in the early 1990s, was ridiculed by the man in the street for his insistence that he could see 'the green shoots of the recovery' of the economy from recession, when at the same time the unemployment figures continued to rise.

During the expansionary phase of the business cycle firms run down their stocks of unsold goods, their order books lengthen, they move to full-time and then overtime working, and eventually they take on more labour. During the contractionary phase order books become shorter, stocks of unsold goods begin to build up, overtime work disappears, some labour works short-time, and eventually some people are made redundant. Thus a rise in the growth rate of real output is followed some time later by a fall in the unemployment rate, and a fall in the rate of growth of real output is later mirrored by a rise in the unemployment rate. This is why the picture presented by the unemployment figures is not identical to that shown by the output figures, and why there is a time-lag.

Inflation and the business cycle

The relationship between changes in prices and in real output is less strong than that between unemployment and real output. Other things being equal, there is a tendency for prices to rise in the expansionary phase of the business cycle as shortages develop of skilled labour, perhaps, and of some raw materials or key components. During the contraction phase prices fall as unsold stocks of goods build up and lower prices are used to try to shift these goods. Given a continuing underlying inflation, prices will rise faster in the expansion and more slowly in the contraction.

The business cycle in perspective

The boom-and-slump pattern of the business or trade cycle has characterized market co-ordinated economic systems for at least two hundred years. (Centrally planned economies have different problems.) The pattern was recognized in the nineteenth century: Karl Marx analysed the business cycle and predicted that its swings would get ever larger and more catastrophic until workers would revolt, unable to take any more. In *Mary Barton* (1848), the novelist Elizabeth Gaskell gives a striking account of the effects of a downturn in trade on the lives of Lancashire cotton workers. As the wife of a Unitarian minister in Manchester, Mrs Gaskell visited the poor and had intimate knowledge of their lives during the 'hungry forties'.

Business cycles are unpredictable in both duration and size but after the Second World War governments felt that they should attempt to reduce the peaks and troughs, particularly because of their impact on employment. This **stabilization policy** had a mixed success and was largely abandoned in the 1970s when persistent and rising inflation, rather than unemployment, became the chief anxiety.

Explanations of the causes of the business cycle fall into three groups. The first group explores the role of investment in capital goods and suggests that fluctuations in investment cause larger fluctuations in output. This idea is explored further in Chapter 19, where it occurs as part of the third macroeconomic model we study. A second group of explanations focuses on the role of money and on the business cycle as a monetary phenomenon. There is a link between the money supply and economic activity—this idea receives more attention in Chapters 21 and 22. A third approach to the business cycle looks at the part played by unexpected shocks to the economy, for example from a change in technology or in relative prices. Since these shocks occur irregularly, this goes some way to explain the irregularity of business cycles.

A brief history of macroeconomic thought

The way philosophers and economists have thought about what would now be called macroeconomic problems strongly reflects the circumstances and times in which they lived, but, equally, the writings of these philosophers and economists have influenced the thinking of their contemporaries and of later generations. As we consider their ideas we need to be aware of their period and to weigh up the extent to which earlier ideas are applicable today.

Outline

Eighteenth- and nineteenth-century thinking on economics can be divided into two main schools: **classical economics** (1770–1850) and **neo-classical economics** (1850–1920). Classical economists were interested in both microeconomics and macroeconomics but neo-classical economists concentrated largely on microeconomic concerns, particularly marginal analysis and equilibrium theory. They accepted the classical economists' views on macroeconomic issues such as unemployment and growth.

In the twentieth century macroeconomic thinking was revolutionized by Keynes, who wrote and spoke widely on economics in the 1920s and 1930s. His ideas were not at first readily accepted but later had a major impact on economics and on government actions until well into the 1970s. He was critical of the policy makers of the time, who were, he thought, in the grip of damaging economic ideas from an earlier era.

In the 1970s and 1980s the focus of macroeconomics and of government macroeconomic policy was strongly influenced by the monetarist school, whose leading light was Milton Friedman.

In this brief survey of the development of ideas in macroeconomics we shall concentrate on the classical economists, point out some of the differences between Keynes and the classical economists, and say a little about monetarism.

The classical economists

The founding father of modern economics was Adam Smith (1723–90), a Scottish philosopher, whose book *The Wealth of Nations* (1776) has had a tremendous impact on subsequent thinking. Smith argued that market economies generally serve the public interest well and that the state should not interfere with the functioning of the economy.

Another very influential work was the *Essay on the Principle of Population as it Affects the Future Improvement of Society*, first published in 1798, by Thomas Malthus (1766–1834). Malthus argued that the combination of normal population growth and diminishing returns in agriculture would lead to starvation, if war or pestilence did not first reduce the population. In those days agricultural output was a far higher proportion of total output than it is today. Two reasons why Malthus's inexorable logic has not yet been proved right in more developed parts of the world are, first, that technological change has raised agricultural yields and, second, that population growth tends to fall as real incomes rise; but the conditions described by Malthus can still be seen in some of the poorest parts of the world.

The Napoleonic Wars finished in 1815 and were followed by recession and unemployment. Malthus became gloomy about the future as the capitalist system seemed unstable. He was the first to identify a lack of effective demand as a problem—the warehouses were full but people would not buy. Incidentally, in 1804 Malthus became Britain's first professor of Political Economy.

David Ricardo (1772–1823), a wealthy stockbroker and Member of Parliament, disagreed with Malthus about the lack of effective demand. He argued that unemployment was the result of wages being too high: if people would accept lower wages they would find work. His view prevailed and was supported by Jean-Baptiste Say (1776–1832), a French industrialist. He put forward the view that general overproduction and prolonged unemployment were impossible. The often-quoted Say's Law is 'supply creates its own demand' or, put another way, the production of goods generates sufficient income to ensure these goods are sold—you may think here of the circular-flow diagram in Chapter 13.

This optimism about the way the free market would solve the problem of unemployment was the conventional wisdom in economics until the 1930s, despite the criticisms of Karl Marx and others.

'The dismal science'

Although the word 'optimism' is used in the previous paragraph, economics was often called 'the dismal science'. The classical economists foresaw a gloomy outcome in the long term. They tended to see a limit to the growth of output, because of diminishing marginal returns. Malthus, for one, foretold starvation and pestilence.

Ricardo was more optimistic about the short term but thought that in the long term profits would fall and wages would be at subsistence level. He did, however, acknowledge that improvements in technology might delay this state.

Karl Marx (1818–83) foretold revolution. He thought that the booms and slumps of the business cycle were the inevitable result of the capitalist system and that, repeated, they would lead to a growing mass of unemployed labour which would become increasingly politically aware. The contradictions of capitalism would eventually lead to a workers' revolution and to the common ownership of the means of production.

The Keynesian revolution

The First World War was followed in Britain by high levels of unemployment which persisted for nearly twenty years. This was unprecedented. The generally accepted opinion at the time, known as the 'Treasury view', was based on the argument of the classical economists that unemployment was due to wages being too high. However, although wages fell, unemployment continued to rise.

John Maynard Keynes (1883–1946) argued, like Malthus, that this unemployment was primarily due to a failure of demand—people were unwilling or unable to buy the goods produced—and that it was possible for an economy to slide into a slump and to stay there. This was the opposite of the classical economists' opinion.

Keynes, however, saw a slump as something the government could cure by a programme of spending: the government could allow its budget to go into deficit while undertaking such spending because increased economic activity would bring higher tax revenues in the future. He argued that the government must look after the short run and the long run would look after itself: 'In the long run we are all dead.'

Keynes's seminal work, *The General Theory of Employment, Interest and Money*, was published in 1936. Although he had been writing and speaking on this theme for some time, and indeed as early as 1931 a cartoon in the humorous weekly *Punch* makes a reference to Keynes's views, publication of the *General Theory* had a major impact on people's thinking. During the Second World War unemployment was hardly a problem but after the war Keynes's ideas gained widespread acceptance and the whole focus of economics changed. Before the 1930s the dominant view was that economic problems represented malfunctions on the supply side of the economy. Keynes stood that view on its head and until the 1970s the main interest was in managing the demand side of the economy to minimize the swings of the business cycle, and thus to maintain low rates of unemployment.

Monetarism

By the 1970s both unemployment and inflation were increasing and the demand-management approach seemed to have no answer, in fact it appeared to be a cause of the persistent inflation. The focus of economics and policy changed again, this time to the role of money and to the supply side of the economy. **Monetarism** is principally associated with Milton Friedman (born in 1912) and other economists of the Chicago school, so called because many worked at the University of Chicago. The monetarist view that 'inflation is always and everywhere a monetary phenomenon' looked back to the quantity theory of money (see Chapter 22) put forward by the classical economists of the previous two centuries.

Controversies continue in macroeconomics, with the attendant debates about the proper role of government, and this is partly what makes the study of macroeconomics so rewarding. Chapters 17, 19, 21, and 22 look at some of the theoretical underpinnings of the subject, starting with the aggregate demand and aggregate supply model, then the Keynesian model, and finally the role of money. The implications for government policy are also examined.

Summary

1. Periodic fluctuations in economic activity have been observed for many decades.

2. Both the unemployment and the inflation associated with the business cycle are causes for concern, which has led to attempts to understand, predict, and control the business cycle.

3. Economic theory has had a powerful influence on the behaviour of governments, but ideas can take a long time to change even when policies are unsuccessful.

4. Classical economists saw the economy as a self-adjusting entity. Unemployment was the result of wages being too high.

5. Prolonged unemployment in the 1920s and 1930s provoked Keynes's analysis of the role of demand. He argued that governments should spend their way out of the slump.

6. The failure of demand management by the 1970s led to another shift of emphasis in macroeconomic thinking and policy. Monetarism reasserted the importance of the money side of the economy.

Key terms

boom	monetarism
business cycle	recession
classical economics	slump
demand management	stabilization policy
depression	trade cycle
lagging indicator	trend

Review questions

1. What happens to (i) the deviation from the trend of real output and (ii) the unemployment rate during each of the four phases of the business cycle?

2. Why might nineteenth-century business cycles have had a more severe effect on the living standards of the unemployed than business cycles in the second half of the twentieth century?

3. What major change in government policy did Keynes advocate in the 1930s and why?

Further reading

- Mabry and Ulbrich, chapter 12
- Lipsey and Chrystal, chapter 27
- Sloman, chapters 13 and 15

CHAPTER 17

The aggregate demand and aggregate supply model

The **aggregate demand and aggregate supply model** is the second model of the economy as a whole with which we deal in this book. It brings together aggregate demand and aggregate supply and is used to show how real output, the price level, and employment are effected by a wide range of influences such as taxes, the money supply, and changes in technology. Because output and income are of equivalent value, as discussed in Chapters 13 and 14, any reference to the level of real output implies a reference to the equivalent level of real income.

The model uses the ideas of demand and supply introduced in the microeconomics part of the book but extends them. In a period of time, usually a year, **aggregate demand** is the total demand for all goods and services in the economy and **aggregate supply** is the total of goods and services supplied in the economy. In macroeconomics we consider the real output of the economy and link that output to the general level of prices in the economy.

Aggregate demand

When we looked at the circular-flow model in Chapter 13 we identified the various forms of spending in the economy and these were referred to again in Chapter 14 when the expenditure method of computing GDP was discussed. In any time period, spending by consumers (C), firms (I), government (G), and net exports ($X - M$) together give total spending, or aggregate demand (AD), at any one price level:

$$AD = C + I + G + (X - M).$$

The notion of a particular **price level** in the economy at any one time may seem odd but it is best thought of as the level of prices as indicated by the **GDP deflator** (see Chapter 15). Over time, as some prices rise and others fall, changes in the GDP deflator will give the overall picture. As the price level changes, spending decisions change so that the aggregate demand for goods and services will change with the price level.

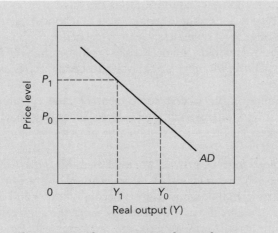

Figure 17.1. The aggregate demand curve

The aggregate demand curve

The **aggregate demand curve** (*AD*) shown in Figure 17.1 shows the relationship between the quantity of **real output** demanded and the price level, with the price level on the vertical axis and real output on the horizontal axis. This relationship depends on the spending decisions of consumers, firms, government, and foreign buyers. It is important to remember that many factors other than price may affect spending decisions but our diagram shows only the influence of the price level—all other factors remain unchanged.

Any change in the price level leads to a **movement along the aggregate demand curve**: in Figure 17.1, at the original price level P_0 the quantity of real output demanded is Y_0. When the price level rises to P_1, the quantity of real output demanded falls to Y_1. Any other changes which affect the quantity of real output demanded will cause the aggregate demand curve to shift—we will come back to this later in the chapter.

(Students new to economics may wonder why diagrams show straight lines when the text uses the term 'curve'. In the absence of any specific information about the relationship between price levels and quantities of real output demanded, for example, we draw a straight line for convenience. This indicates the general nature of the relationship, but does not imply that aggregate demand is necessarily a straight-line relationship between the price level and the quantity of real output demanded.)

Why does the aggregate demand curve slope downwards from left to right?

On first sight the aggregate demand curve looks very similar to any individual demand curve met with in microeconomics but the underlying reasons for its shape and behaviour are rather different. There are three sorts of reason for the downward slope of the aggregate demand curve. The first has to do with financial assets, the second with foreign trade, and the third with interest rates.

The general price level in the economy affects the value of household assets. As the price level rises financial assets (for example savings, cash, and bonds) fall in real value so owners of these assets feel worse off and spend less. Debtors feel better off though and spend more. But since in the aggregate households' financial assets are higher than their debts, spending falls as the price level rises. Conversely, if the price level falls spending rises, because people generally feel better off.

Consumer spending is the largest component of total spending and is the form of spending most sensitive to changes in the price level. This means that total spending responds to price level changes. This response is shown by movements along the aggregate demand curve.

Exports and imports form another part of total spending but foreign trade is influenced by relative price changes between countries. If prices in one country rise faster than prices in another then imports from the second country become cheaper and thus more attractive and are substituted for domestically produced goods. Since the aggregate demand curve shows demand for real output as the price level changes, an increase in imports due to a relative rise in the price level will result in a movement up the aggregate demand curve.

If exports become more expensive for foreign buyers because of a relative rise in the price level then the quantity of goods exported will fall. Again this reduction in the demand for real output due to a relative rise in the price level is shown as a movement up the aggregate demand curve.

Interest rates need to reflect changes in the general level of prices in the economy: when the inflation rate is high the interest rate needs to be even higher, otherwise no commercially-minded individual or institution would lend money to borrowers. Chapter 21 looks at interest rates in more detail.

If firms and consumers see interest rates going up they get worried. They think the cost of borrowing is going up, even though in real terms it may not be, and therefore borrow less. Consumer spending on goods like cars and washing machines falls and firms invest less as the interest rate rises. So as prices and interest rates rise, two components of total spending, consumption (C) and investment (I), are reduced. This is shown by a movement up the aggregate demand curve as the price level rises.

The aggregate demand curve slopes downwards from left to right for the three reasons just described: the effect of changes in the price level on financial assets, foreign trade, and interest rates. So changes in the price level in the economy will lead to movements along the aggregate demand curve, if all other influences on aggregate demand are unchanged. Next we look at the effect of these other influences.

What causes the aggregate demand curve to shift?

Any change which influences aggregate demand other than a change in the price level will cause a **shift of the aggregate demand curve**. Figure 17.2 shows the original aggregate demand curve, AD_0, which shifts to the left at AD_1. At the same price level, P_0, the quantity of real output demanded is now Y_1, rather than Y_0. Similarly, a rightward shift of aggregate demand to AD_2 will lead to a quantity Y_2 of real output being demanded at the price level P_0. There are many possible causes of a shift in aggregate demand and rather than consider each singly we put them into four groups under these headings: fiscal policy, monetary policy, international factors, and expectations.

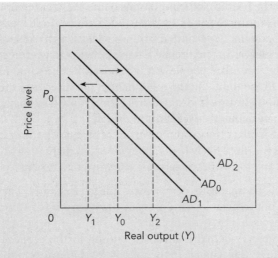
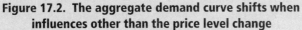

Figure 17.2. The aggregate demand curve shifts when influences other than the price level change

Fiscal policy. The government's actions on its own spending and on taxes are all encompassed by the term **fiscal policy**. Government spending on goods and services feeds straight into aggregate demand. If defence spending falls then aggregate demand falls, which translates into a leftward shift of the aggregate demand curve. Alternatively, as government spending on health services increases—perhaps because of the use of ever more elaborate pieces of medical technology—aggregate demand rises and the aggregate demand curve shifts to the right.

Household spending may be affected by fiscal policy. Lower taxes or higher benefits mean that people have more to spend on goods and services and aggregate demand rises—the aggregate demand curve shifts to the right.

Monetary policy. **Monetary policy** refers to Bank of England and government decisions on the money supply and the interest rate. A greater amount of money in the economy means that spending can be higher and aggregate demand will shift to the right. Interest rate changes affect business and consumer borrowing and spending. If interest rates fall the cost of borrowing falls and borrowing therefore increases, allowing consumer spending and firms' investment to increase, so that aggregate demand shifts to the right.

International factors. Some economies are more involved in international trade than others, which means that international factors will impinge more on aggregate demand in some economies than in others. They are important to Britain. For example, growing incomes in South-East Asia lead to more exports of luxury clothes and whisky from Britain, so that aggregate demand increases and the aggregate demand curve shifts to the right.

The foreign exchange rate affects the prices that overseas customers have to pay for British goods and the prices we pay for imported goods. The ups and downs of the exchange rate in recent years have had an impact on aggregate demand, causing it to shift both to the left and the right.

Expectations. Under the heading of expectations come the ideas people have about what is likely to happen in the future to prices, incomes, and profits; these ideas may well affect people's behaviour in the present. For example, if you expect prices to rise ever faster you may rush out now to buy a new bicycle, on credit if necessary, rather than waiting to buy at an otherwise more convenient time. As other people too are moved by the same impulse the aggregate demand curve shifts to the right. On the other hand if job insecurity increases, people worry about their income in the future and start saving for a rainy day: they postpone major purchases and the aggregate demand curve shifts to the left.

Business confidence is related to an opinion of future profits. The more confident the expectations of future profits the more likely firms are to invest, so increasing the investment element of aggregate demand and causing the aggregate demand curve to shift to the right.

Finally, these effects on aggregate demand are not felt instantly. There are time-lags, and sometimes these are unpredictable; the effects of changes in interest rates, for example, take eighteen months to two years to work through.

To summarize, aggregate demand is total spending in the economy and is drawn as a downward-sloping curve. Any change in the average level of prices in the economy will cause a movement along the aggregate demand curve, while changes in any other factors affecting spending will cause a shift to the right or left of the aggregate demand curve.

Aggregate supply

Aggregate supply is the total of goods and services produced in the economy in a time period at any one level of prices. The **aggregate supply curve** is drawn as a line showing the relationship between various price levels and the associated quantities of goods and services, or real output, produced.

When thinking about aggregate supply we need first of all to distinguish between the short and long run in macroeconomics, where the definitions are different from those for the short and long run used in microeconomics. The **macroeconomic short run** is the time period during which the prices of goods and services change in response to changes in supply and demand but the prices of the factors of production do not: wage rates and salaries are often fixed annually and so change less frequently than prices. Some prices change every day, for example fresh fish prices on the quayside, and others may change dramatically, such as prices for crude oil or coffee beans.

The **macroeconomic long run** is the period long enough for all prices—for goods, services, and the factors of production—to have adjusted fully. In the long run there is full employment because the labour market has adjusted and unemployment is at its natural rate (see Chapter 15). Another way of looking at the distinction between the short and the long run is to say that in the short run some input prices are fixed and in the long run they change.

The aggregate supply curve

Because of these two time-frames, and various views as to their length and importance, there are a variety of aggregate supply curves. We start with the upward-sloping aggregate supply curve shown in Figure 17.3, which is a **short-run aggregate supply curve**. Diagrams illustrating aggregate supply use the same axes as aggregate demand diagrams: the vertical axis shows

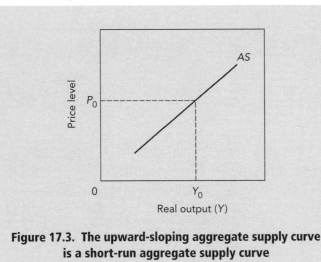

**Figure 17.3. The upward-sloping aggregate supply curve
is a short-run aggregate supply curve**

the price level and the horizontal axis shows the level of real output. At the price level P_0 the quantity of real output supplied is Y_0.

This upward-sloping aggregate supply curve shows that a higher level of prices is associated with a greater quantity of output of goods and services. Does a rising price level cause an increase in real output or does an increase in real output cause rising prices? As Nigel Lawson, a previous Chancellor of the Exchequer, remarked, 'It is always difficult to establish causality in political economy.'[1] Less elegantly, what we have here is a chicken-and-egg situation—which comes first?

Perhaps rising prices encourage suppliers to sell more and enjoy higher profits. Alternatively, perhaps suppliers can only increase output by paying overtime or by paying more for other inputs as they become more scarce. Both are plausible explanations and both are illustrated by the aggregate supply curve rising from left to right.

In the aggregate, or macro, economy more goods and services can only be produced in the short run by using more resources and it is this fact which explains the variety of slopes of the aggregate supply curve which are shown in Figure 17.4. Where the aggregate supply curve is horizontal it is in the 'depression range'. In a depression resources are underemployed—there are spare resources—so increased output can be achieved without any price increases. The last time this happened in Britain was during the 1930s. Normally the economy is on the upward-sloping part of the aggregate supply curve.

However, in the short run every economy may face a physical limit to real output; beyond this point any effort to increase output just leads to higher prices. This is the vertical part of the short-run aggregate supply curve.

The **long-run aggregate supply curve** is also vertical. Remember that in the macroeconomic long run wages and prices have all adjusted (the real wage remains constant) and, in the absence of factors which shift the aggregate supply curve, there is only one level of output which the economy can produce at full employment, whatever the price level. The long-run aggregate supply curve is shown in Figure 17.5.

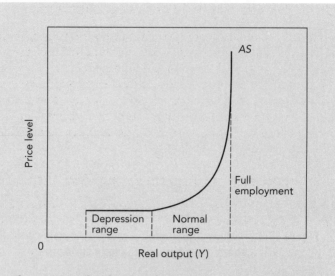

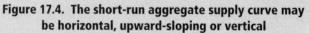

Figure 17.4. The short-run aggregate supply curve may be horizontal, upward-sloping or vertical

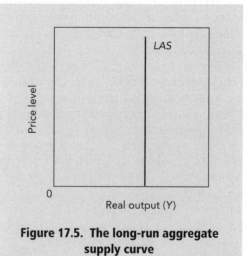

Figure 17.5. The long-run aggregate supply curve

Keynes and the classical economists

So-called Keynesian analysis of the economy tends to assume that the aggregate supply curve is horizontal, or nearly so, so that real output may rise without a rise in prices. The classical economists, on the other hand, and the monetarists more recently, have seen the aggregate supply curve as vertical, so that attempts to move along the aggregate supply curve merely lead to rising prices. The difference of opinion lies primarily in the question of the speed of adjustment of prices and wages—how short is the short run? These different views of the aggregate supply curve lead to opposing views on appropriate government policy, which we discuss in later chapters.

What causes the aggregate supply curve to shift?

As with the aggregate demand curve we look at the aggregate supply curve in two stages. First we look at the link between quantity of real output and the price level, holding all other influences constant—changes in the price level are associated with movements along the aggregate supply curve—and next we consider the effect of other influences on aggregate supply. These cause the aggregate supply curve to shift.

In Figure 17.6 the original aggregate supply curve is AS_0 and the price level P_0 is associated with a level of real output Y_0. Should the aggregate supply curve shift to the left, to AS_1, then the level of real output would be Y_1 at the price level P_0; should the aggregate supply curve shift to the right, to AS_2, the level of real output would be Y_2 at the price level P_0. Factors which shift the aggregate supply curve fall into three main groups: they may be associated with the labour force, with the economy's capital stock, or with technology.

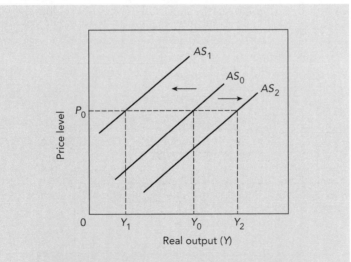

Figure 17.6. The aggregate supply curve shifts when influences other than the price level change

A larger labour force, or a more highly skilled labour force, or a better-educated labour force, will all shift the aggregate supply curve to the right. This leads to growth in real output without rising prices, other things being equal. Additions to the capital stock such as more bridges, more word processors, bigger ships, or more canals as in eighteenth-century Britain, will increase the productive capacity of the economy and therefore shift the aggregate supply curve to the right. Improvements in technology, such as bridges rather than ferries or word processors rather than manual typewriters, also lead to an increase in aggregate supply and a rightwards shift in the aggregate supply curve. Of course, the aggregate supply curve may also shift to the left following an 'adverse supply shock'. Such a shock might be caused by a natural disaster—flood, hurricane, earthquake—or a sudden upward movement in input prices such as the increase in oil prices during the 1970s. Other disturbances include the aftermath of war and the collapse of a country's currency during hyperinflation.

Macroeconomic equilibrium

Up to this point aggregate demand and aggregate supply have been discussed in isolation but if the two curves are put together we can get a picture of the impact on both prices and real output of, for example, changes in technology or changes in defence spending. As shown by Figure 17.7 **macroeconomic equilibrium** occurs when the quantity of real output demanded equals the quantity of real output supplied.

There is only one price level where the quantity demanded equals the quantity supplied: at the equilibrium price level P_e there is a corresponding equilibrium level of real output Y_e.

The price level and the level of real output are two of our key macroeconomic variables; the third is employment. This diagram does not show employment, but real output and employment are closely linked, particularly in the short run. If one rises so does the other, in general,

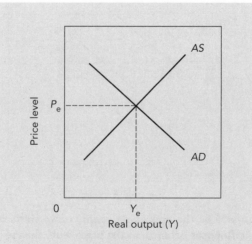

Figure 17.7. Macroeconomic equilibrium

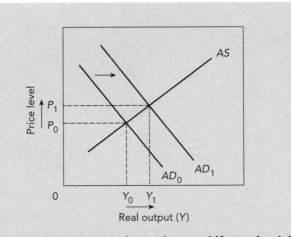

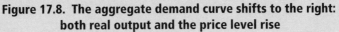

Figure 17.8. The aggregate demand curve shifts to the right: both real output and the price level rise

although there may be time-lags. The aggregate demand and aggregate supply model allows us to study the interrelationships of our three key variables: real output, employment, and the price level.

A new equilibrium

Suppose consumer and business confidence increases and the aggregate demand curve therefore shifts to the right, from AD_0 to AD_1 as in Figure 17.8. Equilibrium real output moves from Y_0 to Y_1 and the equilibrium price level changes from P_0 to P_1; in other words, real output and employment increase, but prices rise too.

Similarly, for example, if exports fall and imports rise due to a change in the exchange rate, then the aggregate demand curve will shift to the left from AD_0 to AD_1 in Figure 17.9, equilibrium real output will move from Y_0 to Y_1, and the equilibrium price level will move from P_0 to P_1. Real output and the price level will fall, while unemployment will increase.

In a third example improvements in technology shift the aggregate supply curve to the right, shown in Figure 17.10 by AS_0 shifting to AS_1, while the aggregate demand curve remains at AD. The equilibrium level of real output increases from Y_0 to Y_1 and the equilibrium level of prices falls from P_0 to P_1. The economy grows and the level of prices falls.

In the fourth example, shown in Figure 17.11, the aggregate supply curve shifts to the left, from AS_0 to AS_1; the aggregate demand curve is unchanged. Equilibrium real output falls from Y_0 to Y_1 and the equilibrium price level rises from P_0 to P_1. In the 1970s the adverse supply shock of rising oil prices led to falling output and employment and rising inflation, as illustrated in Figure 17.11. This alarming combination was dubbed 'stagflation' at the time—a combination of stagnation and inflation.

To paint a happier picture, if we take both Figure 17.8 and Figure 17.10 and put them together in Figure 17.12, it can be seen that rightward shifts of both the aggregate demand and aggregate supply curves may, in theory, lead to growth without inflation. The equilibrium

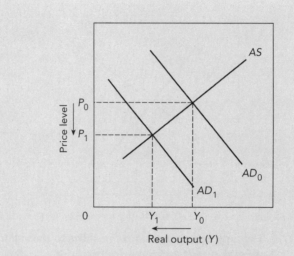

Figure 17.9. The aggregate demand curve shifts to the left: both real output and the price level fall

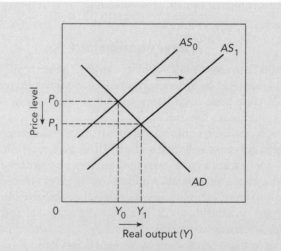

Figure 17.10. The aggregate supply curve shifts to the right: prices fall and real output rises

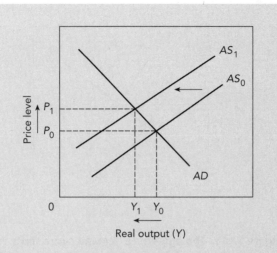

Figure 17.11. The aggregate supply curve shifts to the left: prices rise and real output falls

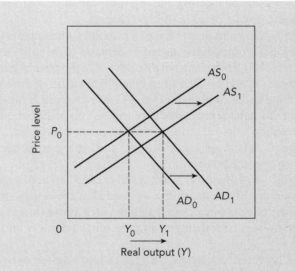

Figure 17.12. Both the aggregate demand curve and the aggregate supply curve shift to the right

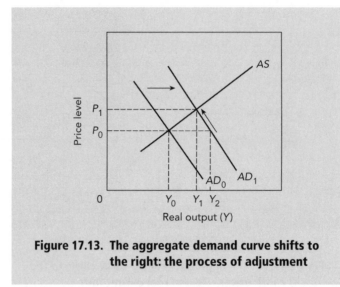

Figure 17.13. The aggregate demand curve shifts to the right: the process of adjustment

price level remains the same at P_0 and the equilibrium level of real output rises from Y_0 to Y_1: this is the goal of many governments. To foster growth without inflation a government needs to find ways of encouraging, or allowing, the aggregate supply curve to shift to the right. Such policies are discussed in greater detail in the next chapter.

Changes to a new equilibrium do not happen instantly; adjustments to the economy may take some time to work through. If the aggregate demand curve shifts to the right, as in Figure 17.13, AD_0 shifts to AD_1. At the original price level P_0 a shortage of goods develops, shown by the distance between Y_2 and Y_0. Firms run down their stocks of unsold goods and start to produce more. In doing so they find that they must pay higher prices for some inputs and may pay more for labour. To remain profitable they will put up prices where possible. As prices rise some customers drop out—in terms of the diagram we move back along AD_1 to reach the higher price level P_1, where aggregate demand and aggregate supply are equal. The economy has reached a new equilibrium.

Of course in the real world there may be any number of influences on aggregate demand and aggregate supply changing at the same time, or in quick succession, so that in the real world equilibrium is unlikely to be attained. What a model such as this does is allow us to study the impact of events and policies on real output, employment, and prices, and so better predict the likely outcome.

This model does, however, lack detail. Chapter 18 looks more closely at aggregate supply and Chapter 19 examines aggregate demand.

The impact of government policies

Both the aggregate demand and the aggregate supply curve may be relatively steep or more shallow but the steepness of either will affect the effectiveness of government policies intended to influence real output, employment, and prices.

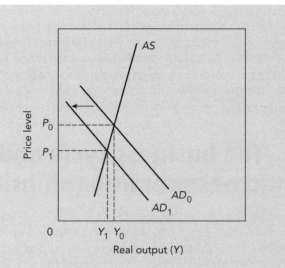

Figure 17.14. A steep aggregate supply curve: price changes are relatively large and real output changes relatively small

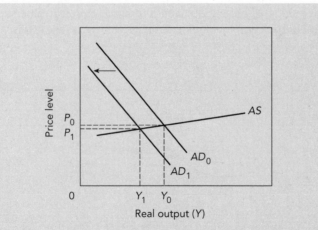

Figure 17.15. A shallow aggregate supply curve: price changes are relatively small and real output changes relatively large

For example, if the aggregate supply curve is relatively steep, as in Figure 17.14, a deflationary government policy which moved the aggregate demand curve to the left would have a much greater impact on prices than on real output and employment. If, however, the aggregate supply curve were relatively shallow, as in Figure 17.15, then a similar policy would have a greater impact on real output and employment than on prices.

This model appears to offer governments some attractive recipes for 'steering' the economy. Equilibrium levels of prices and of output are achieved through the interaction of both aggregate demand and aggregate supply but for many years government policies focused on one or the other, perhaps because of disillusion with the outcomes of previous policies or because of assumptions about the responsiveness of aggregate demand or aggregate supply to changes in the price level. It is important to remember that aggregate demand and aggregate supply *together* determine the average price level and the levels of real output and employment.

The business cycle and macroeconomic equilibrium

Macroeconomic equilibrium does not necessarily occur at full employment; it may be below, at, or above full employment. Figure 17.16 shows real output fluctuating around its long-run trend over the business cycle, as described in Chapter 16. At point A actual real output is below long-run trend real output and there is a recessionary, or deflationary, gap with an equilibrium (Y_a) below full employment (Y_{fe}), shown in part (*a*) of Figure 17.17. At point B equilibrium coincides with long-run trend real output and the economy is operating at full employment, as shown in part (*b*) of Figure 17.17. Finally, at point C equilibrium real output is above the long-run trend real output and there is an inflationary gap, shown in part (*c*) of Figure 17.17, where equilibrium (Y_c) is above full employment (Y_{fe}). The economy moves from one equilibrium to another as the aggregate demand and short-run aggregate supply curves shift. Fluctuations in real output, employment, and the price level are the result.

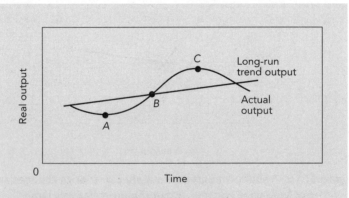

Figure 17.16. Fluctuations in the level of real output over the business cycle

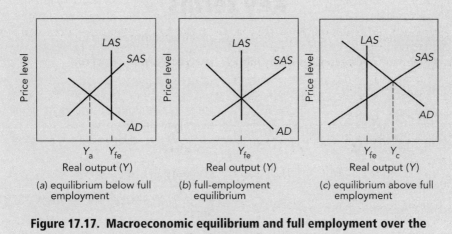

Figure 17.17. Macroeconomic equilibrium and full employment over the business cycle

Summary

1. Changes in the price level will cause movements along the aggregate demand curve. Changes in any of the other factors affecting aggregate demand will cause the aggregate demand curve to shift.

2. Changes in the price level will cause movements along the aggregate supply curve. Changes in any of the other factors affecting aggregate supply will cause the aggregate supply curve to shift.

3. The slope of the short-run aggregate supply curve depends upon the amount of spare capacity in the economy: the horizontal aggregate supply curve is only characteristic of a deep depression; the vertical short-run aggregate supply curve occurs when the economy is at full employment; usually, the economy is operating on the upward-sloping section of the aggregate supply curve.

4. The long-run aggregate supply curve is vertical.

5. The aggregate demand and aggregate supply model shows how real output and the average level of prices interact.

6. The model can be used to look at growth, employment, inflation, and the business cycle.

7. We can also use the model to study the effects of government policies, sudden shocks like the oil price rise of the 1970s, or long-term changes such as population growth.

Key terms

aggregate demand

aggregate demand and aggregate supply model

aggregate demand curve

aggregate supply

aggregate supply curve

fiscal policy

GDP deflator

horizontal aggregate supply curve

long-run aggregate supply curve

macroeconomic equilibrium

macroeconomic long run

macroeconomic short run

monetary policy

movements along an aggregate demand or aggregate supply curve

price level

real output

shifts of an aggregate demand or aggregate supply curve

short-run aggregate supply curve

vertical aggregate supply curve

Review questions

1. For each of the following results draw a diagram to show whether it is caused by a shift in aggregate demand or aggregate supply, or both.

   (i)   Real output falls, price level falls.
   (ii) Real output falls, price level rises.
   (iii) Real output rises, price level falls.
   (iv) Real output rises, price level rises.
   (v)   Real output rises, price level hardly changes.
   (vi) Real output falls, price level hardly changes.
   (vii) Real output hardly changes, price level falls.
   (viii) Real output hardly changes, price level rises.

2. Draw an aggregate demand and aggregate supply diagram to show the effect of an increase in productivity. What might be the causes of such an increase in productivity?

3. Draw diagrams to show:

   (i) the long-run aggregate supply curve;
   (ii) a short-run aggregate supply curve during a depression.

Explain the slope of each curve.

4. In each of the following state whether the aggregate demand curve shifts to the right or to the left.

   (i) Interest rates fall.
   (ii) Taxes rise.

    (iii) Exports rise.
    (iv) The money supply increases.
     (v) Defence spending doubles.
    (vi) The stock market crashes.

Note

1. Nigel Lawson, *The View from No. 11* (London: Bantam Press, 1992), 354.

Further reading

- Mabry and Ulbrich, chapter 12

- Lipsey and Chrystal, chapters 23 and 24
- Sloman, chapter 13

CHAPTER 18

A closer look at aggregate supply

The focus of interest in macroeconomics changed in the late 1970s from aggregate demand to aggregate supply. Attempts to foster growth and maintain high levels of employment through demand management seemed increasingly unsuccessful and there appeared to be a long-run pattern emerging which was better explained by aggregate supply. Policies were introduced which encouraged growth through a rightward shift of the aggregate supply curve, illustrated in Figure 18.1 by the shift of the long-run aggregate supply curve AS_0 to AS_1. This chapter examines some supply-side factors influencing growth; looks at the use of supply-side economics in Britain, the USA, the small island state of Vanuatu, and the former communist country of Bulgaria; and finally considers the links between expectations and aggregate supply.

Growth rates vary over time for one country and vary between countries. Some economies have actually declined in recent years, in some parts of Eastern Europe and sub-Saharan Africa, for example, while others have grown slowly, as in Western Europe, and others have grown fast, particularly in Asia. We need to know which factors contribute to growth, or shift the

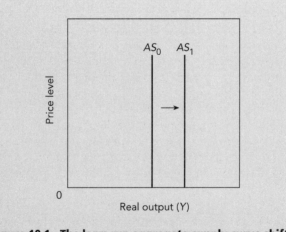

Figure 18.1. The long-run aggregate supply curve shifts to the right when economic growth occurs

aggregate supply curve to the right, and whether there is a formula for success. Can, or should, governments try to play a part?

Finally, a word of warning: a 'dash for growth' may bring few benefits. What matters is that prices are stable, unemployment is low, and real output per head rises in a way that benefits most of the population, not just a lucky few.

Some causes of economic growth

As mentioned in the previous chapter, there are three main causes of economic growth: change in the labour force, increase in the stock of capital, and technological change. We now examine each more carefully.

The labour force

Both the quantity and the quality of the labour force are significant. Taking quantity first, it is obvious that if the size of the labour force increases then, if nothing else changes, the level of output will rise.

The labour force may rise because the population is growing, as in many less-developed countries, or it may rise because changing attitudes to work bring more people into the labour market, or it may rise because of immigration. Immigrants are often particularly hard-working and make a greater than average contribution to output.

The quality of the labour force matters because it affects labour **productivity**, or output per head. This is an area where governments feel they have a role. Basic education is nearly always publicly funded, partly because of the external benefits of education: the individual benefits through higher earnings or greater job satisfaction but all may benefit from that person's greater contribution to output. Higher spending on education should cause a rightwards shift in the aggregate supply curve.

Post-compulsory education is provided in several different ways. It is usually subsidized by the state but is rarely free. Many employers spend money on training their workforce because they expect it to lead to an increase in productivity.

Incentives which encourage people to work harder, longer, or more effectively may also be important. The Soviet Union tried exhortation and honours, as do schools, but most people are expected to respond to money. Here governments may have a role to play. High marginal income tax rates are thought to discourage greater effort at work, and progressive taxes mean that higher-income earners pay more of each extra pound earned in tax. The rich may indeed be discouraged from working harder by high taxes but the disincentive effect on the poor of the way the tax and benefit system works may be more significant. Where benefits are withdrawn as earnings rise low-income earners may face effective marginal tax rates of nearly 100 per cent, and if working involves travel and child care costs as well then the financial incentives are in favour of not working. A wise government tries to minimize the extent of such a **poverty trap**.

The capital stock

If we have better tools we can do a better job, other things being equal. A country which invests a higher proportion of GDP in new plant and machinery is likely to have a higher growth rate. The aggregate supply curve will shift more quickly to the right. A comparison of the relative growth rates since 1950 of the Japanese and US economies illustrates this point.

The reasons why firms invest are complex but two important factors are firms' confidence in future profitability and the cost of investment (the rate of interest). In an economy where people save a smaller proportion of their income, interest rates will be higher to attract savings and this means that firms which borrow money to invest in new plant face higher costs and so invest less. So perhaps government policy should be directed at achieving stable low rates of interest.

Careful government consideration needs to be given to the rules governing the way investment in capital goods can be set off against profits for tax purposes, for such regulations may also influence firms' investment decisions.

Technological change

The rate of adoption of new technology is the third major factor affecting the shift to the right of the aggregate supply curve. Research and development may take place in the public or the private sector, and many governments support research and development, understanding that there may be considerable external benefits. But it is difficult to ensure that new technology is speedily and widely adopted, or that pure research will yield fruitful results.

Innovation, or the adoption of new technology, is more likely in a competitive environment so government policies which reduce monopoly power and which discourage 'featherbedding', or the protection of inefficient industries and restrictive practices, may lead to a faster rate of growth.

Many factors may lead to a rightwards shift of the aggregate supply curve, and therefore to economic growth. Some are effectively beyond government control or influence, others may be affected inadvertently by government decisions, and yet others may be the focus of specific government policies. The next section of this chapter looks at some so-called supply-side policies of the 1980s.

Supply-side economics in Britain and the United States

Supply-side policies aim to shift the aggregate supply curve to the right. They can be used to increase the total factors of production or to encourage greater productivity of existing factors of production. The essence of these policies is to encourage and reward individual enterprise and initiative, to reduce the role of government, and to rely more on market forces and competition and less on government intervention and regulation. Supply-side policies have some paradoxical elements: first, the overall objective is macroeconomic but some supply-side policies focus on individual behaviour, that is they are microeconomic; and secondly, although the intention is to reduce government intervention, some policies are interventionist and involve strict imposition by the government of various regulations. The restrictions by central government of local government activity and spending, and increasing centralization in Britain during the 1980s, are in the latter category.

One element of supply-side policies was to make the labour market more competitive, so making it more responsive to short- and long-term change in the economy. In Britain income tax rates were reduced with the idea of rewarding individual effort more directly. National pay bargaining was discouraged but not eliminated, particularly in the public services, where unions resisted such changes.

The legal framework within which trade unions operated was altered, so that no workplace could be a 'closed shop', where union membership was a condition of employment; the ability of trade unionists to lend support to disputes in another industry by secondary picketing was removed; and strikes could only be called after a secret ballot of all members. Such measures weakened the powers of trade unions and may be linked to both a fall in union membership and a reduction in strikes, although recessions and higher rates of unemployment may also have been significant factors.

Another important element of supply-side policies involved reducing the role of government, both central and local, so that more resources could be released for private sector use. Underpinning this was the idea that because the private sector is more subject to competition it is likely to operate more efficiently. This policy is associated with the cuts to public services of the 1980s and 1990s, with the **privatization** of nationalized industries, and with the **deregulation**, for example, of bus and coach services.

The two strands of this policy, therefore, are privatization and cash limits to public sector spending, such as 'rate-capping' or controlling local authority spending. The 3 per cent 'efficiency saving' imposed on the National Health Service for several years recently is another manifestation of this policy.

These policies have had a mixed effect but they have undoubtedly been successful in halting the seemingly inexorable rise since the 1940s of the size of the public sector relative to national income. There have also been big increases in productivity in formerly nationalized industries, with some of the largest gains, interestingly, occurring just prior to privatization. A more negative result has been the decline in spending on schools, clinics, and hospitals since it is always easier to cut future capital spending than current spending on salaries. However, such infrastructure is important for long-run growth and the Private Finance Initiative, introduced in 1992 to substitute private spending for public spending on such infrastructure projects, has so far failed to deliver the hoped-for results.

Productivity increased faster in the 1980s in Britain than in the 1960s or 1970s though this may not have been entirely the result of the government's supply-side policies, but may also have been due to greater international competition and faster technological progress.

In the United States there was a similar shift in policy emphasis, though the public sector was never as significant a provider of goods and services as in Europe. Supply-side policies were particularly associated with President Reagan, and were often referred to as 'Reaganomics'. These policies had some success: the rate of growth of federal government spending was reduced although military spending rose considerably, tax rates fell dramatically, deregulation was speeded up, and inflation steadied and then fell. However, the United States government spent more than it received in tax revenues and its budget deficits grew so that debt repayments have continued to burden all US governments since.

The tax cuts reduced government receipts but did not stimulate economic growth enough to increase tax revenues. Also government spending was not reduced by very much: welfare payments were cut but large sums were spent on defence. The gap between the rich and the poor increased and this appears to have led to increasing social problems.

The supply side in Vanuatu

As a contrast we now look at a very different economy, that of the small island state of Vanuatu in the South Pacific. Previously called the New Hebrides, Vanuatu gained independence from

Great Britain and France in 1980 and is an archipelago with 68 inhabited islands and a largely Melanesian population. In 1989 the population numbered 143,000 but by 1995 it was estimated to be 168,000. Imports of goods are about three times as great as exports, but the country also earns foreign exchange from its tourist industry and is the recipient of aid from a number of donors. GDP per head was estimated to be US$1,395 in 1995 but it is hard to put a figure on the relatively important subsistence economy.[1] There is no income tax so Vanuatu is an off-shore tax haven with a number of major banks and accountancy firms operating in the principal town.

Strategies in the third national plan (1992) were largely supply-side-orientated: public sector reform, infrastructure investments, and vocational education. John Fallon wrote a consultant's report on the Vanuatu economy for the Australian International Development Assistance Bureau in 1994.[2] He identifies a number of impediments to growth and recommends strategies for development.

The main sources of government revenue are import duties and business licences. Import duties discourage investment by existing businesses since nearly all investment has a very high import content. Business licences are a tax on enterprise and discourage inward investment by expatriates.

The workforce has very low skill levels: only 10 per cent of the population has a secondary education and primary education is neither compulsory nor free, though nearly all children have access to primary education. The economic success of South-East Asia has been built on high-quality primary education and on training on the job. Fallon quotes research by the World Bank which indicates that school-based vocational training, as proposed in Vanuatu's national plan, has been costly and inefficient in other developing countries.

Health problems such as endemic tuberculosis and malaria reduce people's ability to work and their life expectancy. About 70 per cent of the health budget goes towards curative medicine and only 30 per cent towards preventative medicine. A greater focus on prevention might make better use of resources—this of course is not a problem confined to small developing countries but is also true of many wealthy countries.

Another problem not confined to Vanuatu is that traditional attitudes towards women reduce their contribution. One aspect of this is that fewer girls than boys are educated, even at primary level. Finally, political instability in the 1990s has diminished business confidence and significantly reduced investment.

Economic reform in Bulgaria

In many ways supply-side measures are very similar in both developed and developing economies but of particular interest in the 1990s are the economies of Eastern Europe, some of which were already heavily industrialized, but all of which have faced real dislocation as the communist bloc has disintegrated. A recent example is Bulgaria, where the problems of adjustment became particularly acute in the winter of 1996/7. After the collapse of the currency the first step in the recovery was currency stabilization under the strict guidance of the International Monetary Fund (IMF), but studying the other proposals for reform again shows the pervasiveness of supply-side economics.

The Bulgarian economy relied on cheap Soviet energy and raw materials; it was particularly closely integrated into the trading patterns of the communist bloc. The upheavals in Eastern

Europe required a drastic restructuring in Bulgaria which did not take place: since 1990 privatization has been slow and financing the deficits of state-owned enterprises was a major cause of the hyperinflation of 1996 and early 1997. In October 1997 the *Financial Times* reported that about 30 large enterprises still owned by the state were to be sold within the next 15 months, under a fast-track scheme, and that if buyers were not found for these companies they would be liquidated. The companies included 'Soviet-era chemicals and pharmaceuticals manufacturers, a dilapidated Black Sea tourist resort, and Balkan Airlines, the struggling state carrier'.[3] Cash from privatization was seen as an important way of cutting the budget deficit in 1998 and foreign buyers were seen as a good source of the investment necessary for the modernization of industry.

The International Monetary Fund's view

The International Monetary Fund (IMF) takes a close interest in the attributes of successful economies. It distinguishes five determinants of sustained growth, of which the first is the quality of government—growth is impossible if there is a civil war, and difficult if there is widespread corruption. Second, macroeconomic stability (which means stable prices and exchange rates) fosters confidence and large-scale long-term investment. Third, openness to trade with other countries seems to be a particularly important promoter of economic growth. Fourth is the quality of investment and fifth is the skill of the workforce, with universal primary education being very important.[4]

The slope of the aggregate supply curve

The last part of this chapter looks at a number of factors which influence the slope of the aggregate supply curve, because the relative steepness of the aggregate supply curve makes a difference to the effectiveness of policy. You will remember from Chapter 17 that we may draw both a short-run and a long-run aggregate supply curve, and that the short-run curve may be horizontal, upward-sloping with various degrees of steepness, or vertical. The long-run curve is vertical. The extremes of the short-run aggregate supply curve are rare; what is more interesting is the degree of steepness of the upward-sloping short-run aggregate supply curve and the length of the short run, that is, how long it is before the short run becomes the long run.

The answer depends largely on, first, how people's **expectations** of future price and output changes are formed and affect their behaviour, and second, on the speed with which markets adjust to new circumstances.

Adaptive expectations

The **adaptive expectations** theory of how people form their view of future prices suggests that people base their expectations of future inflation on past inflation rates. Economists who support this view of expectations argue that it is a simple rule of thumb and is what many people do in the real world. But it takes time to gather all the information needed to make a judgement about the future so buyers, sellers, and markets may not react quickly to changes in price. This means that a rise in the price level will lead to greater output, in the short run, which implies an upward-sloping aggregate demand curve.

Adaptive expectations mean that when the rate of inflation is rising people will make wrong guesses about the future inflation rate—they will suffer from 'money illusion'. For example, if the inflation rate were 2 per cent two years ago, and 3 per cent last year, we will guess that it will be 3 per cent in the coming year but we will be mistaken because the inflation rate is on a rising trend and turns out actually to be $4\frac{1}{2}$ per cent. So even though people are being relatively sophisticated and trying to take inflation into account, they still guess wrongly and therefore their behaviour is to some extent inappropriate.

Rational expectations

The **rational expectations** hypothesis on the other hand assumes that on average people guess the future correctly. If they get it wrong it is because of some random event which was totally unpredictable. Should people have been forming their view of the future according to adaptive expectations they would quickly realize their error, stop extrapolating the past, and base their view of the future on the state of the economy right now.

If expectations are rational then prices and wages adjust very quickly and we have a much steeper, if not vertical, aggregate supply curve: the short run is very brief with this view of expectations.

Expectations matter because the success of government policy on unemployment and inflation depends on people's expectations. Whatever people expect to happen, their actions will tend to make happen. If a government is to hope to manage an economy successfully, it must convince people that its policies will be effective. One of the reasons for the relatively low rate of inflation in West Germany over many years was that the Bundesbank set monetary policy on a certain course and stuck to it independently of political influence—Germans were keen to avoid inflation since the country had been devastated by hyperinflation in the early 1920s. In Britain the Bank of England has had less independence for decades and inflation rates have varied wildly. Governments have been as credible as the little boy who cried wolf too often, so that until the mid-1990s there was little belief that a government would actually successfully pursue a low-inflation policy in the long term. The announcement by the Chancellor of the Exchequer, Gordon Brown, in May 1997 that in future the Bank of England would set the interest rate independently of the government marks an historic change in British policy and should be seen in the light of the importance of the role of expectations.

The analysis of the impact of expectations, whether adaptive or rational, on the aggregate economy has been as revolutionary in the seventies and eighties as Keynes's ideas were in the thirties, forties, and fifties.

Summary

1. A country's productive potential is influenced by the size, capability, and attitude to work of its labour force; by the size and quality of the capital stock; by the proportion of GDP invested over a long period; and by the rate of adoption of new technology.

2. Supply-side policies attempt to foster economic growth, that is, to shift the aggregate supply curve to the right; they have had a mixed success. Supply-side policies are relevant not only to highly industrialized Western economies but also to tiny developing economies and to former communist economies.

3. How people form their expectations of future price changes influences the slope of the aggregate supply curve and thus the impact of policy on prices, growth, and employment.

Key terms

adaptive expectations

deregulation

expectations

innovation

poverty trap

privatization

productivity

rational expectations

supply-side policies

Review questions

1. How do changes in the size and composition of the labour force affect the aggregate supply curve?

2. Why might real output fall during a period of hyperinflation?

3. Consider each of the following and decide whether it shifts either aggregate demand or aggregate supply, or both, or neither. Draw diagrams to show what effect each will have on prices, real output, and employment.

  (i) a collapse in business confidence
  (ii) widespread flooding
  (iii) the discovery of a major new oilfield
  (iv) a cut in income tax
  (v) the failure of a major export crop
  (vi) an increase in consumer debt
  (vii) the outbreak of civil war

4. Are your answers to Question 3 altered if the aggregate supply curve has a vertical or a horizontal slope?

5. In a small island economy with few exports, what is the likely effect of a doubling of tourist visits? Draw an aggregate demand and aggregate supply diagram to illustrate your answer.

Notes

1. *Vanuatu Facts and Figures*, 1996 edn. (Port Vila, Vanuatu: Statistics Office, 1996).

2. J. Fallon, *The Vanuatu Economy: Creating Conditions for Sustained and Broad-Based Development* (Canberra: Australian International Development Assistance Bureau, 1994).

3. See *Financial Times*, 21 Oct. 1997, 'Survey of Bulgaria', especially the articles by Anthony Robinson (p. 1) and Kerin Hope (p. 2); quotation from the latter.

4. IMF, *World Economic Outlook* (Washington, DC: IMF, 1997) as discussed in Martin Wolf, 'Far from Powerless', *Financial Times*, 13 May 1997, 20.

Further reading

- Mabry and Ulbrich, chapter 13

- Lipsey and Chrystal, chapter 32
- Sloman, chapter 22

CHAPTER 19

A closer look at aggregate demand: the Keynesian model

The third model of the economy studied in this book is known as the **Keynesian model**, because it is based on the ideas put forward by John Maynard Keynes in *The General Theory of Employment, Interest and Money*, published in 1936. Keynes subsequently turned his attention to the wartime and post-war economy and died in 1946; since then many economists have interpreted Keynes's ideas. Although the *General Theory* has been described as a chaotic and obscure book, as a seminal work of economics it still merits attention by the modern student and can be a compelling text.

What we call the 'Keynesian' model is based on others' interpretations of Keynes's writings and focuses on only one part of the material in the *General Theory*. Essentially the model is a tool for analysing the role of aggregate demand in the economy and can be used to explore the various elements of aggregate demand with more subtlety than the aggregate demand and aggregate supply model.

The world Keynes saw about him in the 1930s was one in which prices were generally stable or falling. The Keynesian model describes an economy with a horizontal aggregate supply curve, in which shifts of the aggregate demand curve do not affect the price level. Changes in the price level do not occur in this model so we do not need to distinguish between nominal and real output and can stop using the term 'real output', using 'output' instead.

Since some new students of economics can be confused by dealing with several models of the economy this book adopts the convention used in some other textbooks and from this point on uses the term **aggregate expenditure** when referring to total spending in the Keynesian model. To help distinguish between the two models, the term 'aggregate demand' denotes total spending in the aggregate demand and aggregate supply model.

The simplest version of the model

We deal with the Keynesian model in three stages of complexity. The differences between these versions of the model are best understood by looking back to the diagrams of the circular-flow model introduced in Chapters 13 and 14, where the simplest economy consists of households and firms. A financial sector is introduced with savings and investment, then the government sector is added with taxes and government spending, and finally the economy is opened up to foreign trade with the introduction of imports and exports. Flows out of the circular flow are known as leakages or withdrawals and flows in as injections. The same terminology is used in this chapter, as is the same sequence of increasing complexity.

So the first version of the Keynesian model we look at is one in which there are households and firms and a financial sector, and in which there are no price level changes, or government, or foreign trade. Aggregate expenditure (AE) is made up of spending by households, known as consumption (C), and of spending by firms on capital goods, known as investment (I). The income (Y) received by households goes toward either consumption or saving (S). These all take place within a particular time period, usually a year. So

$$AE = C + I$$

and

$$Y = C + S.$$

The next three sections of this chapter look at consumption, saving, and investment.

Consumption

Most of household income is spent on goods and services. Some households spend all their income and others save some and spend the rest. The proportion of income spent varies between different age and income groups and between different cultures but, in aggregate, the larger part of household income is spent. What is more, in aggregate there is a clear link between the level of income and the level of household spending, or consumption. This relationship between consumption and income is described in mathematical jargon as a function, and so we have the **consumption function**. A function describes the link between one variable — something which may change — and another. (We introduced the production function in Chapter 7.) So the equation

$$C = 5 + 0.7Y$$

says that consumption (C) is related to income (Y) and that as income grows, so does consumption. Importantly, though, it also shows that consumption does not grow by the same amount as income grows, but by less. This is because some of that extra income is saved.

The consumption function shown in Figure 19.1 illustrates these points. The vertical axis shows spending, in this case consumption, and the horizontal axis shows income and output, both represented by the shorthand Y. The consumption function rises from left to right, showing that consumption rises when income rises. In Figure 19.1, when income goes up by 40, consumption goes up by 28.

The increase in consumption as a proportion of the increase in income is 28/40 or 0.7. This figure, 0.7 in the equation above, tells us what proportion of extra income is spent by households and was called by Keynes the **marginal propensity to consume**, often abbreviated to *MPC*. So

$$MPC = \frac{\text{change in consumption}}{\text{change in income that produces the change in consumption}},$$

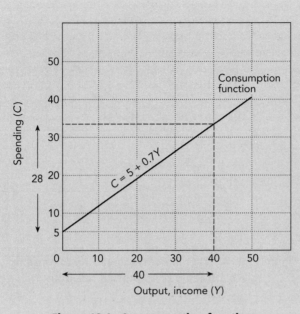

Figure 19.1. A consumption function

or

$$MPC = \frac{\Delta C}{\Delta Y},$$

where the symbol Δ is the Greek capital letter delta and is used to mean 'the change in', so ΔC means 'the change in the level of consumption'.

The consumption function is a straight line with a slope calculated thus:

$$slope = \frac{\text{vertical change}}{\text{horizontal change}}.$$

In this case the vertical change is 28 and the horizontal change is 40, so the slope is 28/40 or 0.7, which is of course the value of the *MPC*. In other words, the *MPC* is equal to the slope, or gradient, of the consumption function.

The equation for the consumption function gives us one other piece of information, that is, how much spending by households is unrelated to the level of income. This is given by the number 5, which shows that even when income is zero a certain minimum level of household spending occurs, financed by borrowing or gifts. In Figure 19.1, 5 is the point on the vertical, or spending, axis, where the consumption function crosses that axis: income is zero but consumption is 5.

Spending by households which is not related to the level of income is called **autonomous consumption**, that is, it occurs anyway and is not affected by income changes.

In using the equation

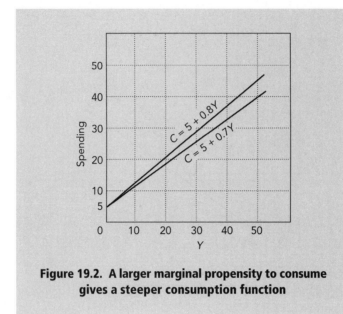

Figure 19.2. A larger marginal propensity to consume gives a steeper consumption function

$$C = 5 + 0.7Y$$

we have taken a particular consumption function. Written in a general form the consumption function looks like this:

$$C = a + bY,$$

where a stands for autonomous consumption and b for the marginal propensity to consume.

The consumption function will not necessarily look just like the one illustrated in Figure 19.1. For example, in an economy where people spend more of their extra income the marginal propensity to consume will be larger than 0.7—perhaps 0.8—and the slope of the consumption function will be a little steeper, as in Figure 19.2. There may also be differences between economies in the level of autonomous consumption. One such difference is shown by the long-run consumption function. Analyses of data on income and household spending over decades in several industrialized economies show that the long-run consumption function starts at the origin, as in Figure 19.3.

Saving

Saving is the part of household income not spent on goods and services. It is a leakage, or withdrawal, from the circular flow of income; therefore, if nothing else changes, an increase in saving will reduce the size of the economy.

Earlier economists linked saving with the rate of interest but Keynes suggested that the level of saving in an economy, like consumption, depends primarily on the level of income. There is a relationship between saving (S) and income (Y) which can be expressed mathematically and which is therefore called the **saving function**. The equation

$$S = -5 + 0.3Y$$

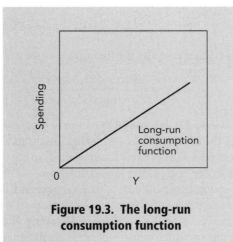

Figure 19.3. The long-run consumption function

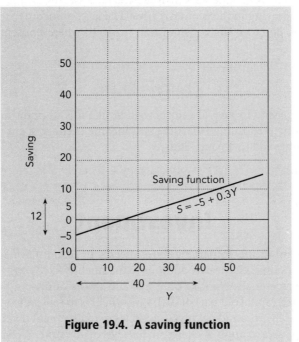

Figure 19.4. A saving function

says that saving grows as income grows but by a much smaller amount. In Figure 19.4 an increase in income (Y) of 40 brings an increase in saving (S) of 12. The proportion of extra income saved is known as the **marginal propensity to save** (*MPS*). In other words,

$$MPS = \frac{\text{change in saving}}{\text{change in income that produces the change in saving}}$$

or

$$MPS = \frac{\Delta S}{\Delta Y}.$$

The slope of the saving function is given by the marginal propensity to save, that is:

$$\text{slope} = \frac{\text{vertical change}}{\text{horizontal change}},$$

which in our example is 12/40 or 0.3. It is useful to compare Figure 19.4 with Figure 19.1 to see how different the slopes of the consumption and saving functions are. In our example 70 per cent of extra income is spent and 30 per cent is saved so the slope of the consumption function is more than twice as steep as the slope of the saving function.

The points where the saving function crosses the vertical and horizontal axes are worth noticing. In Figure 19.4 the saving function crosses the vertical, or withdrawals, axis at a value of −5. This means that when income is zero there is **dissaving** and that the amount of dis-saving is equal to the amount by which consumption is greater than income. If autonomous consumption is 5 then dissaving at zero income is also 5. Similarly, when the saving function crosses the horizontal, or income, axis then there is no dissaving and as income continues to increase the level of saving in the economy rises. The level of income at which saving is zero corresponds to the point on the consumption function where household spending equals income.

In its general form the saving function may be written as

$$S = -a + (1 - b)Y.$$

The marginal propensity to save $(1 - b)$ is written like this to point out its links with the marginal propensity to consume (b). Any extra income is either spent or saved, so the two marginal propensities add up to one. Thus,

$$MPC + MPS = 1.$$

Investment

The term **investment** means something more specific in economics than it does in general conversation. In economics it means additions to the stock of fixed capital and to inventories, which include raw materials, work in progress, and stocks of unsold finished goods. Most investment is in fixed capital but part of such investment is to replace worn-out capital goods: the difference between gross and net investment lies in replacement investment, often repres-ented by a figure for depreciation. A change in the level of investment in an economy from one year to the next can represent a change in any of these elements of investment and may be caused by a wide range of factors. Investment spending fluctuates more than any other element of aggregate demand—economists tend to describe it as volatile. Sir John Hicks, a well-known Cambridge economist and an important interpreter of Keynes's *General Theory*, called invest-ment a 'flighty bird'.

Investment is an injection into the circular flow and in this simple model the level of invest-ment (I) is not related to income (Y). Figure 19.5 shows the investment function I_0, with spend-ing by firms on investment goods on the vertical axis and income and output on the horizontal

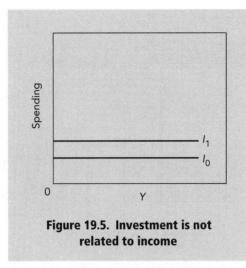

Figure 19.5. Investment is not related to income

axis: if the level of investment rises the line I_0 shifts upwards to I_1. I_0 is horizontal in this diagram because investment is not affected by the level of income; however, investment *is* affected by the rate of interest and by expectations of future profitability, so we turn our attention next to these influences.

Investment and the rate of interest

When firms invest they either use retained profits or they borrow. If they borrow then they have to pay interest on the sum borrowed, and if they use their own money then they are forgoing the interest they would have received had they left that money in the bank. Either way, their decision about the wisdom of investment is affected by the rate of interest.

So when firms invest they need to make profits big enough to cover the interest payments over several years and to pay back the initial cost of the capital equipment. An individual firm may have several different investment projects in mind, with differing levels of likely profitability or rates of return.

Figure 19.6 shows how the rate of interest might affect the investment decisions of a firm. Note that in this diagram investment is on the horizontal axis, unlike the previous diagram, and the rates of interest and of return to investment are on the vertical axis. The firm is faced with four possible investment projects with rates of return varying from 5 per cent to 20 per cent. If the rate of interest is 4 per cent all of these projects will be profitable and will be undertaken. However, if the rate of interest is 11 per cent then only those two with a rate of return above 11 per cent will be undertaken. The firm's investment spending will be considerably reduced. In the aggregate economy the decisions of one firm will be writ large: the level of investment will rise as the rate of interest falls and fall as the rate of interest rises.

We can show investment as a function where the quantity of investment spending is inversely related to the rate of interest, or the price of investment. The downward-sloping line (I) in Figure 19.7 shows, therefore, how much investment will be undertaken by firms at different rates of interest, other things being equal. Figure 19.7 shows, in effect, the demand curve for investment.

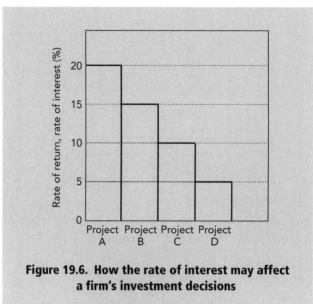

Figure 19.6. How the rate of interest may affect a firm's investment decisions

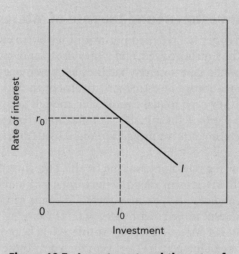

Figure 19.7. Investment and the rate of interest

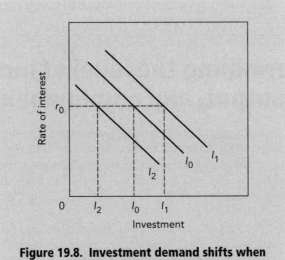

Figure 19.8. Investment demand shifts when business confidence alters

Investment and 'expectations'

The influence of business confidence on investment was another of Keynes's insights. Chapter 12 of the *General Theory* is on **long-term expectations**, which has a meaning quite different from rational expectations and adaptive expectations, mentioned in Chapter 18. Keynes is referring to feelings, hunches, confidence, or the lack of it, in future profitability. Is a change of government imminent? Is the exchange rate stable or volatile? Is war on the horizon, or perhaps a trade war? Many factors may affect the state of long-term expectations. If expectations are confident then investment will increase, other things being equal, and if expectations are poor investment will decrease.

These changes can be shown as shifts of the investment demand curve. In Figure 19.8 investment demand shifts to the right when expectations are good and shifts to the left when expectations are poor. At a rate of interest r_0 the level of investment is I_0 on the investment demand line I_0. If expectations improve I_0 shifts rightwards to I_1 and the level of investment is now I_1 at the same rate of interest, r_0. However, should business confidence take a knock then I_0 will shift leftwards to I_2 and the level of investment when the interest rate is r_0 becomes I_2.

Changes in expectations are the cause of the volatility of investment but by their very nature such changes are very difficult to measure or control. A fall in the rate of interest will not necessarily encourage more investment unless firms are confident that interest rates will not suddenly rise again.

Investment involves taking a risk, or gambling on the future, and bringing ideas of risk and uncertainty into a macroeconomic model was one of Keynes's achievements. The next section of this chapter brings together consumption, saving, and investment to show how these elements determine the levels of income, output, and employment. The classical economists thought that adjustment to full employment was instantaneous, but Keynes recognized that economies need time to adjust to unanticipated events, that people make bad decisions, and that economic systems are not always particularly orderly.

Determining the level of income, output, and employment

This section of the chapter introduces the famous **Keynesian Cross diagram**, also known as the **45-degree line diagram**, which is used to show how changes in any element of the model affect equilibrium income, output, and employment in the economy. We will look secondly at the injections and withdrawals diagram, which may be used in a similar way. The Keynesian Cross diagram uses a device called a 45-degree line and we focus on the important features of this line first.

Look at Figure 19.9. The vertical axis shows total spending, or aggregate expenditure (AE), and the horizontal axis shows income (Y) and output: remember from Chapter 14 on National Income Accounting that in the aggregate economy, income, expenditure, and output are all equal, so two of these may be put on the same axis with no difficulty. Notice that the scale on both axes is the same—an essential feature of the diagram. The 45-degree line is drawn from the origin, 0, at an equal distance from both axes, so cutting the right angle into two. Every point on this 45-degree line shows an equal value of spending, income, and output. The significance of this is that where any other line on such a diagram crosses a 45-degree line it is at a point where spending, income, and output will all be equal.

Combining the consumption function (Figure 19.1) and the investment function (Figure 19.5) gives us aggregate expenditure (AE) in this simplest version of the Keynesian model, which is plotted against income (Y) in Figure 19.10. Notice that investment is added

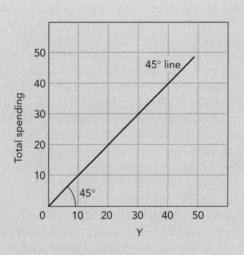

Figure 19.9. A 45 degree line

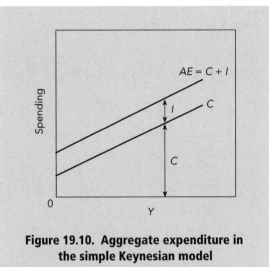

Figure 19.10. Aggregate expenditure in the simple Keynesian model

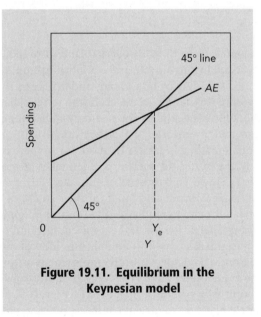

Figure 19.11. Equilibrium in the Keynesian model

to consumption, so investment is shown in the diagram as a layer on top of the consumption function—the vertical distance between any point on the consumption function and the corresponding point above on the aggregate expenditure line gives us the value of investment.

We then superimpose the 45-degree line and achieve in Figure 19.11 a Keynesian Cross diagram for this simple economy. The most important feature of this diagram is the point where the aggregate expenditure line *AE* crosses the 45-degree line: at this point aggregate expenditure is equal to income and output. This is a point of **equilibrium**, the value of which

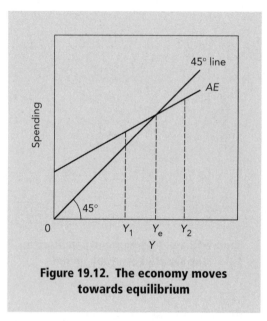

Figure 19.12. The economy moves towards equilibrium

is indicated on the horizontal axis at Y_e. At this particular level of spending in the economy we get equilibrium income, equilibrium output, and equilibrium employment.

At equilibrium, planned spending by households and firms exactly equals the level of output and there is no pressure for change in the economy until something happens either to change spending plans or to frustrate them. The economy adjusts to equilibrium by firms running down or building up their inventories, that is their stocks of unsold goods. In Figure 19.12 at output level Y_1 planned spending is greater than output so there is pressure on producers. They run down their stocks of unsold goods and then take on more labour and begin to increase output towards Y_e. However, if the level of output is Y_2 then it exceeds planned spending by households and firms so producers build up their stocks of unsold goods and subsequently start to lay off labour and to reduce output towards Y_e. Only when output is at Y_e is there no pressure for change, hence the use of the term 'equilibrium'.

Another of Keynes's insights was that this equilibrium level of output, employment, and income has no good reason to coincide with **full employment output**. Figure 19.13 shows a situation in which there is unemployment. The level of output consistent with full employment is Y_{fe} but the economy is in equilibrium at the lower level of output Y_e and there are no economic pressures for change—there may of course be political pressures but these are not enough on their own to change the level of output. Keynes went on to suggest ways in which equilibrium output might be encouraged to rise towards full employment output. These are discussed in the next chapter on fiscal policy.

Finally in this section on equilibrium, we look at the **injections and withdrawals diagram**, which is an alternative way of illustrating the determination of equilibrium income, output, and employment. In the simplest model the only injection to the circular flow is investment and the only withdrawal is saving. Figure 19.14 therefore combines the investment function seen in Figure 19.5 and the saving function seen in Figure 19.4. Where injections equal

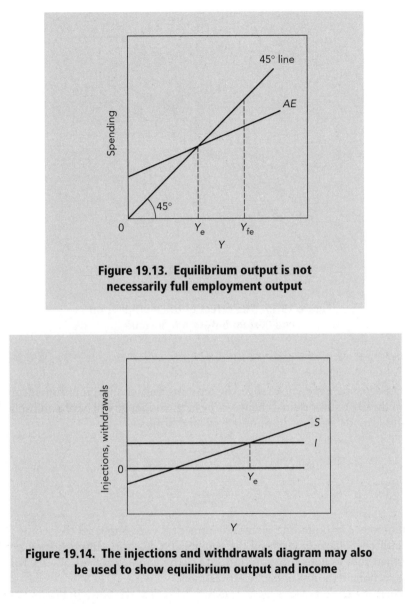

Figure 19.13. Equilibrium output is not necessarily full employment output

Figure 19.14. The injections and withdrawals diagram may also be used to show equilibrium output and income

withdrawals, or in this simple model where investment equals saving, we have an economy in equilibrium: Y_e indicates the equilibrium level of income, output, and employment.

The multiplier

The word 'multiplier' is often used in economics, to the potential confusion of some students; here we are dealing with the **Keynesian multiplier**. If any of the elements of aggregate expenditure

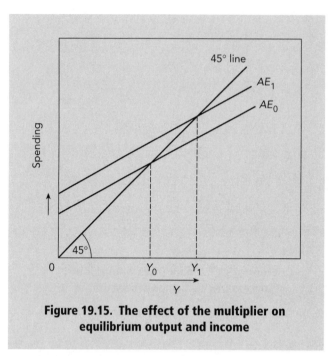

Figure 19.15. The effect of the multiplier on equilibrium output and income

which do not depend on income change, the resulting impact on equilibrium income will be greater than the size of the original change—the original change will have a multiplied effect.

In the simple model we have only households and firms so

$$AE = C + I$$

and

$$C = a + bY.$$

Both autonomous consumption (a) and investment (I) are unrelated to income (Y) and a change in either will have an effect on the equilibrium, but since investment is much more significant than autonomous consumption, and changes more dramatically, we will concentrate in this section on the multiplier and investment.

If investment rises so too does aggregate expenditure. This is shown in Figure 19.15, where the effect of the increase in investment is to shift the aggregate expenditure line upwards from AE_0 to AE_1 and to increase the equilibrium level of income, output, and employment from Y_0 to Y_1. Notice that the vertical distance between AE_0 and AE_1 is smaller than the horizontal distance between Y_0 and Y_1—this shows that the initial spending increase is less than the subsequent increase in income and output.

A similar picture is presented by the injections and withdrawals diagram seen in Figure 19.16. Investment increases so the investment function shifts upwards from I_0 to I_1 and now crosses the saving function at Y_1 rather than Y_0. Again, the vertical distance between I_0 and I_1 is smaller than the horizontal distance between Y_0 and Y_1, indicating the effect of the multiplier.

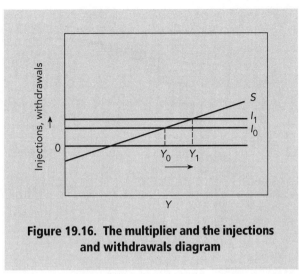

Figure 19.16. The multiplier and the injections and withdrawals diagram

So how does the multiplier work? Take, for example, the impact of foreign investment in Britain. A Japanese car manufacturer decides to build a new factory in Britain to make cars for the European market and pays for its initial investment with money from the Japanese parent company. It buys a green-field site, and builds and equips a large factory. Before it even starts to employ people to make cars a considerable amount of money has been injected into the local economy and this money will have found its way into the pockets of lawyers, surveyors, earth-moving contractors, builders, electricians, computer software designers, catering and cleaning staff, and so on. Some of this money will be saved by individuals but most will be spent and will go into the pockets of decorators, shop assistants, piano teachers, and so on. The recipients of this second round of spending will save some of their income but will spend most of it; and so the money circulates, with each round of spending smaller than its predecessor until at the end the extra spending is very little. It is rather like throwing a stone into a pond—the ripples get smaller the further away they are.

But although throwing a stone into a pond produces ripples it does not produce a permanently higher level of water in the pond, whereas an increase in the level of investment has a multiplied effect on the subsequent level of output and income. Figure 19.17 shows how this builds up. It takes the consumption function used earlier in the chapter,

$$C = 5 + 0.7Y,$$

where the marginal propensity to consume is 0.7 and the marginal propensity to save is 0.3. For every extra pound of income 70p are spent and 30p are saved.

The initial injection of £1 million is followed by £700,000 of spending, which is followed by a further spending round of £490,000, a subsequent round of £343,000, and so on until the final rounds are tiny. The total of all the additions to income and output is 3.33 times as big as the initial £1 million. In mathematical terms what we have here is a geometric progression which sums to 3.33:

$$\frac{1}{1-0.7} = \frac{1}{0.3} = 3.33.$$

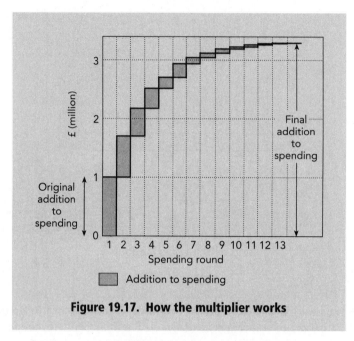

Figure 19.17. How the multiplier works

There are three ways in which we can calculate the value of the multiplier. The first is as follows:

$$\text{multiplier} = \frac{\text{change in equilibrium income}}{\text{change in spending}}, \text{ that is:}$$

$$= \frac{\Delta Y}{\Delta I}.$$

The second way of calculating the value of the multiplier is to use the marginal propensity to consume:

$$\text{multiplier} = \frac{1}{1 - MPC},$$

which in our example above gives

$$\text{multiplier} = \frac{1}{1 - 0.7} = \frac{1}{0.3} = 3.33.$$

The third way is to use the marginal propensity to save, so that:

$$\text{multiplier} = \frac{1}{MPS},$$

which again in our example above gives

$$\text{multiplier} = \frac{1}{0.3} = 3.33.$$

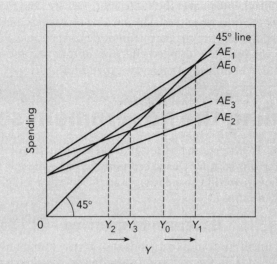

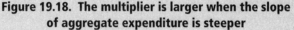

**Figure 19.18. The multiplier is larger when the slope
of aggregate expenditure is steeper**

This last method makes it easy to see that the multiplier is larger if the marginal propensity to save is smaller. For example, if the marginal propensity to save were 0.2 then the multiplier would be 5 rather than 3.33. Similarly, if the marginal propensity to save is larger the multiplier is smaller.

Another way of gauging the size of the multiplier is to look at the slope of the aggregate expenditure line—Figure 19.18 illustrates this point. In this simple model the slope of the aggregate expenditure line is the same as the slope of the consumption function, which is given by the marginal propensity to consume. Where the marginal propensity to consume is larger the slope of both lines will be steeper and the multiplier will be larger than it would be were the marginal propensity to consume smaller.

In Figure 19.18 AE_0 is steeper than AE_2. With a rise in investment AE_0 shifts upwards to AE_1 and equilibrium income and output rise from Y_0 to Y_1. An equivalent rise in investment would shift AE_2 to AE_3 and would change equilibrium output and income from Y_2 to Y_3. The distance between Y_1 and Y_0 is greater than the distance between Y_3 and Y_2, indicating that the multiplier is larger where the aggregate expenditure line is steeper.

Before leaving this section on the multiplier there are some more general points which need to be made. So far we have only considered the effects of an increase in investment but, of course, business confidence is fragile and investment may fall. The effects of a fall in investment will be multiplied in just the same way and will lead to a reduction in income and output greater than the original fall in investment.

The multiplier also works in more complicated models than the simplest version used so far in this chapter. In more complicated models the size of the multiplier also depends on the slope of the aggregate expenditure line, but this slope is influenced by more than just the marginal propensity to consume.

The next section of this chapter makes the model more realistic, and more complicated, first by introducing a government sector and then by opening up the economy to foreign trade. In these more complicated models any change in autonomous spending will shift the aggregate expenditure line and will have a multiplied effect on output and income, but investment remains the most volatile component of aggregate expenditure.

Including the government sector

We now make the model a little more realistic and add the activities of a government, which both taxes and spends. This is still a **closed economy** model—there is no foreign trade. In terms of the circular flow government spending is an injection, or addition to spending, and taxes are a withdrawal, or leakage.

Government spending

We assume that government spending is on goods and services bought from firms and that all taxes are paid by households. In the real world spending on social security benefits can be a significant part of government spending but such transfer payments are ignored in our model and are not included here in the term 'government spending'. A further point of definition is that in this model the word 'government' is understood to include both central and local government.

In the long run the size of government spending will be affected by the size of the economy, but in the short run (which is what this model is dealing with) changes in output and income do not usually affect the amount a government spends on goods and services. How much a government spends depends on how many hospitals it wants to build and what size of army it wishes to run—these are political decisions. So, in this model, government spending is not related to income and output and it is an autonomous element of aggregate expenditure. Figure 19.19 illustrates the independence of government spending and Figure 19.20 shows government spending as part of aggregate expenditure.

Taxes

Taxes are a withdrawal, or leakage, from the circular flow. The level of taxation has a closer link to the size of the economy than government spending, so taxes are assumed here to be related to the size of national income and output. This is again a simplification since political decisions also affect the level of taxation.

Figure 19.21 shows taxes growing as income grows. The relationship between taxes (T) and income can be written as

$$T = tY,$$

where t can be described as the marginal propensity to tax (MPT) and shows the proportion of additions to income which are taken in tax.

Taxes reduce the size of households' disposable income and affect the consumption function, since household spending depends on income after tax. In a model with taxes the slope of the consumption function is reduced, as in Figure 19.22. The size of the multiplier is linked to the slope of the consumption function, thus the multiplier is smaller the greater the proportion of extra income taken in tax. An increase in the tax rate will take more out of the circular

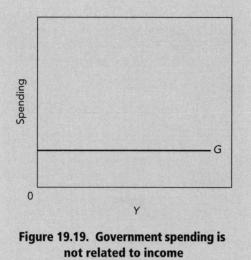

Figure 19.19. Government spending is not related to income

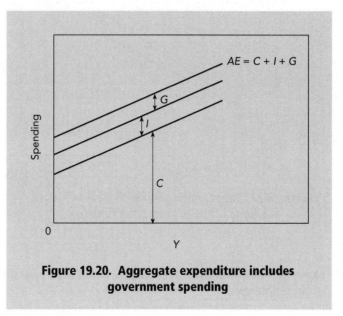

Figure 19.20. Aggregate expenditure includes government spending

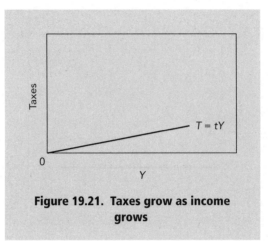

Figure 19.21. Taxes grow as income grows

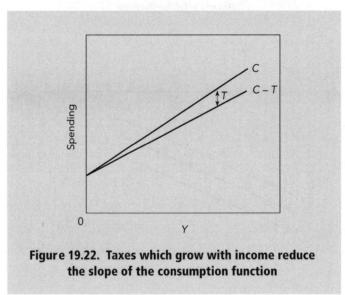

Figure 19.22. Taxes which grow with income reduce the slope of the consumption function

flow, leave less for consumers to spend, and further reduce both the slope of the consumption function and the size of the multiplier.

Since taxes affect the consumption function they also affect aggregate expenditure, reducing the slope of the aggregate expenditure line so that it swivels to a lower position, as shown in Figure 19.23.

Finally, note that there is no reason why the level of government spending should automatically be equal to the level of taxes.

This section may be summarized in symbols as follows:

$$AE = C + I + G$$

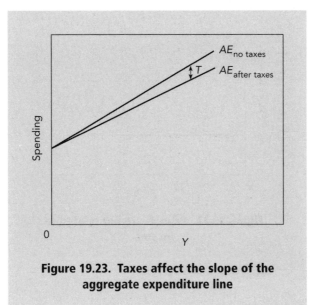

Figure 19.23. Taxes affect the slope of the aggregate expenditure line

but

$$C = a + b(Y - T)$$

and

$$T = tY.$$

Opening the economy to foreign trade

An **open economy** is an economy open to trade with other countries. We now add foreign trade to the model and treat it in a similar manner to the government sector: exports are an injection to the circular flow and imports are a withdrawal.

Exports

Exports are an addition to aggregate expenditure because they are an addition to spending on domestically produced goods and services. The quantity of exports sold abroad depends on incomes abroad, not on domestic income, and is therefore unrelated to the size of the economy. Figure 19.24 shows that exports (X) are independent of income and output (Y).

Imports

Imports rise as domestic incomes rise; they are therefore dependent on the size of the economy. Figure 19.25 illustrates the relationship between imports (M) and income and output (Y). There is a **marginal propensity to import** (MPM), which is the proportion of each addition to national income spent on imported goods and services, so the imports function may be written as

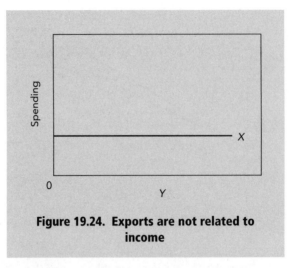

Figure 19.24. Exports are not related to income

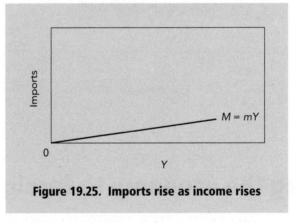

Figure 19.25. Imports rise as income rises

$$M = mY,$$

where m is the marginal propensity to import and gives the slope of the imports function.

Net exports

The British economy is a very open economy; that is, exports and imports are relatively large in proportion to GDP. Both exports and imports have grown from about 20 per cent of GDP in 1950 to 30 per cent of GDP in the 1990s. The comparable figures for the United States are 6 per cent to 12 per cent over the same period. But **net exports**, that is exports less imports or $(X - M)$, are very small in relation to GDP. There is no reason why exports and imports should be of equal value in any particular time period.

Net exports affect the level of aggregate expenditure. Figure 19.26 shows how aggregate expenditure looks in an open-economy model. First, exports raise the level of aggregate expenditure, and then imports reduce the slope of the aggregate expenditure line.

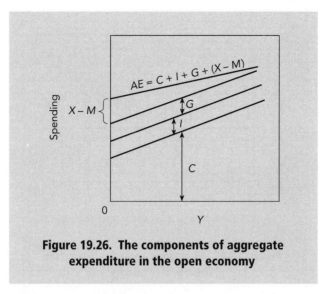

Figure 19.26. The components of aggregate expenditure in the open economy

Our model with households and firms, a government, and foreign trade, may be summarized as follows:

$$AE = C + I + G + (X - M)$$
$$C = a + b(Y - T)$$
$$T = tY$$
$$M = mY.$$

Investment (I), government spending (G), and exports (X) are all independent of income (Y), as is the part of consumption indicated by a. All these forms of spending are known as **autonomous spending**.

The injections and withdrawals diagram

In the more complicated model described above the injections are all forms of autonomous spending and the withdrawals are all linked to income. Figure 19.27 shows how the equilibrium level of income and output, Y_e, occurs where injections and withdrawals are equal. Note that in equilibrium it is not necessary for each injection to be equal to its corresponding withdrawal but for total injections to be equal to total withdrawals. Thus in equilibrium

$$I + G + X = S + T + M.$$

The slope of the withdrawals function is given by adding together the slopes of each of the withdrawals, that is the marginal propensities to save, tax, and import:

slope of the withdrawals function = $MPS + MPT + MPM$.

The multiplier in the more elaborate model

As shown in Figure 19.26, the slope of the aggregate expenditure line is reduced as the number of withdrawals from the circular flow increases. This means that, other things being equal, the

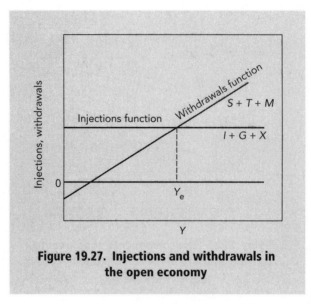

Figure 19.27. Injections and withdrawals in the open economy

multiplier is smaller in an open economy with a government sector than it is in the simplest version of the model.

Linking the Keynesian model to the aggregate demand and aggregate supply model

At the beginning of this chapter the Keynesian model was described as a way of analysing the role of aggregate demand in the economy and we have examined the various elements of total spending, seen how each is or is not linked to income, and seen how changes in total spending might affect the level of income, output, and employment. All this has been in the context of constant prices. The aggregate demand and aggregate supply model, on the other hand, examines how changes in the price level influence the levels of real output and employment. It is possible to link these two models and to use one to illuminate the other.

We look first at the familiar aggregate expenditure diagram shown in Figure 19.28, where spending is on the vertical axis and real output on the horizontal axis. There are two parts to aggregate expenditure: autonomous spending and **induced spending**. Autonomous spending occurs independently of income or output and includes the first part of the consumption function (a), investment (I), government expenditure (G), and exports (X). The other forms of spending are related to income, hence induced spending—the major part of consumption ($b[Y - T]$), and imports (M).

For any particular price level there will be a particular level of autonomous spending and therefore a particular aggregate expenditure line. If the general level of prices in the economy changes then the level of autonomous spending (shown as the starting point of the aggregate

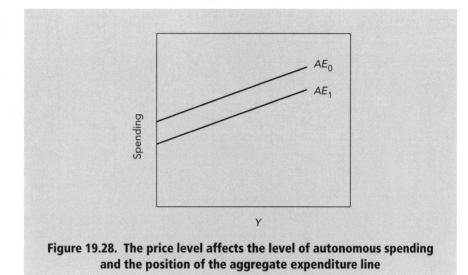

Figure 19.28. The price level affects the level of autonomous spending and the position of the aggregate expenditure line

expenditure line on the spending axis) changes too, and we have a different aggregate expenditure line. So in Figure 19.28 AE_0 indicates total spending at one price level and AE_1 indicates total spending at another price level.

Why does a change in the price level affect autonomous spending and the position of the aggregate expenditure line? This territory is explored more deeply in later chapters on money but, briefly, if the price level rises and the quantity of money in the economy stays the same, people feel worse off—and are worse off—because their money buys less. So if the price level rises autonomous spending falls. Again, if the price level rises relative to other countries' price levels, imports seem cheaper and exports become more expensive for foreigners to buy so exports fall and imports rise, which also means that aggregate expenditure is reduced.

This is shown in the upper part of Figure 19.29 as a downward shift in the aggregate expenditure line from AE_0 to AE_1 as the price level rises. The effect of this shift on equilibrium income and output is shown by the move from point A to point B, that is from Y_0 to Y_1.

The lower part of Figure 19.29 shows aggregate demand as the quantity demanded of output plotted against the price level. P_0 is the original price level and is associated with a level of demand for output shown by point A'. When the price level rises to P_1 there is a movement along the aggregate demand curve to point B' and the quantity Y_1 of real output is demanded. So the aggregate expenditure line shifts down from AE_0 to AE_1 when the price level rises from P_0 to P_1, and this is shown as a movement along the aggregate demand curve AD, from A' to B'.

Similarly, should the price level fall from P_0 to P_2, AE_0 will shift upwards to AE_2 because autonomous consumption will rise as people feel better off, exports will rise, and imports fall. This shift in aggregate expenditure can be shown as a movement down the aggregate demand curve below from point A' to point C'. Equilibrium income and output change from Y_0 to Y_2. Each point on the aggregate demand curve in the lower diagram can be linked to an equilibrium point in the upper diagram where an aggregate expenditure line crosses the 45-degree line.

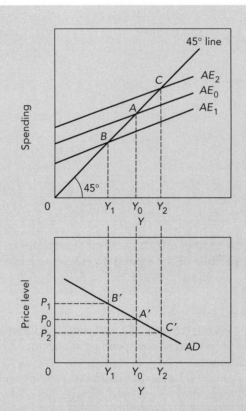

Figure 19.29. Linking aggregate expenditure in the Keynesian model with aggregate demand in the aggregate demand and aggregate supply model

It is important to remember that these changes in the price level are taking place against a background of all other influences on the economy remaining unchanged—an essential feature of economic models. These models can give us considerable insight into the workings of the economy but to be easy to deal with they need to be used to examine the impact of one change at a time. This means that in the real world things are not so simple and the outcome is not so predictable, because changes do not happen in convenient isolation. The Keynesian model in particular seems to offer governments a number of possibilities for intervention to foster growth and higher employment, but remedies based on a simple model are unlikely to have the intended effect. The next chapter examines some government policies based on Keynesian ideas on the economy.

Summary

1. The Keynesian model links aggregate expenditure and the level of income, output, and employment in the economy. The model assumes that prices do not change.

2. The largest part of aggregate expenditure is household spending, or consumption. The consumption function shows how consumption is influenced by income and by decisions whether to spend or save that income.

3. There are three injections into the economy: investment, government spending, and exports. None of these is affected by the level of income.

4. There are three withdrawals or leakages from the economy: saving, taxes, and imports. Each of these grows as income grows.

5. Any change in one of the injections has a multiplied effect on the level of income, output, and employment. The size of the multiplier is affected by the proportion of any increase in income which is withdrawn as saving, tax, or imports. The greater these marginal propensities, the smaller the multiplier.

6. The Keynesian model can be linked to the aggregate demand and aggregate supply model.

Key terms

45-degree line diagram

aggregate expenditure

autonomous consumption

autonomous spending

closed economy

consumption function

dissaving

equilibrium

full employment output

induced spending

injections and withdrawals diagram

investment

Keynesian Cross diagram

Keynesian model

Keynesian multiplier

long-term expectations

marginal propensity to consume

marginal propensity to import

marginal propensity to save

net exports

open economy

saving function

Review questions

1. In Atlantis the marginal propensity to consume is 0.8 while in neighbouring Erewhon the marginal propensity to consume is 0.6. Draw a diagram to illustrate the difference between the two countries' consumption functions.

2. In which country is the multiplier larger, other things being equal?

3. Explain how both business confidence and the rate of interest influence the level of investment. Draw appropriate diagrams to illustrate your answer.

4. A number of large building societies demutualize (become banks) and many savers and borrowers receive an allocation of shares. Is this an increase in income or wealth? How will it be reflected in the consumption function? Illustrate with a diagram.

5. How would a rise in exports affect equilibrium national income?

Further reading

- Mabry and Ulbrich, chapter 14

- Lipsey and Chrystal, chapters 21 and 22
- Sloman, chapter 16

CHAPTER 20

Fiscal policy

Fiscal policy brings us into the interesting area of what governments choose to do to influence the economy. In the 1950s and 1960s fiscal policy was seen as the most important way of controlling the economy—governments were influenced by Keynes's view that the level of spending in the economy determined the levels of output and employment (see Chapters 16 and 19). Since both government spending and taxing decisions have an impact on aggregate expenditure economists and politicians thought that the government could influence and perhaps control employment, output, and prices.

As discussed in Chapter 19 the links between government spending (G), taxation (T), and aggregate expenditure (AE) are these:

$$AE = C + I + G + (X - M)$$

and

$$C = a + b(Y - T),$$

so that an increase in government spending or a reduction in taxes will lead to a higher level of aggregate expenditure, other things being equal. Similarly, a cut in government spending or an increase in taxation will reduce aggregate expenditure. In this model the level of aggregate expenditure has a direct impact on the equilibrium levels of income, output, and employment.

Does a budget deficit matter?

Government spending and taxing decisions are presented in the budget. If government receipts, largely from taxes, are higher than government spending there is a **budget surplus** and if spending is higher than receipts there is a **budget deficit**. (Note that in this context government spending includes transfer payments such as state pensions, unemployment benefits, and other social security benefits, whereas in the Keynesian model government spending does not include transfer payments.)

The UK has had a budget deficit for most of the post-war period: there have been budget surpluses only in the years 1969, 1970, 1987, 1988, 1989, and 1990. Budget deficits matter for a number of reasons but in the UK we tend to feel more relaxed about them than people do in the United States, where the budget deficit is frequently a big political issue.

How does the UK government finance a deficit? It may do so either by borrowing from the Bank of England or by borrowing from the public, either via National Savings or by selling government securities. The larger the deficit the more money the government needs to borrow and the more money the government borrows the higher the rate of interest rises, other things being equal.

The **national debt** is the accumulated debt of central government deficits over many years. **Public sector debt** is the national debt plus the debts of local government and public corporations such as the nationalized industries and the BBC. As discussed in Chapter 15 inflation benefits debtors by reducing the real value of the debt so the government has benefited from the inflation of the past fifty years.

The government's **fiscal stance** indicates whether the government is trying to expand the economy, that is to increase employment, or trying to 'take the heat out of the economy' as journalists say, which means trying to reduce the likely level of inflation. The first is called expansionary or reflationary, and the second is contractionary or deflationary.

The fact that the government runs a budget deficit does not mean that it necessarily has an **expansionary fiscal policy**—it is not necessarily trying to increase output and employment if there is a budget deficit. Nor does a budget surplus necessarily indicate a **contractionary fiscal policy**.

What we need to know is the impact that the current size of the public sector deficit (or surplus) is having on aggregate expenditure. What matters is whether the deficit (or surplus) is rising or falling. A complicating factor is that the budget deficit gets larger in the contraction phase of the business cycle as tax revenue falls and social security payments rise, and smaller in the expansion phase as tax revenue rises and benefit payments fall. A relatively large deficit may therefore be the result of the government's wish to increase employment or it may simply be the result of the economy being in a recession.

Automatic stabilizers

This brings us to **automatic stabilizers**. These are taxes from which the revenue rises as national income rises—most taxes in fact—and forms of government spending that fall as national income rises. Many transfer payments are in this group: they affect household income and spending and are not part of government spending on goods and services. Automatic stabilizers reduce the size of the multiplier and help smooth out the up-and-down swings of the business cycle.

Discretionary fiscal policy

Automatic stabilizers cannot prevent the swings of the business cycle, they can only help reduce the impact of those swings. The government may also decide to change the level of government spending on goods and services, or to change the level of taxation, and thus directly to alter aggregate expenditure. This is called **discretionary fiscal policy**.

An argument for the government's attempting such macroeconomic manipulation is provided by the destabilizing effect of changes in investment, which is the most volatile part of aggregate expenditure. The multiplier makes the effects of changes in investment on income, output, and employment larger, so a government might wish to counteract these effects by changing the levels of government spending or of taxation.

In the 1930s not only was investment spending low but so also was consumer spending: the incomes of many households were reduced by unemployment and many others saved a higher

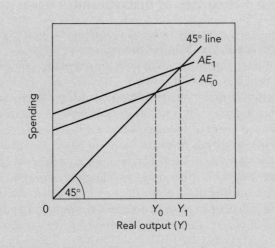

**Figure 20.1. Fiscal policy may be used to increase
equilibrium income, output, and employment**

proportion of their income because they were anxious about possible unemployment. Keynes argued that increased government spending in these circumstances would lead to increased income and employment, taking the economy out of the slump. President Roosevelt's New Deal in the United States put these ideas into effect.

In Figure 20.1 an increase in government spending will shift the aggregate expenditure line upwards from AE_0 to AE_1 and will lead to a higher level of output and employment, shown by the move from Y_0 to Y_1 on the horizontal axis. Similarly, reducing taxes will put more money in consumers' pockets, shift the aggregate expenditure line upwards, and increase output and employment.

However, the impact of the cut in taxes is not as great as the impact of an equivalent increase in government spending. This is because the cut in taxes has the effect of increasing consumers' incomes but not all of that increase is spent, because the marginal propensity to consume is less than one—part of the extra income is saved.

So if a government in the same year increases both its spending by £10 million and its tax receipts by £10 million, thus not changing the size of the budget deficit or surplus, then the expansionary effect of the government spending increase will outweigh the contractionary effect of the tax increase. This phenomenon is known as the **balanced budget multiplier**. A little algebra, found in more advanced texts, shows that the balanced budget multiplier is always equal to 1, which means that it is smaller than the ordinary Keynesian multiplier, and that the increase in output and income is equivalent to the increase in government spending.[1]

In summary, if the government wishes to expand the economy it may raise government spending or cut taxes; if it wishes to counteract the inflationary effects of a boom it may reduce government spending or increase taxes. This may seem to be straightforward, but in practice the implementation and effect of such policies has turned out to be fraught with difficulties.

Some difficulties of discretionary fiscal policy

Difficulties in managing the economy by using discretionary fiscal policy fall into two main categories: problems of size and problems of timing.

Problems of size involve judgements about both the size of the required fiscal adjustment by the government and the likely size of its impact. The economic statistics on which a government bases its policy decisions are often revised upwards or downwards over later months and getting economic forecasts right is notoriously difficult. A rise in government spending may have the unintended effect of reducing other elements of aggregate expenditure. For example, if the government spends more on health or education, private spending in these areas is likely, sooner or later, to fall. Similarly, if an increase in government spending results in the government needing to borrow more and interest rates rise, then firms will invest less. This is known as **crowding out**—government spending 'crowds out' private spending. Another complication is that an increase in taxes will not only cause consumers to spend less but also to save less. All this means that it is extremely difficult to forecast the impact of changes in fiscal policy.

The second major problem associated with discretionary policy involves timing and the unpredictable length of **time-lags**. There is a time-lag before a problem is recognized, a second time-lag while a suitable action is decided upon, a third time-lag while the action is put into effect (and it can be months before announced changes in tax rates come into effect), and finally a fourth time-lag as the multiplier effect works through.

Frank Paish, of the London School of Economics, used to tell students that attempting to control the economy by means of fiscal policy was like driving a car along a straight but hilly road without being able to see anything but through the rear-view mirror, with uncertain time delays after using the brake and accelerator pedals, and with seats which made it impossible to tell if the car was going uphill or downhill.

Imagine you are driving such a car. As you drive you realize that you are now going downhill but the brake does not at first work. Anxiously you step harder on the brake, only for it finally to work when you now appear to be going uphill. So you accelerate but again there is no immediate response and by the time the accelerator takes effect the car starts to speed alarmingly downhill.

Your problems would be even worse if the rear window were misty, the misty rear window being analogous to the unreliability of the statistics on which discretionary fiscal policy decisions are made.

Fine-tuning the economy

With the benefit of hindsight it seems that discretionary fiscal policy has often made the slumps deeper and the booms greater, so that what was intended as stabilizing policy was actually destabilizing. Figure 20.2 illustrates this point: line A shows economic activity fluctuating over the course of the business cycle; line B shows the intended effect of discretionary fiscal policy on the economy, smoothing out the peaks and troughs of the business cycle; and line C shows the unintended outcome of discretionary fiscal policy. Such use of fiscal policy was often described as **fine-tuning** the economy, in a reference to fine-tuning a car engine of the period to make it run as efficiently as possible. The heyday of fine-tuning in the UK was the 1950s and 1960s, the era of 'Stop–Go' policies which are now thought to have led to lower

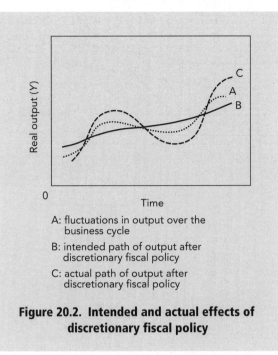

A: fluctuations in output over the
   business cycle

B: intended path of output after
   discretionary fiscal policy

C: actual path of output after
   discretionary fiscal policy

**Figure 20.2. Intended and actual effects of
discretionary fiscal policy**

business confidence, a lower level of investment, lower productivity, and slower growth of
the economy.

Fiscal policy and prices

Apart from a reference to the impact of fiscal policy on interest rates, the money side of
the economy has been ignored in this discussion of fiscal policy. All of the above discussion
has taken place in the context of the Keynesian model of Chapter 19, in which prices
are assumed to be constant, that is, the aggregate supply curve is horizontal. The effects
of expansionary fiscal policy could then be shown by Figure 20.3, where, in the upper part
of the diagram, an increase in government spending or a reduction in taxes shifts aggregate
expenditure upwards from AE_0 to AE_1, leading to a higher equilibrium level of output at
Y_1. The lower part of the diagram shows how aggregate demand shifts to the right from AD_0
to AD_1, with the price level remaining constant at P_0. In both diagrams the level of output
and income rises from Y_0 to Y_1. This picture is only possible if the aggregate supply curve is
horizontal.

Figure 20.4 shows what happens in more usual circumstances when there is an upward-
sloping aggregate supply curve. As in Figure 20.3 expansionary fiscal policy shifts the aggregate
demand curve to the right, from AD_0 to AD_1, but this shift of aggregate demand leads to a
movement up the aggregate supply curve, AS, so that the price level rises from P_0 to P_1 and
the level of output and income rises from Y_0 to Y_1. In these circumstances expansionary fiscal
policy both has a crowding-out effect and causes a rise in the price level.

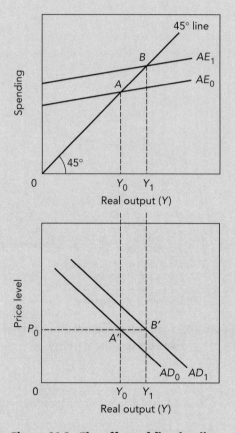

Figure 20.3. The effect of fiscal policy on aggregate demand

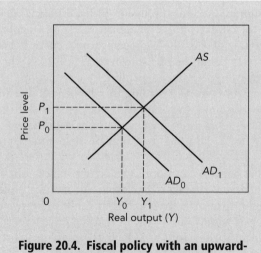

Figure 20.4. Fiscal policy with an upward-sloping aggregate supply curve

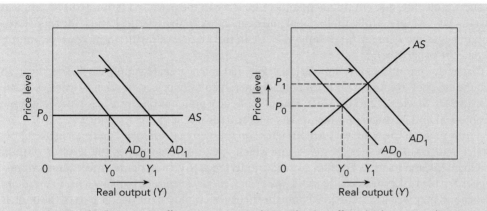

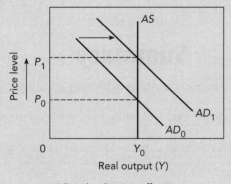

Figure 20.5. The effectiveness of expansionary policy depends on the slope of the aggregate supply curve

When is fiscal policy most effective?

One of the reasons why expansionary fiscal policy may be less effective than hoped is due to the possible crowding-out effects of government spending. If firms' investment spending is very sensitive to changes in the interest rate then crowding out will be greater than if investment is less sensitive to interest rate changes.

Another factor is the steepness of the aggregate supply curve: the steeper the aggregate supply curve the less effective is expansionary fiscal policy. Figure 20.5 shows how fiscal policy is most effective when the aggregate supply curve is horizontal and least effective when the aggregate supply curve is vertical. In part (a) the aggregate supply is horizontal because unemployment levels are high. Expansionary fiscal policy shifts aggregate demand from AD_0 to AD_1, which results in an increase in output, income, and employment from Y_0 to Y_1 and no increase in the level of prices. In part (b) the same shift in aggregate demand leads to a smaller increase in output, income, and employment and an increase in the price level from P_0 to P_1, while in part (c), where there is full employment and aggregate supply is vertical, the same rightwards shift of aggregate demand leads only to a rise in the price level, with no increase in output, income, or employment.

Classical economists and monetarists argue that the aggregate supply curve is vertical, so that the effect of expansionary fiscal policy is merely to raise prices, in other words it is worse than useless. So we need to consider instead monetary policy and its impact on the economy: Chapters 21 and 22 discuss money and its role, and the use of monetary policy.

At this point in the book we turn our backs on the aggregate demand and aggregate supply model, and on the Keynesian model, in which spending determines the level of output, employment, and income. Focusing on this model tends to give students a misleading impression. The title of Keynes's major work was *The General Theory of Employment, Interest and Money* and here we have considered only the theory of employment; a large part of the book is about money and the rate of interest. Keynes considers the psychology of the speculator and gives an insider's account of the Stock Exchange; Robert Skidelsky, in his biography of Keynes, describes Keynes as 'the poet of money'.[2]

Summary

1. A budget deficit is not necessarily something to be worried about.

2. Automatic stabilizers reduce the peaks and troughs of the business cycle.

3. Discretionary fiscal policy is difficult to use as intended because of poor information and uncertain time-lags.

4. Attempts to fine-tune the economy are thought to have exacerbated business cycle fluctuations.

5. Crowding out and rising prices reduce the effectiveness of expansionary fiscal policy.

6. Fiscal policy is most effective when the aggregate supply curve is horizontal.

Key terms

automatic stabilizers

balanced budget multiplier

budget deficit

budget surplus

contractionary fiscal policy

crowding out

discretionary fiscal policy

expansionary fiscal policy

fine-tuning

fiscal stance

national debt

public sector debt

time-lags

Review questions

1. Suppose the economy is operating at well below full employment. What fiscal policies might a government use to increase employment?

2. Which would be your choice among these policies? Would inflation or crowding out reduce the effectiveness of your policy? In what circumstances would your policy work best?

3. What is the difference between an 'automatic stabiliser' and 'fine-tuning' the economy?

4. Why might crowding out occur?

Notes

1. For some algebra showing the balanced budget multiplier equal to 1 see Sloman, 530. Alternatively, M. Parkin, M. Powell, and K. Matthews, *Economics*, 3rd edn. (Harlow: Addison-Wesley, 1997), 752 gives the same result.

2. 'If Marx is the poet of commodities, Keynes is the poet of money': Robert Skidelsky, *John Maynard Keynes: The Economist as Saviour 1920–1937* (London: Macmillan, 1997), 543. This second volume of Skidelsky's major study of Keynes's life and work contains many insights. Chapter 15, 'Firing at the Moon', is a very readable and rounded account of the *General Theory*.

Further reading

- Mabry and Ulbrich, chapter 15

- Lipsey and Chrystal, chapters 24 and 27
- Sloman, chapter 17

CHAPTER 21

Money (1)

Most of the macroeconomic theory we have studied so far has dealt with what is called the real side of the economy, that is with output and employment; now we look at the money side of the economy and study how financial markets interact with the real economy. First we examine the role of money in the economy.

For a start, the amount of money in the economy can have a big effect on aggregate demand and, as you know from Chapter 17, changes in aggregate demand affect prices, output, and employment. But there is controversy about how the amount of money—the **money supply** —influences the economy. Some economists argue that changes in the money supply have a large effect on aggregate demand and that changes in aggregate demand principally affect the price level rather than output and employment—this is the **monetarist** position. On the other hand, economists of a more Keynesian persuasion argue that changes in the amount of money in the economy have an uncertain effect on aggregate demand. They argue that any changes in aggregate demand have a more significant influence on output and employment than on the price level. Also, they believe that the amount of money in the economy is often the result of, not the cause of, changes in the real economy.

These are important issues which have influenced many countries' economic policies and the living standards of millions of people. Before we can explore these ideas we need to be clear about first, the purposes of money and second, what we mean by the term 'money'.

Why use money?

Most people's everyday use of money is to pay for goods and services, but there are many examples, old and new, of occasions when money is not used. Modern examples of occasions where goods and services are exchanged without the use of money, to what is generally understood to be mutual advantage, include baby-sitting circles, swapping football stickers, LETS (Local Economy Trading System) schemes, and ritual gift exchanges at birthdays, Christmas, and weddings. The usual term for such moneyless transactions is **barter**, which is often thought to be associated more with so-called primitive societies but is alive and well down your street.

Accounts of barter tend to emphasize its disadvantages, which can be significant, and tend to imply that it is outmoded. A famous example is that given by W. S. Jevons, in *Money and the Mechanism of Exchange* (1875), which describes the bad luck of Mademoiselle Zélie, a French opera singer on a world tour, when she gave a concert in the Society Islands (part of French Polynesia). Mademoiselle Zélie's fee was one-third of the takings and amounted to three pigs, twenty-three turkeys, forty-four chickens, five thousand coconuts, and piles of lemons, oranges, and bananas. Unable to eat all this, and unable to take much of it with her,

Mademoiselle Zélie had to feed the pigs and poultry with the fruit and to forgo a large part of this significant fee. Perhaps she should have given a feast.[1]

The grandfather of one of the authors was a country doctor in northern New Hampshire, USA; he died in his thirties, in 1926. His poorer patients would often pay him in kind rather than in money. So, in the early 1990s, while staying in their grandmother's house, his descendants discovered a few large tins of maple sugar in the bottom of the kitchen cupboards, the last few of many such tins given in payment by farmers. This supply of maple sugar had been used in cooking for many years. Maple sugar is a valuable commodity but was obviously not all needed at the time, nor for the next seventy years, and though still sweet it eventually lost its delicious flavour and tasted nastily of metal—wasted, as was Mademoiselle Zélie's fee.

Barter needs a 'double coincidence of wants'; in the case of Mademoiselle Zélie and of the country doctor there seems not to have been such a coincidence. Both were left with more or less perishable goods, in quantities far greater than their needs, in payment for services rendered. Both would have preferred money.

A barter economy is wasteful of time and effort—in economists' jargon there are high transactions costs associated with barter—which makes the economy much less efficient. The use of money overcomes such problems and the primary role of money is as a **medium of exchange**.

But money has other functions. Money acts as a *unit of account*, enabling comparisons to be made: the value of one good may be compared with that of another, or the national income of one country may be compared with the national income of another country.

Money also acts as a *store of value*—it can be saved. Of course money is not the only store of value: houses, works of art, and precious jewels are other ways of storing value or wealth for use in the future.

Finally, money is a *standard of deferred payment*. People need to be able to sign contracts for goods and services produced in the future and such contracts are most usefully expressed in terms of money.

So, there are four functions of money: a medium of exchange, a store of value, a unit of account, and a standard of deferred payment. Next we look at what we mean by the term 'money', which is not as straightforward as it might seem.

What is money?

We are all familiar with our own notes and coins, and this is what immediately comes to mind when thinking of money. Many people will have used foreign notes and coins and will have seen ancient coins in a museum or book, but in both the ancient and the modern world people have used many things other than coins or bank notes as money.

In a famous article on 'The Economic Organisation of a POW Camp', R. A. Radford describes how cigarettes were used as money.[2] Radford wrote from experience—he had been a prisoner of war in Germany.

On the island of Yap, in the central Pacific, a stone currency was still in use in the 1980s. Large stone wheels, the largest up to twenty feet in diameter, were used to pay for major purchases such as land, canoes, and permission to marry. Since stone wheels have their disadvantages as pocket money, necklaces of stone beads strung around a whale's tooth, large sea shells, and beer are all in use to pay for smaller items. Yap is a United States trust territory so the US dollar is increasingly used alongside the traditional forms of money.

Pigs, cows, jewellery, sugar, coffee, and nylon stockings have all been used as money.

A common, but not necessary, feature of most forms of money in simpler economies is that the money itself has an intrinsic value. Animals can be eaten, cigarettes smoked, jewellery worn, and so on. These are all examples of **commodity money**, as are the gold, silver, and copper coins in use in Britain in the nineteenth century. However, because such commodity money is expensive, it suits most countries better to use **token money**, whose intrinsic value is much less than its face value. Our 'silver' coins no longer contain silver to the value of the coin because there are better uses for a precious metal and everyone accepts that token money is legal tender, as they do **IOU money** such as banknotes promising to pay £5 or £50.

What are the features of an ideal form of money?

Whatever is used as money must be in a form generally *acceptable* as a means of payment, if it is to be used as a medium of exchange. Money must also be *durable*; this is where stone wheels score highly and maple sugar less well. Money used as a store of value must not deteriorate over time. Money must also be *convenient*, preferably portable, because as money changes hands it must be small and not too heavy. Stone wheels are useless in this respect but seashells may be good.

A further attribute of an ideal form of money is that it must be easily *divisible*, which is one reason why animals are not much used as money. A £50 note may be an embarrassment in a corner shop, as is a £10 note at a jumble sale, because it may be impossible to get change for them.

Money needs to be *uniform* in weight and appearance, particularly if it is commodity money with an intrinsic value. When English money was silver—commodity money—coins of equal value had to be of equal weight.

Gresham's law states that 'bad money drives out good'; the origins of this saying give a good example of the importance of a uniform currency. Sir Thomas Gresham (1519–79) was a merchant and financial adviser to Elizabeth I. Silver coins had been defined as having 925 parts of silver per 1,000, but during the two previous reigns sterling had been debased and coins had been issued with only 250 parts of silver per 1,000. Where two coins had an equal face value but one had a much lower intrinsic value, that is, a lower silver content, the better coin was melted down for its silver. Only the debased coins remained.

A further attribute of money is that it must be *scarce* or in restricted supply, particularly in the case of commodity money, and in the case of paper money it should be too difficult for individuals to produce for themselves. Finally, money should possess *stability of value*; this is particularly important when money is being used as a store of value and as a standard of deferred payment. The results of inflation, when money loses its value, can be socially and economically damaging and present a good argument for control of the money supply by the central bank or the government.

Narrow money and broad money

We return to what is meant today by money and how money is defined for the purposes of managing the money supply. Cash (notes and coins) is money, current accounts in banks are money, but after this the definitions get blurred.

A narrow definition of money, **narrow money**, includes cash and money in accounts that can be spent directly with a cheque book or debit card. **Broad money** includes narrow money as well as money in bank and building society deposit accounts. Unfortunately, there are several different broad money definitions in use, which arose largely as a result of the government's rather unsuccessful attempts to control the money supply in the 1980s.

A distinction between the narrow and broader forms of money lies in the concept of **liquidity**, or how easy it is to get at your financial assets and turn them into cash. Obviously, the cash in your pocket and the money in your current account can be used instantly—these are **liquid assets**. Less liquid, for example, are savings in a Post Office account that requires one month's notice of withdrawal.

Narrow money is liquid; other forms of money are less liquid. Financial assets range from the completely liquid to the illiquid and there is a trade-off between liquidity and the rate of return on the asset. Completely liquid assets pay no interest, or at best a very low rate of interest, while ninety-day accounts and five-year bonds, where money is tied up for a specified period, pay a higher rate of interest to the owner of the asset.

Measuring the money supply

In the UK currently the narrowest measure of the money supply is known as M0 (also known, confusingly, as 'the wide monetary base') and the broadest measure is called M4; in many European countries and in the United States the broadest money is known as M3, so care is needed when making comparisons. The general rule is that 'M' stands for 'money supply' and the larger the figure after it the broader is the definition of the money being measured.

The size of the money supply depends on a variety of factors such as the size of the economy, the institutional framework, and government and central bank policy. Some of these are discussed in Chapter 22, but for now we take the money supply as given and turn our attention to the demand for money.

The demand for money

The demand for money is the desire to hold money rather than to spend it or to purchase other financial assets with it. The demand for money is the result of its roles as a medium of exchange and as a store of value. The demand for money is a stock, not a flow. (Stocks and flows are first discussed in Chapter 15.)

When Keynes considered the demand for money he identified three reasons, or motives, for holding money. The first of these is called the transactions motive, and the money thus held is known as the **transactions demand for money**. This is the most important of the three motives for holding money and comes from money's function as a medium of exchange.

When you go to buy your lunch, or a newspaper, you need ready cash. You will expect to buy quite a lot of food in a week in one form or another and it would not suit you to have to go to the pawnshop with your grandmother's earrings or to sell your Yorkshire Water shares whenever you need cash for day-to-day spending. You are likely to have that money in your purse or pocket. You may be in the habit of going to the bank once a week to draw out more cash but in that case you are just transferring money held in your bank account to your pocket or purse. You hold enough money for this form of spending so that you minimize the inconvenience associated with each transaction or purchase.

The second reason why people hold money is known as the precautionary motive. Money held for this purpose protects you against an unforeseen, or uncertain, need for money. Travellers beyond the reach of a convenient banking system often carry large amounts of US dollars or pounds sterling with them just in case something unexpected happens. Similarly, if you run an old car, it seems prudent to have a bit of extra money available if the MOT test is imminent—you do not know what any necessary repairs might cost and they could be expensive. The **precautionary demand for money** is much smaller than the transactions demand and, for simplicity, is often combined with the transactions demand.

The third reason for holding money is called by Keynes the speculative motive and is for many students the hardest of the three motives to grasp, largely because the words used are more obscure and the motive itself less familiar. The speculative motive gives rise to the **speculative demand for money** (sometimes known as the asset demand). People who are comfortably off and have money to spare for more than everyday purchases have a choice about what to do with the surplus. They may leave the money earning little or no interest in their pockets or current accounts (identified by Keynes as **idle balances**), or they may purchase some kind of financial asset, upon which they expect to earn some kind of return some time in the future. Since there is always some element of uncertainty about the rate of this return in the future—such a purchase is more or less risky—this use of money can be called speculation, although in normal speech people would reserve the word only for the purchase of the most risky financial assets. However, the speculative demand for money involves people *holding on to* money which they might otherwise have used for speculations, and is not the money used for speculation; it is in this looking-glass definition that most of the confusion arises.

The speculative demand for money is linked to the function of money as a store of value. In some circumstances people will prefer to store their wealth as money rather than to purchase government bonds or other less liquid financial assets; maybe the price or the rate of return are unstable, or maybe the rate of return is too low to compensate for the loss of liquidity. Keynes called this preference for money over less liquid financial assets **liquidity preference**.

So, there are three motives for holding money and three kinds of demand for money: the transactions, precautionary, and speculative demands.

What influences the size of the demand for money?

Holding money has a cost. There is a price risk because if prices rise money buys less—it becomes less useful as a store of value—which is why in inflationary times people like to buy goods, such as houses and antiques, whose prices rise with inflation. The opportunity cost of holding money is the rate of interest forgone, which is why less liquid financial assets tend to have a higher rate of interest.

The quantity of money held by households and firms, or the demand for money, is affected by prices, by real expenditure, and by opportunity cost. These three can be linked to three important macroeconomic variables: the price level, real GDP, and the interest rate. We will deal with each in turn.

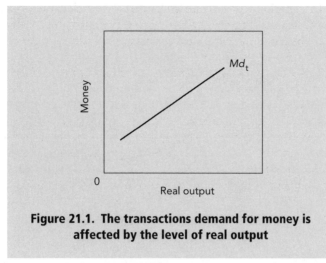

Figure 21.1. The transactions demand for money is affected by the level of real output

The price level

What matters to people is what their money will buy, or its real value. Real money is independent of the price level but nominal money is held in proportion to the price level: the higher the price level the higher the quantity of nominal money demanded, other things being equal.

Real output

The demand for real money is affected by the size of real output: if real output rises then more goods and services are produced, and more buying and selling goes on. Both real aggregate income and real aggregate expenditure rise.

Real output primarily affects the transactions demand for money. Figure 21.1 illustrates the relationship between the two as the line Md_t, with real output on the horizontal axis and the amount of money held on the vertical axis.

The rate of interest

The **rate of interest**, or the opportunity cost of holding money, affects the speculative demand for money: if the rate of interest is high then the opportunity cost of holding money is high and less money is held in idle balances, other things being equal. The relationship between the speculative demand for money and the rate of interest is shown in Figure 21.2. Notice that in this diagram the amount of money held is shown on the horizontal axis (unlike in Figure 21.1) and the rate of interest is on the vertical axis—the result is the downward-sloping demand curve Md_s, with price (the rate of interest) on the vertical axis and quantity on the horizontal axis.

How do we incorporate the other demands for real money, the transactions and precautionary demands? Neither are particularly sensitive to the rate of interest so will not much alter the slope of the speculative demand curve. At any one level of output there will be a money demand curve (Md_0) plotted against the rate of interest, as in Figure 21.3, and as real output rises this demand curve will shift rightwards to Md_1.

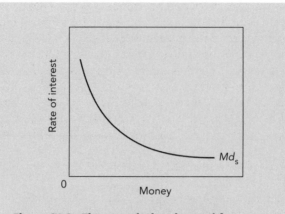

**Figure 21.2. The speculative demand for money
is affected by the rate of interest**

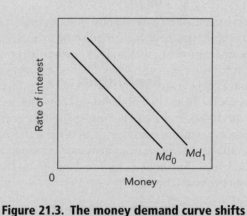

**Figure 21.3. The money demand curve shifts
to the right as real output rises**

What about the effect of changing prices? If 'nominal' is substituted for 'real' in all these diagrams they work just as well. The effect of rising prices is to increase the nominal demand for money at each rate of interest, so the money demand curve shifts to the right, from Md_0 to Md_1, as prices rise and money loses its value.

Interest rates

The next section puts the demand and supply of money together and shows how the rate of interest is determined; but first we consider interest rates in the real world.

The rate of interest is not the price of money; money is the medium of exchange and you cannot buy pounds with pounds. Nor is interest a payment for using money. It is rather the price paid for borrowing money or the reward for lending money. By paying interest on borrowed money people can use resources they have not yet earned enough to pay for. Having the use of resources now is generally worth more than the future use of those resources, so it can be worthwhile paying to borrow money.

Although we talk about the interest rate as if there were only one, in fact there is a family of interest rates, with different rates for different circumstances, all in operation at the same time. One of the main reasons for this variety of interest rates is that the income of banks and other financial institutions comes from charging a higher rate of interest to borrowers than they pay to depositors (savers). But there are other reasons too for the range of interest rates at any one time.

In March 1996 Barclaycard sent a notice to all its cardholders announcing that its monthly interest rate would be reduced from 1.63 per cent to 1.61 per cent. Rather a tiny change, you might think, but actually quite significant in terms of competition with other credit card companies and the amount of interest paid by more heavily indebted cardholders over several months. Most interest rates are quoted as annual rates and are therefore easy to compare, but here a monthly interest rate was quoted, which is much less frightening for thoughtless borrowers. Although this is normal for credit card companies, it also tends to mislead the less mathematically aware, who imagine that the annual rate is twelve times the monthly rate and do not realize that interest is compounded over the twelve months and that the actual rate is thus a higher figure than they think. Barclaycard's annual rate of interest in this case was reduced from 21.4 per cent to 21.1 per cent, while the rate at which commercial banks were lending to their most reliable large customers at this time was 7 per cent.

Credit card interest rates tend to be higher than most other interest rates, although the highest rates of all are charged by loan sharks, lending to the poor and desperate. One factor affecting the rate of interest charged is the degree of **risk** run by the lender that the borrower will not repay the money borrowed; credit card companies extend credit widely and therefore run quite a risk.

Another factor which may influence risk is the length of time over which the loan is being made. In general, a longer time period increases the risk of default and therefore the rate of interest payable.

A third element of risk faced by the lender is that the money may lose some of its value while the borrower is using it—not because money gets worn out, but because the price level may change and the money's purchasing power be less by the time the loan is repaid. This risk is obviously greater in inflationary times and when loans are made over a longer period. The lender needs to be compensated for the expected loss in value over the time period of the loan so interest rates are higher the higher the expected rate of inflation, and the best guide to the expected inflation rate is the current inflation rate.

Nominal interest rates are therefore affected by the inflation rate. The real interest rate reflects all influences, other than inflation, on the rate of interest. The **real interest rate** is the **nominal interest rate** minus the rate of inflation.

To summarize, the factors affecting the level of an interest rate are whether it is a borrowing or a lending rate, the risk of default, expected inflation, and the time period of the loan.

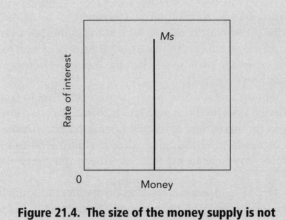

Figure 21.4. The size of the money supply is not affected by the rate of interest

The rate of interest and money market equilibrium

The size of the money supply is controlled, more or less effectively, by a country's central bank—in Britain this is the Bank of England. The central bank actually tries to control the **nominal money supply**, which does not guarantee that it can control the **real money supply**. The relation between the two forms of money supply is as follows:

$$\text{real money supply} = \frac{\text{nominal money supply}}{\text{price level}}.$$

To make our analysis easier, we will assume that there is no change in the price level, that is, that the nominal is the same as the real. Simple monetary theory holds that the supply of money is not influenced by the rate of interest but by institutional factors, briefly mentioned earlier in this chapter. Figure 21.4 illustrates this lack of a relationship between the rate of interest and the money supply. With the rate of interest on the vertical axis and the quantity of money on the horizontal axis, the money supply (Ms) is shown as a vertical line.

However, as described earlier in this chapter, the demand for money is affected by real output and the rate of interest. Using the same axes as Figure 21.4, Figure 21.5 shows the demand for money (Md). To arrive at equilibrium in the **money market**, we put the demand for money and the supply of money together in Figure 21.6. Only at the rate of interest r_e are the demand and supply of money equal: it is only at the rate of interest r_e that the money market is in equilibrium.

Equilibrium in the money market is achieved by adjustments of the exchange rate and of the interest rate. The exchange rate is outside the scope of this part of the book and we focus here on the role of the interest rate.

Changes in the interest rate affect the speculative demand for money. At the equilibrium interest rate people want to hold money in just the same quantity as the money market

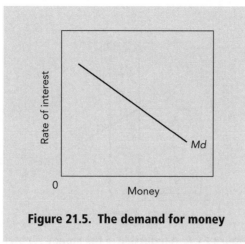

Figure 21.5. The demand for money

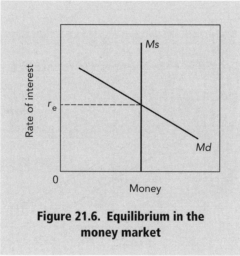

**Figure 21.6. Equilibrium in the
money market**

supplies. If the rate of interest is higher people would rather hold less money and will, for example, buy more government bonds. This increased demand for bonds will drive up their price, which will have the effect of lowering the interest rate. There is an inverse relationship between the price of bonds and the rate of interest—one rises and the other falls. As the price of bonds rises they become less attractive, and holding money more attractive, until the interest rate is back to its equilibrium level.

This process will work the other way round too, of course. If the demand for money is greater than the supply people will sell bonds to acquire money; this will drive the price of bonds down and the rate of interest up, to the point where the demand and supply of money are again equal.

A shift in either the demand or the supply of money will have an effect on the rate of interest. The central bank may reduce the money supply either by selling government stock or by

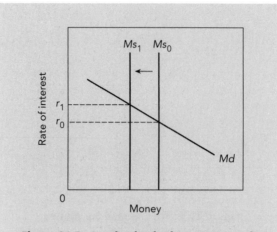

**Figure 21.7. A reduction in the money supply
leads to a higher rate of interest**

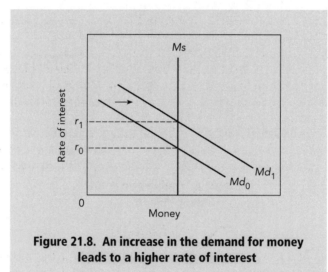

**Figure 21.8. An increase in the demand for money
leads to a higher rate of interest**

putting restrictions on the banks; Figure 21.7 shows what happens. With a fall in the money supply, the money supply line Ms_0 shifts to the left, to Ms_1, and the equilibrium rate of interest rises from r_0 to r_1. This higher rate of interest is necessary to induce people to buy bonds rather than continuing to hold the same amount of money in idle balances. On the other hand, an increase in the supply of money would result in a fall in the equilibrium interest rate.

So far we have assumed a given level of output which has determined the position of the money demand line, Md_0. If output rises then people need more money to carry out transactions at each rate of interest—the demand for money rises; in Figure 21.8 the demand for

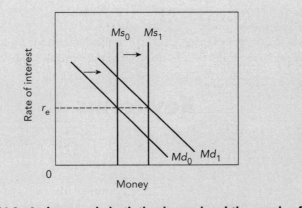

**Figure 21.9. An increase in both the demand and the supply of
money may lead to no change in the rate of interest**

money line Md_0 shifts rightwards to Md_1 and the equilibrium interest rate rises from r_0 to r_1. On
the other hand, a fall in output with an unchanged money supply would lead to a leftwards
shift of the money demand line and a fall in the rate of interest.

Finally, Figure 21.9 shows the utopian state of affairs in which output rises and the money
supply increases sufficiently to maintain the same equilibrium rate of interest. After the rise
in output the money demand line shifts rightwards from Md_0 to Md_1, the rise in the money
supply is shown by the rightwards shift of the money supply line from Ms_0 to Ms_1, and the
equilibrium rate of interest remains at r_e.

Utopia is all very well but in the real world things can be much more difficult. The next chapter continues to examine the role of money in the economy, building towards a discussion
of monetary policy both as a tool for managing the economy in the short term and as a way of
fostering longer-term stability and economic growth.

Summary

1. Money's primary use is as a medium of exchange, but it also functions as a store of value and
a unit of account.

2. IOU money, token money, and commodity money may all be used. The last can take many
different forms.

3. The demand for money is made up of the transactions demand, the precautionary demand,
and the speculative demand. The transactions demand is related to the size of the economy and
the speculative demand to the rate of interest.

4. A change in the level of output will cause the money demand curve to shift and a change in
the rate of interest will cause a movement along the money demand curve.

5. The many rates of interest in an economy at any one time reflect the varieties of risk faced by lenders.

6. Equilibrium in the money market occurs when the demand for money is equal to the supply of money. The rate of interest is determined by money market equilibrium.

Key terms

barter	money supply
broad money	narrow money
commodity money	nominal interest rate
Gresham's law	nominal money supply
idle balances	precautionary demand for money
IOU money	rate of interest
liquid assets	real interest rate
liquidity	real money supply
liquidity preference	risk
medium of exchange	speculative demand for money
monetarist	token money
money market	transactions demand for money

Review questions

1. Why are each of the following unsuitable for use as money?

    (i) houses
    (ii) bananas
    (iii) cats
    (iv) bird of paradise feathers

2. In each of the following circumstances say whether you would choose to increase or decrease the 'idle' cash in your bank account.

    (i) Last year's inflation rate was 12 per cent.
    (ii) Interest rates are higher this year than last year.
    (iii) Your salary is increased by 15 per cent.
    (iv) You expect interest rates on financial assets to rise soon.
    (v) You expect inflation to rise next year.

3. Explain why the interest rate falls when

(i) the inflation rate falls;
(ii) the money supply increases.

Notes

1. Jevons's account of Mademoiselle Zélie's fee is referred to in G. Davies, *A History of Money* (Cardiff: University of Wales Press, 1994), 13–14. Yap stones are also discussed by Davies (36–8).

2. R. A. Radford, 'The Economic Organisation of a POW Camp', *Economica*, 12 (1945), 189–201.

Further reading

- Mabry and Ulbrich, chapter 16

- Lipsey and Chrystal, chapter 26
- Sloman, chapter 18

CHAPTER 22

Money (2)

This chapter continues our study of money in the economy, looking first at how changes in the money supply affect output and prices. Next the role of banks in expanding the money supply is outlined, and the UK's financial institutions described, before the final section discusses monetary policy.

The **quantity theory of money** links money, output, and prices. It is one of the best-known parts of economics, ranking in the popular consciousness with supply and demand, and with Keynesian ideas on the management of the economy. Perhaps because the quantity theory of money is relatively well known it is often misunderstood and misapplied, and therefore deserves a careful consideration by students of economics.

Money, output, and prices: the quantity theory of money

The quantity theory of money is associated with classical economics and with monetarism. David Hume (1711–76), the great Scottish philosopher, gave a clear account in the eighteenth century but the quantity theory of money is said to be at least five hundred years old and some even suggest that it dates from Confucius (551–479 BC), the Chinese philosopher.

The quantity theory of money says that changes in the nominal money supply lead to equivalent changes in the price level and in money wages, but have no effect on output and employment. In other words, money affects the money side of the economy, but not the real side. This is sometimes described as the 'crude quantity theory'.

A shorthand version of the quantity theory is the **equation of exchange**,

$$MV = PY,$$

where M stands for the money supply, V for the velocity of circulation, P for the price level, and Y for real output. PY, or the price level multiplied by real output, gives us the nominal value of output. All of these should be familiar concepts except for the **velocity of circulation**, which gives an idea of how frequently money changes hands in a year, or how fast money circulates around the economy. If money circulates quickly less of it is needed to sustain a particular price level, but if circulation is sluggish more is needed to sustain the same price level. The equation above is a truism, not a theory; all it is saying is that the amount of money used equals the amount of money spent.

Two assumptions of the quantity theory of money

The equation becomes a theory if two assumptions are made. The first assumption is that changes in the velocity of circulation are so small that V can be treated as constant, with a characteristic and fixed value for each economy. The second assumption is that real output (Y) is not affected by the amount of money in the economy and therefore may also be treated as constant. So, if V and Y do not change then any increase in M, the money supply, will feed straight through to P, the price level. The percentage change in the money supply will equal the percentage change in the price level. The quantity theory of money is thus a theory of inflation—one of the oldest theories of inflation.

You might well argue that holding the velocity of circulation and the level of real output constant are big assumptions to make, and ask, 'Is there any evidence for the crude quantity theory?' In fact, figures from many countries do show a link between changes in the money supply and changes in the price level. On a small scale, R. A. Radford, in his article on the use of cigarettes as money in the German prisoner-of-war camp, notes the same phenomenon: after the arrival of Red Cross parcels containing cigarettes, prices of other goods rose in terms of cigarettes, the generally accepted currency.[1]

On an international scale, when a comparison is made of the rates of growth of the money supply in many countries and their rates of inflation, two things become obvious. One is that there is a link between the two rates, both when inflation rates are high and when they are low, and the other is that it is not a strong link. This suggests that the crude quantity theory is too crude, and that there must be other factors besides the growth of the money supply which affect the rate of inflation.

Does the measure of the money supply used make a difference? In Britain, at least, no clear picture emerges. In the 1970s and early 1980s there appears to be a similar pattern for the growth rate of broad money and the inflation rate, but with a time-lag of about two years. After the early 1980s the pattern changes and if there is any link between the two rates the time-lag would seem to have disappeared. From the early 1980s there is a closer link between the rate of growth of narrow money and the inflation rate. Pity the economic forecaster.

The quantity theory leaves an important question unanswered. While there seems generally to be a link between money and prices, what is the direction of causation? Does an increase in the money supply lead to rising prices or do rising prices lead to an increase in the money supply? In Britain in the 1970s, the rate of growth of broad money did appear to lead to later, and similar, changes in the inflation rate. Otherwise the picture is not clear.

What happens if *V* and *Y* are not constant?

As discussed earlier, for the quantity theory to have any predictive power it is necessary to assume that the velocity of circulation, V, and real output, Y, are both constant in the equation

$$MV = PY.$$

However, real output is only constant at full employment. The aggregate demand and aggregate supply model explored in Chapter 17 may help our analysis here, because it links real output and the price level.

Consider Figure 22.1, which shows a typically upward-sloping aggregate supply curve (AS), with the price level (P) on the vertical axis and real output (Y) on the horizontal axis. An increase in the supply of money will lead to a reduction in the rate of interest, which will lead to an increase in aggregate demand, shown by the rightwards shift of the aggregate demand curve from AD_0 to AD_1 (see pp. 184–186 above). Following this increase in the supply of money the price level rises from P_0 to P_1 and real output also increases from Y_0 to Y_1.

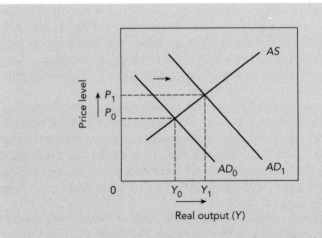

Figure 22.1. An increase in the money supply may lead to both rising prices and an increase in real output

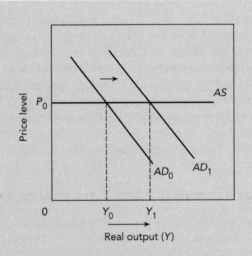

Figure 22.2. Significant spare capacity in the economy may mean that an increase in the money supply leads to increasing real output and no rise in prices

A Keynesian analysis, that is, short term and with lots of spare capacity in the economy, is illustrated in Figure 22.2. Here the aggregate supply curve is horizontal and the rightwards shift of the aggregate demand curve leads only to an increase in real output, from Y_0 to Y_1. Prices remain unchanged at P_0.

The classical view of the economy, in which aggregate supply is vertical, and unaffected by changes in the price level, is shown in Figure 22.3. Here an increase in the money supply again leads to a rightwards shift of the aggregate demand curve but the only result is an upward

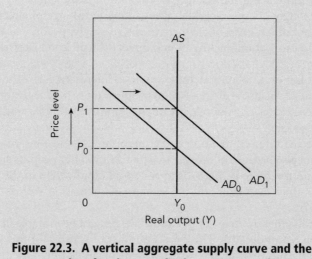

Figure 22.3. A vertical aggregate supply curve and the results of an increase in the money supply

movement in prices, from P_0 to P_1. Real output is unaffected at Y_0. You should recognize the quantity theory of money in action here.

The quantity theory seems more appropriate in the long run or when the economy is at full employment, that is, in circumstances when the aggregate supply curve is vertical.

The other assumption behind the quantity theory is that the velocity of circulation changes so little that it can be treated as constant. It is not easy to measure the velocity of circulation, and conclusions about its behaviour are usually drawn from observing how other elements of the equation of exchange behave. In fact, the speed with which money circulates around the economy does vary, and can be unpredictable.

Another problem with the velocity of circulation is familiar: are we interested in the velocity of broad money or the velocity of narrow money? Analysis of figures for the velocity of circulation in the United States from 1929 to 1989 show that the velocity of circulation of broad money was relatively stable; in contrast, the velocity of circulation of narrow money rose steadily from the mid-1940s until it took a sharp dip in the mid-1980s, but then began to rise again.

In Britain, on the other hand, the velocity of circulation of both broad and narrow money has shown considerable variation in the last twenty-five years, particularly in the 1970s and early 1980s. More recently the velocity of circulation of narrow money had been rising and the velocity of broad money falling, until the mid-1990s when both fell. The velocity of circulation is obviously far from stable, and cannot be assumed to be constant in the equation of exchange.

A number of factors affect the velocity of circulation. How frequently wages and salaries are paid is one important influence; the less frequently people are paid, the more money is held, on average, in current accounts or in jam jars on the mantelpiece. Money lying idle is not circulating around the economy. The long-term trend in Britain has been for more and more people to be paid monthly rather than weekly, which means that the velocity of circulation should have fallen, other things being equal.

A second factor influencing the velocity of circulation is the efficiency of the payments mechanism. Surprisingly, cheque clearing takes as long in this age of electronic banking as it has for decades, but other forms of payment are increasingly speedy. The ever-growing use of debit cards, credit cards, standing orders, and direct debit all lead to a rise in the velocity of circulation.

A third influence is the rate of interest; for example, as interest rates rise the opportunity cost of holding money in idle balances also rises, and people want to hold less money. Other things being equal, as interest rates rise the velocity of circulation rises, and as interest rates fall the velocity of circulation falls.

Finally, the expected rate of inflation can be important, not just because of its influence on interest rates, but also because of the way in which it may alter people's spending habits. If people expect inflation rates to be high, or to rise more rapidly than in the recent past, they will spend sooner rather than later and the velocity of circulation will rise. This happened in Britain in the 1970s.

The evidence shows that the velocity of circulation has not been stable in either Britain or the United States in recent decades. There are a number of reasons for this instability, which makes estimates of the future behaviour of the velocity of circulation difficult.

The crude quantity theory of money—the percentage change in the money supply equals the percentage change in the price level—is too crude because it relies on the assumption that both real output and the velocity of circulation are constant. These assumptions are obviously unwarranted, but it is still true to say that the money supply matters; changes in the money supply will, to a greater or lesser extent, affect the price level, output, and employment, depending on the time period and the level of spare capacity in the economy.

We now need to consider why the supply of money might change. We start by examining the role of the commercial banks and how their activities affect the money supply.

How banks create money

Banks are not charitable institutions; they need to make profits and these profits are made by paying depositors a lower rate of interest than is charged to borrowers. So the more money a bank can lend out, the more income it earns.

Banks were originally safe places where the wealthy could store their gold and silver coins. Bankers got very good at cultivating a really safe and reliable image and soon discovered that their customers never all arrived at once demanding all their bags of gold and silver. Bankers also realized that they could make a little money for themselves on the side by lending some of their depositors' money to others whose needs for money were more pressing, so long as, most importantly, they kept more than enough money in their reserves to satisfy any likely demands by depositors for cash.

Thus was born the idea of the **reserve ratio**, sometimes known as the cash ratio or the liquidity ratio. This is the proportion of a bank's total deposits held in reserves and not lent out. In the absence of any regulations the size of this reserve ratio depends on the behaviour of the depositors and the prudence of the banker. A bank can make larger profits but court disaster by having a lower reserve ratio; the whole edifice is built on confidence. If confidence collapses there is a 'run on the bank' (all the depositors try to withdraw their money at once), the bank cannot pay, and many depositors lose their money.

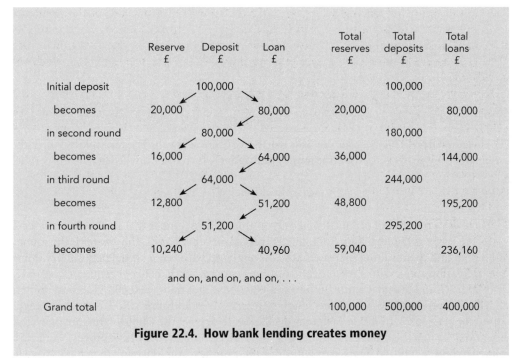

	Reserve £	Deposit £	Loan £	Total reserves £	Total deposits £	Total loans £
Initial deposit		100,000			100,000	
becomes	20,000		80,000	20,000		80,000
in second round		80,000			180,000	
becomes	16,000		64,000	36,000		144,000
in third round		64,000			244,000	
becomes	12,800		51,200	48,800		195,200
in fourth round		51,200			295,200	
becomes	10,240		40,960	59,040		236,160
		and on, and on, and on, . . .				
Grand total				100,000	500,000	400,000

Figure 22.4. How bank lending creates money

The size of the reserve ratio may be important in terms of the stability of the bank, but it is also highly significant in terms of the money supply. Merely by taking deposits and lending to borrowers, banks increase the supply of money; how is this so? Study Figure 22.4, which shows how an initial deposit of £100,000 leads to total deposits of £500,000, given a reserve ratio of 1 to 5. Put another way, the reserve ratio is 20 per cent, that is, 20 per cent of deposits are kept in bank reserves and the remaining 80 per cent are lent to borrowers.

The left side of Figure 22.4 shows the steps by which the extra £400,000 of deposits are created. Of the initial deposit of £100,000, the bank puts £20,000 into its reserves and then has a further £80,000 which it may lend to a suitable borrower, and will lend, if the bank is to maximize its income. The second round in the money creation process starts with £80,000 being lent and deposited in another bank account. The second bank now adds 20 per cent of £80,000 to its reserves (£16,000) and lends the remaining £64,000 to another borrower, who will deposit that £64,000 in the next bank in the chain, leading to the third round of lending and another increase in total reserves. Notice that with each round the figures are becoming smaller, and that the sequence is forming a geometric progression.

The right side of Figure 22.4 shows the running totals after each round of bank lending brought about by the initial deposit of £100,000. The final figure at the bottom is arrived at by using the formula for the sum of an infinite geometrical progression—luckily, we do not have to work it all out in an infinitely painstaking way, round by round.

To find the total value of deposits, given the initial deposit of £100,000 and the reserve ratio (*RR*) of 20 per cent, we apply this formula:

$$\text{total deposits} = \text{initial deposit} \times \frac{1}{RR}$$

$$= £100{,}000 \times \frac{100}{20}$$

$$= £100{,}000 \times 5$$

$$= £500{,}000.$$

The original deposit has become deposits worth five times as much. The multiple by which the original deposit grows is known as the **money multiplier**, which is one divided by the reserve ratio:

$$\text{money multiplier} = \frac{1}{RR}.$$

There are a number of points to make about this process. One is that the lower the reserve ratio, the larger is the final figure of total deposits or, in other words, the greater is the money multiplier and the resulting increase in the money supply from any initial deposit. Try doing the calculation above with a reserve ratio of 10 per cent rather than 20 per cent; $1/RR$ becomes 100/10 or 10, and the final figure becomes £1,000,000 rather than £500,000. A second point is that banks may decide to keep excess reserves (reserves over and above those required by regulations or prudence), or individuals may decide not to deposit the whole of the sum of money borrowed, so that the money multiplier may be reduced. Finally, the whole process works just as well in reverse; should depositors withdraw their money from the bank then banks have to call in loans, and the size of the money supply is reduced.

So, given that the size of the money supply is strongly influenced by the tension between the caution of bankers on the one hand and their desire to maximize profits on the other, does this matter for the economy? Does the money supply need to be controlled in some way?

As discussed at the beginning of this chapter, changes in the money supply can influence prices, output, and employment, and therefore instability in the rate of change of the money supply can have serious consequences. Banks may decide to keep excess reserves—reserves above the necessary reserve ratio—in circumstances of uncertainty, when they do not see opportunities to make profitable and secure loans. Such circumstances are most likely during the downswing and trough of the business cycle, when the natural behaviour of banks will lead to a reduction in the money supply, which in turn will lead to a reduction in aggregate demand and therefore worsen the output and employment effects of the recession. Similarly, during the upswing and boom periods of the business cycle the effects of the money-creating activities of the banks may increase inflationary pressures in the economy. Finally, economic instability is associated with lower long-term growth rates in an economy, so there are good reasons for a government or for a central bank to try to achieve monetary stability. The last section of this chapter looks at how monetary policy can be used to control the money supply, but before that we need to understand the financial revolutions of the 1980s and 1990s in Britain.

Financial deregulation in Britain

In the past there were clear demarcation lines between different financial institutions in Britain; each type of institution, be it a bank, a building society, an insurance company, a stockbroker, or a discount house, had a distinctive role and operated within a set of strict regulations. One of the functions of these regulations was to restrict the entry of new firms and so to reduce competition in the financial sector. The City of London was the first European financial centre to face **deregulation**; since the 'Big Bang' in 1986 a wave of reform has increased competition between institutions and changed the nature of specialist institutions.

The impact of this deregulation continues into the 1990s and its most familiar effect is probably the changing role of the building societies. Until 1986, building societies were mutual societies, owned by the depositors and the borrowers, which concentrated on lending money for house purchase. A building society may now act as a bank, lending money for a much wider range of purposes, and may become a publicly owned company, with shareholders rather than members; this process is inelegantly known as 'demutualization'.

In early 1997 the discount houses lost their monopoly over dealing with the Bank of England and in May 1997 the incoming Labour government announced that the Bank of England would henceforth operate independently of government control—this is a particularly important change. One result of financial deregulation has been to make control of the money supply by the Bank of England much more difficult; any discussion of monetary policy in Britain needs to make clear the time period to which it is relevant.

The role of the Bank of England

The Bank of England is the UK's central bank. All countries have a central bank and they have two very important roles. One is to oversee the whole monetary system and the other is to act as the government's agent, both as its banker and in carrying out monetary policy.

The Bank of England was founded in 1694 by London merchants to lend money to the state and to deal with the national debt. It was nationalized in 1946 and freed from overt government control in 1997. The Bank of England has never acted wholly independently of the government and after nationalization was subservient to the government, unlike the Federal Reserve in the USA or the Bundesbank in Germany.

Apart from the general functions of any central bank, mentioned in the first paragraph of this section, the Bank of England has a number of specific roles, some of which are changing as this book is being written. First, it issues banknotes in England and Wales, and is responsible for their printing. Second, the Bank acts as a bank to the British government, to other British banks, and to overseas banks with sterling deposits. Third, the Bank is the lender of last resort, ensuring that the banking system never runs out of money. The Barings Bank failure in 1995 was an interesting case where the Bank of England did not bail out a bank in difficulties. Fourth, the Bank operates the country's monetary and exchange rate policies. Monetary and exchange rate policies are closely linked, but in this chapter we will deal only with monetary policy, touching on exchange rate policy in Chapter 24.

Two previously important functions of the Bank of England are in the process of change, after government announcements made in May 1997. The Bank has for many years supervised the conduct of banks and other financial institutions, and was therefore an important guarantor of confidence in the banking system. This role seems to have become more difficult in recent years—a recent example of the failure of the Bank of England's supervisory role was the collapse of Barings Bank. This supervisory role will pass to a new regulator, the Financial

Services Authority. For over three centuries the Bank of England has managed the government's borrowing and the national debt; this function has now passed to the Treasury.

Other UK financial institutions

The **discount houses** were a unique feature of the British financial system. They acted as intermediaries between the Bank of England and other banks, which could not borrow directly from the Bank of England. Discount houses have always been particularly flexible, borrowing for very short periods, often overnight, and lending for slightly longer periods, up to three months. They have broadened the range of their activities in recent years and lost their special privileges in January 1997. The **commercial banks** are the high street, or retail, banks such as Barclays Bank or Lloyds Bank, and the overseas banks operating in Britain.

Other financial institutions in Britain include the **merchant banks**, which specialize in organizing finance for industry. The merchant banks also play an important role in advising companies on mergers and take-overs. **Building societies** specialize in loans for house purchase, but they are now increasingly turning themselves into high street banks. **Finance houses** provide consumer credit, such as car loans and hire-purchase arrangements.

Monetary policy

Monetary policy is the deliberate attempt to control the money supply, or to control interest rates, or to restrict the amount banks can lend to their customers. As with fiscal policy, there is no general agreement amongst economists or politicians about the effectiveness of monetary policy.

Monetary policy can be used conservatively, or cautiously, to provide 'sound money', so that rising prices do not confuse market signals. The current Governor of the Bank of England, Eddie George, has argued for several years that controlling inflation is the best way to encourage steady, long-term growth in the UK economy. Alternatively, monetary policy can be used to 'fine-tune' the economy, in rather the same way as fiscal policy might be used. We examine next the tools of monetary policy, looking first at ways of controlling the money supply.

Controlling the money supply

An earlier section of this chapter outlined the links between the commercial banks' reserve ratios and the money supply. If bank lending were reduced then, other things being equal, the size of the money supply would be reduced. One way in which bank lending may be reduced is by requiring banks to hold a greater proportion of their assets as reserves. This method of altering the money supply has not been used in Britain since 1981, but is still commonly used in other countries.

Open-market operations are a second method of influencing bank lending, and thus the money supply. The Bank of England sells government securities such as Treasury bills or bonds, and as these are bought by the banks money flows into the Bank of England, leaving the commercial banks with less money with which to make loans. Interest rates rise because loanable funds are more scarce. By the reverse process, the money supply is increased when the Bank of England buys securities. Money goes to the commercial banks from the Bank of England in payment for the securities, increasing the banks' reserves and making it possible for banks to lend more. Interest rates fall as more money becomes available for borrowing.

Controlling the interest rate

The Bank of England can choose the rate of interest at which it lends to other banks. This rate then affects other interest rates. Until 1972 the Bank's lending rate was called Bank Rate, and was announced every Thursday, with all interest rates following suit. Changes in Bank Rate were very newsworthy. From 1972 until 1981 this rate was called the Minimum Lending Rate, which differed from Bank Rate in that other banks did not have to follow the lead of the Bank of England, although they usually did so.

Formal announcements of the Minimum Lending Rate are no longer made, but the interest rate at which the Bank of England lends to other banks still has a knock-on effect on other interest rates.

Controlling credit

A third form of monetary policy consists of regulations controlling credit, or the lending of money. British governments used to like to keep interest rates low to encourage investment, but they were then faced with an excess demand for borrowing money. So various rationing schemes were imposed, such as ordering banks to restrict their lending and imposing hire-purchase controls.

Another way of controlling lending is to require banks to leave higher reserves with the Bank of England, thus reducing commercial bank lending. None of these methods of controlling credit is currently in use in Britain, being out of keeping with the spirit of deregulation of recent years.

How effective is monetary policy?

The tools of monetary policy are aimed at influencing the money supply or the interest rate. Expansionary monetary policy increases the money supply and reduces the interest rate, other things being equal; this is shown in Figure 22.5. Contractionary policy, shown in Figure 22.6, decreases the money supply and increases the interest rate, other things being equal.

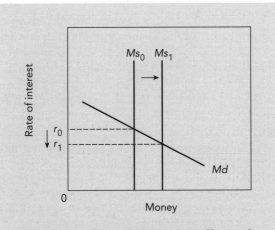

Figure 22.5. The money market effects of expansionary monetary policy

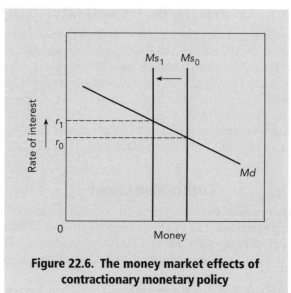

Figure 22.6. The money market effects of contractionary monetary policy

However, several difficulties may make the outcome of monetary policy less certain than this pair of diagrams might imply. The first is that the velocity of circulation may change; a change in the velocity of circulation may reinforce, or act against, the effect of the change in the money supply.

A second uncertainty lies in the behaviour of the banks, which may decide to delay their response to increases in their reserves; they may not lend more immediately if they expect interest rates to rise later. On the other hand, if the money supply falls banks have to reduce their lending fast.

A third problem can be illustrated by the aggregate demand and aggregate supply diagram in Figure 22.7. As explained earlier in this chapter and illustrated in Figures 22.1, 22.2, and 22.3, an increase in the money supply will shift the aggregate demand curve to the right, from AD_0 to AD_1. If the aggregate supply curve (AS) is steep, the impact of a change in the money supply will be felt largely on prices, rather than on output and employment. The price level rises significantly from P_0 to P_1, while output rises much less, from Y_0 to Y_1. If the aggregate supply curve were vertical, the change in the money supply would merely be reflected by a change in the price level, with no change in output.

A fourth potential area of uncertainty with monetary policy lies in the responsiveness of both the demand for money and investment demand to changes in the rate of interest. Both will affect the extent of the shift of aggregate demand in response to a change in the money supply. Aggregate demand will shift further, and monetary policy will be more effective, when both the demand for money and investment demand are more responsive to changes in the rate of interest.

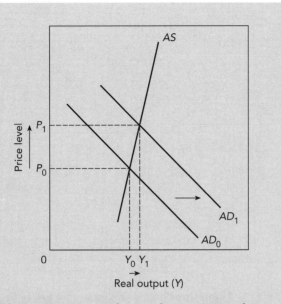

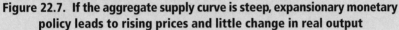

Figure 22.7. If the aggregate supply curve is steep, expansionary monetary policy leads to rising prices and little change in real output

Fiscal policy or monetary policy?

One long-running debate between the Keynesian and monetarist schools of thought centres on whether fiscal or monetary policy is more effective in shifting aggregate demand. Extreme Keynesians have argued that only fiscal policy is effective, while extreme monetarists have argued that only monetary policy is effective. Research has shown that both positions are too extreme; both fiscal and monetary policy affect aggregate demand.

Discussion of fiscal policy in Chapter 20 suggested that fiscal policy is more effective when investment demand is less responsive to changes in the rate of interest, because the crowding-out effects of expansionary fiscal policy are less. In the section above, monetary policy is described as being more effective in the opposite circumstances, when investment demand is more responsive to changes in the rate of interest. In other words, it would seem that fiscal policy is most effective when monetary policy is least effective, and vice versa. What happens if fiscal and monetary policy are used together?

To examine this question we will take the example of expansionary policy, that is, policy aimed at increasing output and employment. The constraint on the effectiveness of fiscal policy in shifting aggregate demand is due to the impact of crowding out. Crowding out occurs when a government borrows money to finance greater public spending, and the greater demand for money drives up the interest rate, which in turn reduces the level of private sector investment. If the money supply were to increase at the same time, by a suitable amount, then the rate of interest would not rise and crowding out of private expenditure would not happen.

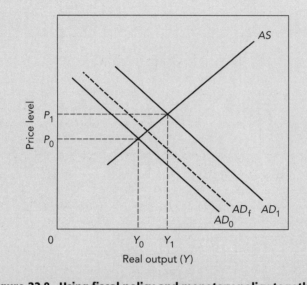

Figure 22.8. Using fiscal policy and monetary policy together has a larger impact on aggregate demand

Put simply, expansionary fiscal policy accompanied by expansionary monetary policy could mean that aggregate demand shifts further to the right. What happens to prices would depend on the slope of the aggregate supply curve, that is, on the amount of spare capacity in the economy. This is illustrated in Figure 22.8, where aggregate demand shifts from AD_0 to AD_1, aggregate supply (AS) is upward-sloping, the price level rises from P_0 to P_1, and output rises from Y_0 to Y_1. Expansionary fiscal policy on its own would only shift aggregate demand to the dotted line AD_f. Fiscal policy and monetary policy working together are more effective than either working in isolation.

Should monetary policy be interventionist?

The history of discretionary fiscal policy has not been glorious, for all the reasons given in Chapter 20—lack of reliable information, unpredictable time-lags, and so on. The same tends to be true of actively interventionist monetary policy. Although pressure groups and anxious politicians frequently call on the government or the Bank of England to react to current economic indicators and alter the rate of interest, for example, there are many who argue that the best role for monetary policy is to provide the stability which is more likely to foster long-term growth.

The discussion of the rate of interest and monetary policy so far has concentrated on domestic considerations only, as though Britain were a closed economy. Although such an approach makes things easier to understand it can be misleading, for the exchange rate and the interest rate are closely linked. For example, in September 1992 the turbulence of the domestic interest rate was not the result of attempts to manage the UK economy in any way, but was instead a reflection of the turbulence of the foreign exchange markets and the ultimately futile attempt by the UK to stay within the European Exchange Rate Mechanism. Chapter 24 examines exchange rates in more detail.

Summary

1. The quantity theory of money links money, output, and prices. In its crude form it links the rate of growth of the money supply to the rate of growth of prices. It is one theory of inflation. The quantity theory may be summed up by the equation of exchange, $MV = PY$.

2. The quantity theory of money works best when the velocity of circulation is stable and when there is full employment, or in the long run.

3. Everyday bank lending practices—credit creation—influence the size of the money supply. The larger the banks' reserve ratio, the smaller the money multiplier.

4. The scope and role of UK financial institutions have changed in the last two decades, and continue to change. Financial deregulation has been one cause of such changes.

5. Monetary policy involves attempts to control the money supply or interest rates. It may be deliberately interventionist, attempting to influence aggregate demand, or it may be used to promote long-term stability.

6. Interventionist monetary policy is most effective in circumstances where fiscal policy is least effective. Fiscal and monetary policy used together are likely to have the greatest impact on aggregate demand in the short term.

Key terms

building societies

central bank

commercial banks

discount houses

equation of exchange

finance houses

deregulation

merchant banks

monetary policy

money multiplier

open-market operations

quantity theory of money

reserve ratio

velocity of circulation

Review questions

1. Would you expect interest rates to rise when

    (i) the price of bonds falls?
    (ii) the demand for money increases?
    (iii) consumer prices rise?
    (iv) the money supply falls?

2. In what circumstances would you expect an increase in the money supply to

    (i) raise the price level?
    (ii) increase output?

Draw diagrams to illustrate both of these cases.

3. Why is it difficult to control the money supply?

Notes

1. R. A. Radford, 'The Economic Organisation of a POW Camp', *Economica*, 12 (1945), 189–201.

2. Changes in the financial sector continue: the *Financial Times* and *The Economist* are excellent sources of up-to-date information and comment. The financial pages of serious newspapers are also good sources.

Further reading

- Mabry and Ulbrich, chapters 16 and 17

- Lipsey and Chrystal, chapters 26 and 27
- Sloman, chapter 19

CHAPTER 23

A review of inflation

Reducing inflation has been a top priority of many politicians (apart of course from staying in power) in many different countries. But persistent inflation is a relatively new phenomenon. In Britain the average price level has risen every year since 1945 and prices are now twenty times higher than they were in 1950, a greater rise than occurred over the previous three hundred years. This chapter looks at some ideas about the causes of inflation and at some of the policies which have been used to control inflation. Earlier sections of this book deal with measuring inflation (Chapter 15) and with the effect on people's behaviour of inflationary expectations (Chapter 18).

Some theories of inflation

The first theory of inflation is the **quantity theory of money**, which holds that changes in the price level are the result of changes in the money supply; this is discussed at the beginning of Chapter 22.

Then there are the demand-pull and cost-push explanations of inflation. The **demand-pull** approach suggests that if the economy is near or at full employment an increase in aggregate demand will cause higher prices, rather than a significant increase in output. This is illustrated in Figure 23.1, which uses the aggregate demand and aggregate supply model, with the price level on the vertical axis and real output on the horizontal axis. Aggregate supply is shown by the nearly vertical line AS. Aggregate demand shifts from AD_0 to AD_1 and the equilibrium price level rises from P_0 to P_1, while the equilibrium level of real output rises only a little from Y_0 to Y_1.

There are a number of possible causes of such an increase in aggregate demand: they include growth in the money supply (leading to a reduction in interest rates and an increase in autonomous spending) and increased government spending on goods and services, financed by a budget deficit. In both cases the increase in spending may be followed by an increase in prices, which may well be followed by an increase in wages, which will lead to a further increase in prices, and so on, round and round and up and up the infamous **wage–price spiral**.

Cost-push inflation starts off differently. There are two versions, one being that an increase in the prices of imported goods and raw materials makes manufacturing costs rise, and these increased costs are then passed on in higher prices to consumers. The other is that powerful trade unions negotiate higher wages for their members which are not matched by compensating productivity gains, and that the increased costs of production are passed on to the consumer in higher prices. Both versions of the cost-push explanation of inflation are only possible in imperfect markets, where there is an element of protection and a lack of competition. Again, a wage–price spiral may ensue, as employees justify higher wage demands on the grounds of an increase in the cost of living.

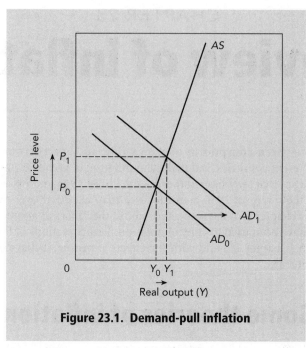

Figure 23.1. Demand-pull inflation

The initial stage of the cost-push argument is illustrated in Figure 23.2, which uses the same model as Figure 23.1 but shows that the increase in costs causes the aggregate supply curve to shift to the left. An increase in costs means that less will be produced at any particular price level and the aggregate supply curve, AS_0, shifts to AS_1; the aggregate demand curve, AD, does not move, but there is a movement along the aggregate demand curve so that the new equilibrium price level is higher at P_1, and real output falls to Y_1.

Examples of both demand-pull and cost-push inflation can easily be found, but a wage–price spiral can only be established if the money supply continues to expand.

The Phillips curve

An interesting angle on inflation is given by the **Phillips curve**. This is usually understood to show a relationship between the rate of unemployment and the rate of inflation, but the original Phillips curve linked the rate of change of money wages and the rate of unemployment. This famous piece of research was published in the November 1958 edition of *Economica* and is an instructive read for modern students of economics.[1]

A. W. Phillips analysed data on wages and unemployment in Britain between 1861 and 1957 and found a relationship between the two. Figure 23.3 shows the curve he fitted to the data for 1861 to 1913; the vertical scale shows the average rate of change of money wages in a year and the horizontal scale shows the average unemployment rate during a year. The article discusses the various sources of data used, the way these sources change over the years, and

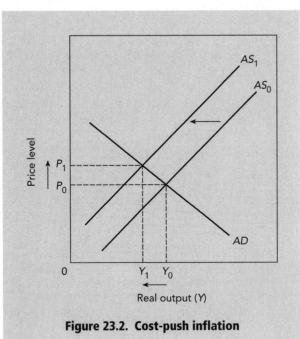

Figure 23.2. Cost-push inflation

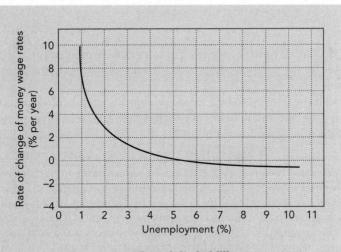

Figure 23.3. The original Phillips curve

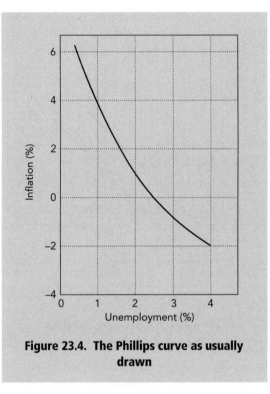

Figure 23.4. The Phillips curve as usually drawn

some of Phillips' assumptions and exclusions; in essence, the data are not very reliable and the older they are, the less reliable they are. The same curve was fitted to the data for later years but by the period 1948 to 1957 a better fit was achieved by lagging the unemployment data by seven months.

On the face of it there seems to be a strong relationship between the percentage change of money wage rates and the unemployment rate; it is an inverse relationship, in which one variable goes up as the other goes down. Phillips' cautious conclusion was as follows:

> Ignoring years in which import prices rise rapidly enough to initiate a wage–price spiral, which seem to occur very rarely except as a result of war, and assuming an increase in productivity of 2 per cent a year, it seems from the relation fitted to the data that if aggregate demand were kept at a value which would maintain a stable level of product prices the associated level of unemployment would be a little under $2\frac{1}{2}$ per cent. If, as is sometimes recommended, demand were kept at a value which would maintain stable wage rates the associated level of unemployment would be about $5\frac{1}{2}$ per cent. . . . These conclusions are of course tentative. There is need for much more detailed research into the relations between unemployment, wage rates, prices and productivity.

Economists and policy makers were excited about this piece of work and much further research took place.

The Phillips curve was subsequently usually drawn with the inflation rate on the vertical axis, rather than the rate of change of money wages, and is shown in Figure 23.4. It seems to suggest that the aims of a low inflation rate and a low unemployment rate are incompatible and suggests instead that there is trade-off between the two—as unemployment falls inflation rises and vice versa. Since low unemployment and stable prices are both important macro-economic goals, this analysis presents policy makers with a dilemma, rather than an answer. Governments in the late 1950s and the 1960s, it seemed, had to choose between expanding demand and reducing unemployment on the one side, while accepting that prices would rise faster, or on the other side, keeping price increases down but accepting a higher rate of unemployment.

However, in both Britain and the United States, the anguished memories were of the high unemployment of the 1930s, rather than of alarming levels of inflation. So by and large, policies were adopted which kept unemployment down, rather than restraining price increases. The Phillips curve quickly entered popular consciousness and has remained there, as have some other fragments of economic theory. It was particularly popular with politicians of the period because it gave them the illusion that they had a reliable recipe for manipulating the economy.

Unfortunately, there have been many years since 1970 when unemployment and inflation have risen together, and the trade-off between the two implied by the Phillips curve seems to have disappeared. Milton Friedman, an eminent economist of the Chicago school and associated most notably with monetarism, suggested that people's behaviour had changed because they had begun eventually to expect rising prices. He argued that in the long run there was no trade-off between inflation and unemployment, and that the link between the two shown by the Phillips curve was a short-run relationship, arising out of the swings of the business cycle.

Friedman suggested that there were a series of short-run Phillips curves, which moved up and down the long-run curve at the natural rate of unemployment. This is illustrated in Figure 23.5. This diagram has the same axes as the standard Phillips curve in Figure 23.4, but here a succession of short-run curves (SR_1, SR_2, SR_3, and SR_4) are shown. The height of each short-run Phillips curve depends on the underlying growth of the money supply and the expected inflation rate. Low expected inflation would be associated with SR_1, for example, and high expected inflation with SR_4.

The long-run relationship between inflation and unemployment is shown by the vertical line, *LR*, positioned at the **natural rate of unemployment**. In other words, there is no trade-off between inflation and unemployment in the long run, which implies that attempts to manipulate the economy to reduce unemployment will only tend to increase expectations of inflation, and will have no long-term beneficial effect on the level of unemployment. Should the natural rate of unemployment change, the long-run Phillips curve would shift to the right or to the left. In Figure 23.6 a rise in the natural rate of unemployment moves the long-run Phillips curve to the right, from LR_0 to LR_1. Both have their own family of short-run curves.

Friedman's analysis fitted the data of the 1970s much better. The implication of his argument was that should a government wish to shift the short-run Phillips curve downwards, from SR_4 in Figure 23.5 to SR_3 for example, then it must convince people that inflation would be lower in the future. It may do this by strict control of the money supply.

We have considered a number of explanations of the causes of inflation: the quantity theory of money; the pull of increased aggregate demand; the push of increased costs of production; the Phillips curve and its implied trade-off between unemployment and inflation; and the influence of expectations of inflation. What do these theories suggest might be effective remedies for inflation?

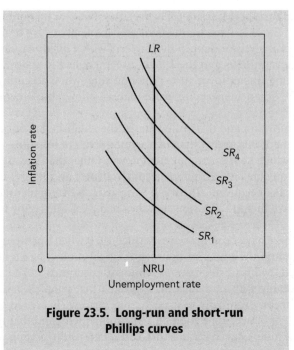

Figure 23.5. Long-run and short-run Phillips curves

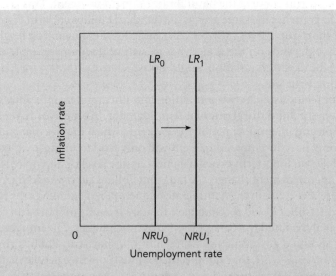

Figure 23.6. The long-run Phillips curve shifts to the right as the natural rate of unemployment rises

How may inflation be reduced?

Monetarists saw the cause of inflation as excess demand, fed by too much money. Reducing the government budget deficit and strictly controlling the money supply were their essential remedies. But this approach has some difficulties in practice. As discussed in Chapter 22, the money supply has proved hard to control and there was uncertainty about which measure of the money supply it was most useful to monitor. Even if the money supply is controlled, the velocity of circulation may be unpredictable and increases in the velocity of circulation may undermine the results of efforts to control the money supply.

Another difficulty lies in the political and, for some, moral unacceptability of high unemployment. If expectations of inflation are revised downwards only very slowly, and this seems to be the case, then a very long period of high rates of unemployment may be necessary before low inflation rates are achieved. It also seems that an economy may not return to its previous natural rate of unemployment once inflation is eliminated. Long-term unemployment puts many out of the labour market and therefore increases the natural rate of unemployment.

Some who argue that prolonged high unemployment is unacceptable put forward an **incomes policy** as the best way of controlling inflation. There are various forms of incomes policies, but in essence they involve restrictions on pay rises, sometimes backed by the law. Critics argue that first, incomes policies have been shown not to work—various forms of incomes policy were used in Britain between 1965 and 1979, by governments of both the left and the right. In practice an incomes policy only lasted for up to three years and was invariably followed by a catching-up period of rapid pay rises. Another criticism is that an incomes policy leads to a misallocation of resources since growing firms cannot attract new labour by paying higher wages. Such policies distort the labour market and make the economy less efficient the longer they are in force. Interestingly, no British government that has introduced any form of incomes policy has subsequently been re-elected.

Since leaving the European Exchange Rate Mechanism in 1992, British governments have resorted to a policy of aiming at a low inflation rate by manipulating interest rates. The government has announced the desired rate of inflation and the Bank of England has altered its base lending rate as thought necessary to achieve that inflation rate. A rise in interest rates will lead to leftward shift of the aggregate demand curve, other things being equal, as consumers borrow less and spend less, and as firms reduce their investment spending. Interest rate rises may also affect the exchange rate (see the next chapter) so that exports fall and imports increase, again shifting the aggregate demand curve to the left. However, unpredictable time-lags may make the effect of this policy rather uncertain. Figure 23.7 shows how a rise in interest rates may exert a downward pressure on prices as the aggregate demand curve shifts leftwards from AD_0 to AD_1.

Although anti-inflation policies have had their difficulties, it seems that in many industrial economies in the 1990s the rate of inflation is becoming lower. A few commentators now suggest that inflation has been cured, and need no longer be a concern. It took several decades for the British public to adjust its ideas and actions to inflation, and now most people expect prices to rise. If persistent and high levels of inflation are a thing of the past, how long will it take for expectations and behaviour to change?

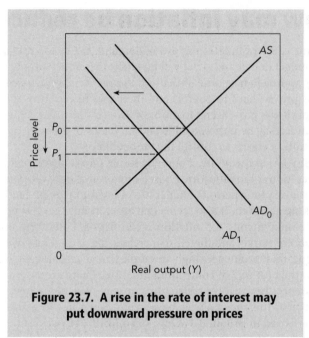

Figure 23.7. A rise in the rate of interest may put downward pressure on prices

Summary

1. Explanations of inflation include demand-pull, cost-push, and the quantity theory of money.

2. The usual version of the Phillips curve demonstrates the trade-off between inflation and unemployment, but this seems only to hold good in the short term.

3. The long-run Phillips curve shows no trade-off between unemployment and inflation and is vertical at the natural rate of unemployment.

4. Policies intended to reduce the inflation rate include attempts to control the supply of money and to halt the wage–price spiral. Incomes policies have generally been unsuccessful. Policies to break inflationary expectations by achieving long-term monetary stability seem to have been more successful.

Key terms

cost-push

demand-pull

incomes policy

natural rate of unemployment

Phillips curve

quantity theory of money

wage–price spiral

Review questions

1. What is a wage–price spiral? Why might it occur and how might it be halted?

2. Explain the trade-off between inflation and unemployment shown by the short-run Phillips curve.

3. Why is the long-run Phillips curve vertical?

4. Explain why a rise in interest rates may be an anti-inflationary tool. Use an aggregate demand and aggregate supply diagram to illustrate your explanation.

Note

1. A. W. Phillips, 'The Relation between Unemployment and the Rate of Change of Money Wage Rates in the United Kingdom, 1861–1957', *Economica*, 25 (1958), 283–99.

Further reading

- Lipsey and Chrystal, chapter 30
- Sloman, chapters 14 and 21

CHAPTER 24

The open economy: international trade and the exchange rate

International economics is a large and important area of study. This book makes no attempt to summarize all the main theories for reasons of space; however, there are some key ideas of which students need to be aware. For example, it is not possible to consider monetary policy without paying some attention to the importance of the links between the interest rate and the exchange rate. The approach taken here is to review some of the main themes in international trade theory from a historical perspective and to examine briefly some current policies.

The benefits of international trade

National pride is often involved in popular thinking about trade and payment for trade. This is an area where there can be damaging misconceptions in people's minds, which may lead to poor policies.

The first derives from **mercantilism**, a way of thinking about trade which pre-dates the classical economists of the eighteenth and nineteenth centuries. In the days when trade was paid for in gold, people felt that the purpose of international trade was to export more than was imported and to accumulate gold so that the nation became richer. Mercantilists argued that if imports were greater than exports then imports should be restricted. But David Hume, writing in the 1740s, argued that as the quantity of gold in a country changes so does the price level (here you will recognize the quantity theory of money), so that the real wealth of a country would be unaffected by piling up gold.

Later, in *The Wealth of Nations* (1776), Adam Smith explained that restrictions on imports would reduce economies of scale and gains from specialization, so making a country poorer. Then, writing in 1817, David Ricardo demonstrated how the **law of comparative advantage** worked and why **free trade** was to the ultimate benefit of all. As applied to international trade the law of comparative advantage is as follows: countries should specialize in producing what they are most efficient at producing; they may then trade these goods for those produced most efficiently by other countries. This is common sense but the law goes further, stating that trade is still beneficial to both parties even when one country is more efficient at producing everything than another, so long as each country concentrates on producing and trading what it produces most efficiently. (See Further Reading at the end of this chapter.)

These arguments lay behind the Free Trade movement of the nineteenth century, a period of a great flowering of trade and prosperity. Interestingly though, mercantilist ideas are still influential and you may well recognize them. These ideas lie in the feeling that trade must be a zero-sum game, in which the gains by trade of one country are counter-balanced by the losses of another. But the evidence is to the contrary. In the 1920s and 1930s trade restrictions were imposed by countries trying to protect domestic jobs but these restrictions led to a collapse in world trade and to greater unemployment. After the Second World War the General Agreement on Trade and Tariffs (GATT) attempted to establish freer trade, because it was recognized that trade restrictions were damaging to world prosperity. Removing trade restrictions is an ongoing and difficult process; the most recent GATT negotiations are known as the Uruguay round and took place between 1986 and 1993. GATT was replaced by the World Trade Organisation in 1995.

An example of mercantilist ideas still holding sway in the 1990s is the thinking which led the United States to put pressure on the Japanese to reduce their exports to the USA, because these goods were seen as undercutting prices in the United States, leading to higher unemployment and a growing trade deficit. This ignores the facts that consumers in the United States prefer to buy cheaper and better Japanese goods rather than their higher-priced domestically produced versions, and that using lower-priced imported components would mean that American goods could be more competitively priced in international markets. As nearly always happens a few large producers campaigning for their own protection are a more effective lobby group than the many consumers who might benefit from low-priced imports.

Paying for international trade

There are economic benefits from international trade in goods, services, and factors of production, but such trade needs an efficient means of payment. The balance of payments, the exchange rate, and the chosen exchange rate mechanism are three aspects of financing international transactions. Such transactions will work best, first, if businesses have easy and reliable access to foreign exchange and, second, if there is a relatively stable relationship between domestic and international prices.

The balance of payments accounts

The **balance of payments** accounts record a country's international trade and its international borrowing and lending. There are three parts to the accounts. The first, the **current account**, shows the value of imports and exports of goods and services. The UK frequently has a deficit on the current account, that is, the value of imports is often greater than the value of exports. International trade in goods is known as **visible trade** and international trade in services, such as insurance, is known as **invisible trade**; for the UK there is usually a deficit in the trade in goods and a surplus in the trade in services. However, the surplus in invisibles is usually smaller than the deficit in visibles, hence the overall deficit on the current account. How can this overall deficit continue?

This question brings us to the second element of the balance of payments, the **capital account**, which records international borrowing and lending. The third element is the balance for official financing, which shows the overall increase or decrease in a country's holdings of foreign currency reserves. A deficit on the current account is adjusted on the capital account, or by changes in the official reserves. These three elements make up the overall balance of payments, which always balances, by definition.

This raises the question, if the balance of payments always balances why do people talk of balance of payments problems, or even crises? Since the Second World War there have been several British balance of payments crises. A 'balance of payments problem' usually means an imbalance on the current account and the identification of a 'problem' is largely a matter of judgement. McAleese considers that a 'country can be said to have a balance of payments problem when the current account is in deficit for a sustained period of time in conditions of free trade and "full" employment'.[1]

The current account balance matters because, first, it affects aggregate demand and, second, it affects the level of a country's international indebtedness. The USA has had a series of current account deficits since the early 1980s and has changed from being a major international creditor (lending money overseas) to being the world's largest debtor (borrowing money from other countries).

If exchange rates can adjust freely then balance of payments problems will sort themselves out, although changes in the exchange rate bring their own difficulties. Britain's balance of payments crises have occurred when exchange rates were fixed, for example in 1967, and some have been followed by a devaluation of the pound, a brutal readjustment of exchange rates.

Exchange rates

The **exchange rate** is the price of foreign currency in terms of domestic currency and reflects, in the long run, the relative purchasing power of two currencies. In the short run an exchange rate may also reflect speculative forces and relative interest rates. Exchange rates can be fixed, floating (or flexible), or managed. These exchange rate regimes have evolved over time and each has its advantages and disadvantages, as is shown by the following brief history of exchange rate regimes, starting with the gold standard of the nineteenth and early twentieth centuries.

The gold standard

The UK adopted a **gold standard** in 1819 when the Bank of England was required by law to exchange all currency for gold. Other major countries followed suit and by 1879 the gold standard was the international monetary system. The UK was dominant in international trade, had highly developed financial institutions, and became the centre of the international financial system based on the gold standard. This was a **fixed exchange rate** regime where each currency had a fixed price in gold and was convertible into gold. Paper money had to be backed with gold reserves, which promoted price stability.

Currency chaos and depression

During the First World War many countries left the gold standard and financed their military spending by printing money; inflation followed. The American dollar became widely used for international payment. Currencies continued to float after the war, that is, exchange rates adjusted freely, but the continued fall in the value of sterling and the fear of inflation led Winston Churchill, then Britain's Chancellor of the Exchequer, to go back to the pre-war gold standard in 1925. Other countries followed but the old relationships between currencies no longer reflected true relative values and the system did not work as smoothly as before the war. The Great Crash of 1929 led to a collapse of banking systems around the world and convertibility into gold was abandoned. Currency blocs were formed, such as the sterling area covering the British Empire, but world trade collapsed with the increasing protection of domestic markets against imported goods during the depression of the 1930s. This dreadful experience led policy makers to devise a better system after the Second World War.

The Bretton Woods system

The **Bretton Woods system** is named after the location of the luxurious Mount Washington Hotel in New Hampshire, USA, where representatives of the wartime allies met in 1944 to devise a workable international monetary system. The result was an **adjustable peg** system which lasted until the early 1970s, when it was in turn abandoned. The Bretton Woods system arranged for each currency to be convertible at a fixed rate into the American dollar, which was itself fixed to a particular quantity of gold. To that extent the system was based on gold. A major difference from the old gold standard was that there were arrangements for individual currencies to alter their exchange rate in terms of dollars.

Exchange rates could only fluctuate within 1 per cent of the official exchange rate, but if this led to chronic and persistent balance of payments problems then adjustments could be made. Necessary devaluations were, however, usually badly delayed and such delays led to currency speculation and the loss of a country's reserves. The Bretton Woods system broke down following the US inflation during the Vietnam War; the gold–dollar link was broken in 1971.

Floating exchange rates

Leaving the Bretton Woods system behind, most countries adopted a **floating exchange rate**, but this is not universal. Some peg their currency to an **anchor currency**, usually that of their dominant trading partner: for example the Austrian schilling is pegged to the German Deutschmark. Others have pegged their currencies to a trade-weighted basket of currencies, a system used by both Australia and New Zealand in the 1970s and early 1980s, but then abandoned for a floating exchange rate. Other countries have attempted to create their own monetary sub-system, such as the European Exchange Rate Mechanism and the movement towards European Monetary Union. This is because floating exchange rates have disadvantages as well as advantages.

In theory a floating exchange rate does not require intervention from a country's central bank to maintain its value and may fluctuate according to market forces in the currency markets. In practice, the major currencies—the American dollar, the Japanese yen, and the German Deutschmark—do not float entirely freely because their central banks do intervene in certain circumstances. The foreign exchange rate is seen as an important influence on a country's economy and there are advantages in stability.

Increasingly currency markets have been subject to speculative buying and selling, which has led to sudden and large changes in the value of some currencies. The resulting dislocation and uncertainty causes serious problems for importers and exporters, discourages trade, and may lead both to second-best investment decisions and to heavy transactions and hedging costs. An adverse change in the exchange rate after an export contract has been signed can turn a profit into a big loss and lead to bankruptcy.

A **managed exchange rate** means that an exchange rate is kept within a band around a pre-set value. The central bank will intervene in the foreign exchange markets, buying or selling the currency to stabilize its value. Future exchange rates are therefore more predictable than when freely floating so businesses face fewer difficulties and uncertainties. The European Exchange Rate Mechanism is essentially of this nature and has come about partly out of a desire to remove difficulties constraining trade between European Union member countries.

Fixed exchange rates give certainty so businesses face much lower transactions and hedging costs. However, a fixed exchange rate may impose heavy burdens on the central bank when trying to support its value; large fluctuations in official financing may test the limit of a country's currency reserves.

Exchange rates and the domestic economy

Fiscal and monetary policy aimed at the domestic economy has an effect on the balance of payments and on the exchange rate. Equally, international factors affecting the balance of payments and the exchange rate will impinge on the domestic economy.

The exchange rate and imports and exports

Changes in the exchange rate will alter the level of a country's imports and exports, after varying and often uncertain time-lags. As the exchange rate rises, imported goods become cheaper and the level of imports rises, while at the same time exports become more expensive and the level of exports falls; the balance of trade worsens. As the exchange rate falls, exports rise and imports fall so the balance of trade improves. The impact on output and employment is examined in Chapter 19 and the impact on the price level is discussed in Chapter 18.

The exchange rate, the money supply, and the interest rate

When a central bank buys currency to support an exchange rate this action will reduce the domestic money supply, with consequent effects on the domestic economy. When the central bank sells currency in the foreign exchange market the domestic money supply will increase.

If there are no restrictions on currency flows a higher interest rate set for domestic reasons will, other things being equal, attract foreign buyers of the currency. This will lead to a rise in the exchange rate and affect imports and exports, leading to a reduction in aggregate demand and reinforcing the deflationary effect of the original interest rate rise.

The exchange rate and expansionary fiscal and monetary policy

If a government adopts expansionary fiscal or monetary policy to increase output and employment, the results will differ according to whether the exchange rate is fixed or floating. With a fixed exchange rate fiscal policy is powerful in the short term, but in the long term prices rise and there may well be pressure for a devaluation. Monetary policy has no effect because money leaves the country to maintain the exchange rate, cancelling the increase in the money supply and leaving the interest rate unchanged.

The opposite is the case if the exchange rate is floating. Expansionary fiscal policy is ineffective because it leads to an increase in the interest rate, money flows in from overseas, the exchange rate rises and this reduces aggregate demand. Complete crowding out occurs and output and employment are unchanged. On the other hand, monetary policy is powerful in the short term and output and employment rise, but in the long term prices rise too and the 'real' economy is unchanged.

This framework goes some way to explain the changes in focus of government policies during the post-war period. During the 1950s and 1960s, when exchange rates were fixed, fiscal policy was the preferred tool. In the 1980s and 1990s, when exchange rates have floated to a greater or lesser extent, monetary policy has been preferred.

Summary

1. Popular ideas on international trade are often misconceived.

2. The balance of payments accounts record a country's international trade and its international borrowing and lending.

3. A continuing deficit in the current account leads to greater international indebtedness, which, sooner or later, leads to a reduction in the relative value of a country's currency.

4. Exchange rates show the value of one country's currency in terms of another. The history of exchange rates in the nineteenth and twentieth centuries shows the advantages and the disadvantages of both fixed and floating exchange rates.

5. A country's exchange rate has an impact both on its domestic economy and on attempts to manage that economy. With a fixed exchange rate fiscal policy is more effective; with a floating exchange rate monetary policy is more effective.

Key terms

adjustable peg

anchor currency

balance of payments

Bretton Woods system

capital account

current account

exchange rate

fixed exchange rate

floating exchange rate

free trade

gold standard

invisible trade

law of comparative advantage

managed exchange rate

mercantilism

visible trade

Review questions

1. Explain the following terms: floating exchange rate, anchor currency, invisible trade, gold standard.

2. If Country A's inflation rate is higher than that of Country B, what should happen to the exchange rate of their two currencies?

3. Explain how a country's exports may be affected by the combination of a high domestic interest rate and a floating exchange rate.

Note

1. D. McAleese, *Economics for Business* (Hemel Hempstead: Prentice-Hall, 1997), 525. Chapter 17 gives a full account of the gains from trade, including the law of comparative advantage.

Further reading

- Mabry and Ulbrich, chapter 18

- Lipsey and Chrystal, chapters 28, 29 and 34
- Sloman, chapters 14, 23, and 24

Index